GENDERING POETRY

DA

Return to L
Fines ar

i.m. Mum and Dad

GENDERING POETRY

CONTEMPORARY WOMEN AND MEN POETS

VICKI BERTRAM

Pandora
LONDON, CHICAGO, SYDNEY

First published in 2005 by Pandora Press
An imprint of Rivers Oram Publishers Limited
144 Hemingford Road
London N1 1DE

Distributed in the USA by
Independent Publishers' Group
814 North Franklin Street
Chicago, Ill 60610

Distributed in Australia by UNIReps
University of New South Wales, NSW 2052

Set in Sabon by
NJ Design, Fordingbridge, Hants, and
printed and bound in Great Britain by
T. J. International Ltd, Padstow, Cornwall

British Library Cataloguing in Publication Data
A catalogue record for this book is available from the British Library

ISBN (cloth) 086358 433 0
ISBN (paperback) 086358 434 9

CONTENTS

Poets needs must be
Or men or women—more's the pity.

Elizabeth Barrett Browning
Aurora Leigh

PREFACE

Sex and gender matter in poetry. As a genre, poetry has proved especially resistant to this idea. It is not that sex and gender *determine* content or meaning but rather that they play a significant and neglected part in the way poets write and readers read. The ongoing denial of this facilitates the continuance of a critical tradition that prioritises and naturalises men's writing and concerns.

Much contemporary poetry by both women and men explores gender constructions and relations between the sexes. By concentrating on *men* and *women* poets, the aim is to demolish the idea that sex and gender are only relevant to women poets' work. By foregrounding women poets, the balance of most mainstream poetry criticism, where women occupy a marginal position, if, indeed, they are included at all, is redressed.

The focus is on lyric poetry, definition of which has always been broad and vague. Over the last few decades many of the poets included here have responded to postmodernist attacks on the humanist subject by stretching the form into new modes. Nevertheless, the term still describes the vast majority of the poems here discussed. *The Oxford Dictionary of Literary Terms* gives this definition of lyric:

> Any fairly short poem expressing the personal mood, feeling, or meditation of a single speaker (who may sometimes be an invented character, not the poet).

I have chosen to write almost exclusively about poets who are resident in, and publish in, Britain and Ireland, partly because of the lack of critical material available on this contemporary work. But I have gone this route because I also believe that there is an intricate connection between poetry and culture. Indeed, one of the sub-themes pursued here is an investigation of this link as it relates to gender.

A brief word about methodology. Lyric poetry *requires* close textual analysis. This is not to say that close reading is sufficient by itself. The limitations of the practice are clear: it may de-contextualise the writing, eliding the social, cultural, or political resonances that surrounded its composition; or invite an overly subjective interpretation. But there is nothing to rival its most valuable attribute—thoughtful attentiveness to language. Lyric poetry deals in nuance, ambiguity, emotion, tone, making it vital to sustain respectful attention to the text while also remaining alert to the ideas and challenges of contemporary theoretical interests.

The difference between 'theory' and 'criticism' is primarily one of scale. While theory sets up hypotheses, or generalisations, on the basis of a broad analysis, criticism focuses on a specific text, author or delineated theme. It is difficult to generalise about lyric poetry, even about the work of one individual poet since, almost by definition, each poem is a work in itself, each is unique, particular. On the other hand, it is relatively easy to make a poem 'fit' a specific theory because, as argued in chapter 1, poems offer their readers considerable scope for interpretative freedom. This kind of analysis—where the poem is read according to the theory—does little to 'open it up' in the ways I value as a reader of criticism. It does not, for example, help me explore why particular images have been juxtaposed, or the effect of such juxtapositionings. On the other hand, theoretical work has been indispensable in highlighting the assumptions and blind-spots embedded in the sort of 'close reading' practice alluded to above. I have tried to import these (often political) insights within a close reading practice.

The aim at all times is to be reader-friendly, using accessible language and poets whose works are generally available for further consultation. With readings of an individual poet's work, material is usually restricted to one of their published collections, so as to make it easier for readers to consult the full texts. Quotations are kept short, to ensure that they are acceptable under the disputed terms of the 'Fair Dealing' agreement (which provides an exception to the rights of copyright, for the purposes of criticism or review).

The book is intended for a broad range of readers and will succeed if it stimulates argument and discussion about the relevance of sex and gender in poetry. My wish is to stir things up rather than impose interpretations on poems that are, in the end, usually more subtle and flexible than any criticism can ever hope to be.

INTRODUCTION
POETRY AND CRITICISM:
THE CONTEMPORARY MOMENT

Undoubtedly gender does play an important part in the making
of any art, but art is art and to separate writings, paintings,
musical compositions, etc. into two sexes is to emphasise
values in them that are not art.[1]

Elizabeth Bishop, whose words open this introduction, resisted the
segregation of poetry on the basis of sex. Many of today's women
poets, who acknowledge her importance, also share her scepticism,
preferring to claim that poetry transcends sexual difference.[2]

Yet if women are unsure, men seem certain that there is something *different* about women poets' writing. In studies of
contemporary poetry published over the last two decades, the
women are often grouped together in a chapter of their own. For
example, the title of Alan Robinson's last chapter, devoted to women
poets, is 'Declarations of Independence: Some responses to feminism'.[3] In his discussion of four poets he focuses on their attitude
towards feminism and womanhood. In Robinson's view, women's
poetry is 'distinctively other than the masculine tradition in its
thematic concerns and point of view'. (p.163) In *his* survey of the
field, Peter Childs tries to avoid accusations of tokenism by having
one chapter on 'recent male anthologies' and another on 'recent
anthologies by women'.[4] But while the first chapter covers a broad
range of issues from Thatcherism to philosophy, the second takes
feminism as its central theme. Keith Tuma includes only one woman
in his series of 'brief readings' of British experimental poets, and

this reading—of Geraldine Monk—is substantially briefer than all the others. Tuma prefaces it thus:

> Pity poor Geraldine Monk, extracted here from a whole host of British women experimentalists—including Denise Riley, Wendy Mulford, Caroline Bergvall, Maggie O'Sullivan, Grace Lake, Paula Claire, Carlyle Reedy and Fiona Templeton— inevitably to be made to carry a discussion of the issues confronting feminist poetry in Britain. She might equally well be made to represent some of the possibilities of performance and performance writing.[5]

His use of the passive voice makes it sound as if he had nothing to do with the matter.

The same categorising operates in reviews too. While the grouping of women poets together *could* be used to positive effect—to foreground shared emphases, or highlight instances of dialogue and allusion between one poet and another—what usually happens, as in these examples, is that the focus falls exclusively on feminism, and the poems are discussed only in relation to 'issues' that the critic associates with feminism. (More often than not, moreover, feminism is assumed to entail an exclusive focus on women's oppression, and hostility towards men.) The dangers of this isolationist approach are obvious: it creates and sustains the impression that women poets' only subject is their womanhood; it also keeps gender-conscious critique firmly in one chapter, thus ensuring none of the men poets is explored with questions of sexual politics or gender in mind.

The alternative strategy, integration, is not necessarily more successful. Rejecting a separatist model, David Kennedy declares his intention to avoid 'consigning women poets to a literary ghetto and...perpetuating conceptions of poetry by women as a kind of cultural sideshow'.[6] But his book contains very little discussion of women poets' work. The angle he takes on topics effectively occludes gender difference. So, for example, his exploration of postmodernist poetics, despite quoting Linda Hutcheon's emphasis on its appeal to the 'excentric...those who are marginalized by a dominant ideology...[writers] working as they do from both inside and outside a culturally different and dominant context' (p.82), fails to include any women poets. Women apparently do not form part of this marginality, while three male white poets from the north of England do.[7] A similarly gender-blind definition of 'political' must account for the absence of women poets from Tom Paulin's *Faber Book of Political Verse*. R. P. Draper's ambitious survey volume, *An Introduction to Twentieth-century Poetry in English*, provides a fine example of how the inclusion of a chapter for the women can backfire. He includes a 23-page chapter, 'Women's Poetry', which discusses the work of Adrienne Rich, Sylvia Plath, Stevie Smith, Elizabeth Bishop, U. A. Fanthorpe, Carol Ann Duffy and Amy Clampitt. This is followed by two chapters (57 pages) devoted to 'Regional, National and Post-Colonial' poetries; despite sub-sections on Irish, Welsh, Scottish, Caribbean, Canadian and Australian poetry, only three women are mentioned throughout these sections.[8]

It is not surprising, then, that women express considerable ambivalence about the significance of their sex to their writing, when any emphasis of it so frequently produces such limited expectations of subject matter. Carol Ann Duffy has clearly felt her sex to be a handicap, implying constraint over her range as a poet (see chapter 2 for fuller discussion of this). Eavan Boland aims, ambitiously, to 'humanize femininity', thus attempting to overturn humanism's determinedly masculine conception of the subject.[9] It has even been suggested that younger women poets are reluctant to acknowledge the importance of women from the generation before them.[10]

But if this uneasy impasse is the situation today, profound changes have taken place since 1974, when North American poet and critic Louise Bernikow published the anthology *The World Split Open: Four Centuries of Women Poets in England and America, 1552–1950*.[11] She opened her introduction with a brief anecdote, describing the reaction of 'a venerable professor of English literature' when asked about women poets:

He: 'Women don't make good poets.'
I: 'Why not?'
He: 'Because women are good at accumulation of detail...'
He is holding his arms in front of his body, forming a circle with them. He has shaped a pregnant belly.

'...and not at the sharp, thrusting...'
He is making sharp, thrusting motions with one of his arms.
'...sensibility that is required for good poetry.'
This is the sort of person who has written literary history. (p.3)

Bernikow goes on to outline the main reasons for the disappearance and neglect of women poets' writing, in an essay that
remains one of the best introductions to this area. The criteria she
uses for her selection are significant. She chooses not the most
successful poems, but

[t]he poems that are not often printed, the poems on being a
woman, the poems on traditionally 'unfeminine' subjects, the
poems that sometimes don't quite make it on purely esthetic
grounds, whatever those grounds are, but make attempts that
are interesting and often revolutionary. (p.xxi)

She includes poems by Queen Victoria and by suffragettes impris-
oned in Holloway, as well as a generous selection of Blues singers
(including Bessie Smith and Ida Cox) and songs from American mill-
and mine-workers. Her anthology challenges the much narrower
conventional versions of poetic tradition in England and America:
'The native poetic traditions of America are not necessarily those
that emerge from the pages of the *Atlantic Monthly* or *Poetry*
magazine, nor from the presses of book-publishing houses.' (p.47)
    As this quotation—and the selection of poems—indicates, it
somehow proved easier to open up American poetic tradition. In
Britain in 1974 Elizabeth Jennings, Kathleen Raine and Laura
Riding Jackson were the only living women poets with any recognition; perhaps not coincidentally—the latter two had very firm
views about the innate inferiority of female poets.[12] Poetry happened
in universities; aspiring young poets gathered under the tutelage of
an older, established male figurehead, who acted as patron and
champion. Women were just not part of this scene. Eavan Boland
has described her own experiences as a would-be poet at Trinity
College, Dublin, in the mid-1960s. She remembers that 'there were
no women poets, old or young, past or present in my immediate
environment.'[13] When she had a baby, she discovered not only that

she was no longer seen by others as a writer but as a wife and mother, but also that the daily realities of her life, which she felt moved to write about, were not considered appropriate material for poetry. Domesticity was not a fit subject for the genre, which was, after all, one of the highest art forms. Its magnificent tradition and arcane rules ensured that only the most determined embarked on such a challenging undertaking. Yet at precisely the same time Boland was dutifully practising the shape and tone of the model 'patriarchal poem'(p.48), startling developments were taking place in Britain. The threesome that later became known as the Liverpool poets (Adrian Henri, Roger McGough, Brian Patten) was attracting unprecedented numbers to their readings, and large-scale public poetry events like the Poetry Olympics and Poetry International, which brought politics into the picture, were being planned. But there was almost no overlap between this emergent, accessible, popular, often political poetry and the literary intellectual strain. Poets like Seamus Heaney and Ted Hughes did not participate in these lively events. And while the accessible, political work generated far more popular interest and book sales, the literary, intellectual tradition continued to wield far greater influence as the 'purer' form, bolstered by prestigious and powerful institutions like Faber and Faber and Oxbridge. This is still the case today.

The parallel existence of two different versions of 'poetry' finds its corollary in the general public's views about the genre. As Helen Carr has commented,

> Poetry is regarded in our culture in strikingly contradictory ways, and those contradictions are intimately bound up with gender. Poetry is seen both as a prestigious, elite and esoteric form, and as a private, intimate, intensely subjective one. And whilst considered in the former way women may feel intimidated, in the latter, they (and less privileged men) can regard poetry as a place in which they are enfranchised.[14]

Academic critique of poetry does its best to avoid any mention of emotion. Partly this is because emotion is suspect in these days of 'sophisticated' theoreticised approaches to literature;[15] partly, it is because poetry threatens to unravel the carefully constructed objectivity of literary studies. Once you admit the part played by subjectivity it becomes impossible to present your argument with academic authority. This, coupled with copyright law which can make it prohibitively expensive to quote from some poems, results in an odd critical field. To start with, there is not much criticism available. Many are put off by the impossibility of matching the techniques of exegesis they have been taught to their experience of reading poems; others are put off by the fear of arcane rules about metrics, syllabics and 'truncated dactylic dimeters'.[16] (As, traditionally, one of the highest art forms, often likened to religion, it is not implausible to draw a comparison between poetry critics and priests. As privileged interpreters, neither are above using esoteric language to keep out the riff-raff.) Particularly during the last decade, academic criticism has been preoccupied with postmodernism's influence over poetry. The focus is invariably on the literary 'pure' strain, rather than the more popular tradition, now swelled by the virtuoso performance work of a number of younger poets. Within the academy, the most widely discussed poetry is the long-neglected experimental writing that is related to the L-A-N-G-U-A-G-E poets in North America, and exists mainly on the web, and in private publications or published by small presses. It seems likely this is because the work responds well to—indeed, is often produced in reaction to—post-Structuralist theoretical critiques. As Suzanne Juhasz suggested back in 1977, 'the poem that is thought of as "really poetry" is usually the work that responds well to criticism.'[17] Ironically, while the critical approaches currently in favour are preoccupied with the complex construction of the *subject*, they pay little attention to the *critic's* subjectivity.

Lyric poetry is inevitably problematic in a climate such as this, and the revered lyric tradition of English poetry may well account for the continuing separation between popular and elite poetry, which characterises the British poetry world. Lyric poetry is a strange hybrid; existing on a crepuscular boundary between private and public worlds, its roots lie in the personal, but it transforms this originary matter, and then offers it up to the world at large. John Sutherland encapsulates its hybrid nature by referring to poetry's 'published privacies'.[18] The clarity of the public/private division has been eroded in recent years; to take one example, the kind of domestic material to which the genre seemed hostile in the 1960s now features regularly in poetry by both men and women. Because of the continuing influence of Romantic conceptions of the poet as sagacious man apart, and because of its status as high art, poetry is also public discourse, granted the authority and *gravitas* reserved for society's most revered forms of speech: alongside religious and legal discourse. The Victorian gendering of the public sphere as male, and the private as female, still polices the boundaries, so that male poets' ventures into domestic landscapes carry different associations and produce very different effects.

However much academics emphasise postmodernism, it is still a minority interest beside entrenched beliefs about humanist and Romantic ideologies, both of which continue to exert a profound influence over attitudes and expectations about poetry in Britain. The lyric's preoccupation with individual human experience allies it with a humanist world view, however much that 'individual' in question may be hedged round with quotation marks and irony. But humanist conceptions of the subject, which have shaped our notions of the literary subject, are determinedly masculine. This means that women face particular problems when they attempt to create versions of the subject that convey aspects of experience or perspectives allied to *female* subjectivity. Many find it difficult to establish sufficiently authoritative female subjects within a tradition that treats femaleness as aberrant, and views its very specificity as, in itself, signalling the limits of its relevance. Such attitudes make it extremely difficult to create a female lyric voice whose authority is accepted as transcending its femaleness to speak of general insights or truths.

It was during the Romantic period that a number of changes took place relating to ideas about the poet. Christine Battersby has claimed that, prior to this, there was no assumption that the sublime was restricted to male writers.[19] Elisabeth Bronfen has traced significant shifts in conceptions of the muse to the same period: previously a supernatural visitant, communicating through the poet—who was merely her vessel—it was the Romantics who transformed the idea of the muse into her physical embodiment as a woman whose presence and beauty inspires the poet.[20] The effect of such developments continues to resonate.

THE POETRY ESTABLISHMENT

Some women poets' work can be characterised as accessible or popular and others literary or intellectual. But the work of *feminist critics* writing on women poets tends to have little contact with mainstream poetry criticism, which, in its turn, seems almost untouched by feminist thought. This has implications for the future critical reputations of today's women poets. What those who have worked to retrieve women's literary texts from contemporary obscurity discover is that, in the writers' lifetimes, they were well known, well received, even well networked.[21] However popular and respected during their lifetimes, women poets are particularly prone to fall through the net of literary history.[22]

That the feminist critics who produce valuable work on contemporary women poets have little contact with those individuals and institutions who devote their attention to pure, literary, intellectual poetry, with a capital P, is hardly surprising. The 'poetry establishment' is composed of powerful individuals, although it is not easy to show exactly how it exerts such power. For years writers from the north of Britain used to complain at the Oxbridge mafia's stranglehold on poetry publishing. To give one recent example, Middlesbrough-based poet and editor Andy Croft delivered an attack on the establishment's condescension towards 'amateur' poets:

> Visitors are not always welcome in the Republic of Poetry, its citizens are treated as subjects and its borders are heavily policed....This is a culture happy to reproduce itself, effortlessly recycling the self-confirming judgements of publishers and the London prize-giving circuit, as it establishes the criteria which set 'professional' poets apart from their audience.[23]

Northern-based poets are not the only ones to feel excluded. Black British poets get little attention from this establishment, and performance work is largely ignored, despite the large audiences it attracts. Humorous poetry like that of John Hegley generates little or no critical discussion; nor do poems that have their roots in oral tradition, whether ballads, lullabies, folksongs or the tales descended from west-African griots (travelling poets who circulate poems and stories orally). So it is not only women whose work is ignored by this powerful group. Nor is it that *all* women are excluded; as Rebecca O'Rourke observed in 1990,

> Women, like black and working-class writers, are not so much denied excellence as mediocrity; we must be geniuses or nothing. The playgrounds of poetry, its teething rings and testing grounds are closed to us, swamped with men and boys of indifferent talents.[24]

The establishment's approach to poetry may be characterised by the heavy emphasis it places upon literary tradition, as though, in order to be worthy of the name, poetry must address itself to the past; must engage with, allude to, answer or quarrel with, the poets of the past. This establishes a self-replicating tradition which, to a degree, also determines appropriate subject matter and discourse. Such an approach effectively guarantees the centrality of a particular tradition: shoring it up by co-opting each new generation into its sphere of influence. This emphasis on allusion and internal dialogue may serve quite conservative, conservationist ends. Where routes to reputation are as narrow as in the world of poetry, if those in influential positions remain wedded to this tradition, they are poorly equipped to understand or appreciate poetry that takes different traditions and different models as its point of reference. Such poetry remains, therefore, outside the establishment. This is fine in so far as it goes—the performance promoters *Apples & Snakes* don't need the approval of the editors of *P. N. Review*—but to secure a place in literary history, it is still necessary to win the respect of key individuals.

However, there are signs of change within the academic critical establishment, and within the mainstream poetry world: the tensions were visible during discussions about who (if anyone) should become Poet Laureate on the death of Ted Hughes.[25] The unquestioned dominance of liberal-humanist approaches has recently given way to an interest in the impact of postmodernism. But any overtly politicised critique is still rare, as are thematic studies that foreground content. Literary tradition and philosophy dominate as the favoured emphases. And women poets continue to generate little criticism at all.

Part of the explanation lies in the different reading interests of men and women who do not, on the whole, read the same books. While this is obvious to publishers' marketing departments and to general readers, it is not a popular idea in academic circles. And when it comes to 'literature', critics often try to disguise this fact by claiming that 'great' literature should appeal to, and be read by, all.[26]

In the case of poetry, special prohibitions have operated: until the twentieth century, women were permitted to write on certain acceptable subjects—namely, love and religion.[27] Louise Bernikow made the following blunt claims in 1974:

> Writing about 'other' subjects has always meant deep trouble. The gap between what interests women and what interests men has locked women poets into a paralyzing contradiction from which some have emerged and to which others have succumbed. Women's lives bore men. The reality of those lives, especially the embarrassing subject of women's bodies, frightens men. Male approval, the condition of a poet's survival, is withheld when a woman shapes her poetry from the very material that contradicts and threatens male reality.[28]

One of the things I hope to investigate in what follows is whether such a depressing claim still holds true. Do men read women poets?

Certainly, examination of the ratio of male-to-female poets on publishers' lists indicates that women are in the minority. In 1990 Rebecca O'Rourke announced her intention 'to bring an abacus into the hushed house of poetry and count women, and women's poems and women's concerns'.[29] The results of her enquiry are reproduced here in table 1.

Debbie Taylor's research, conducted in 2000, indicates a small increase in the number of women.[30] I have converted these statistics to a pie chart, illustrated in table 2.

It is worth noting that, amidst all the talk of the current ubiquity of women poets, even the publisher with the best showing still has less than half of its publications by women.

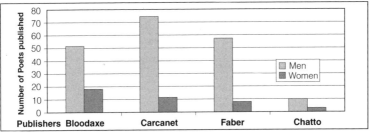

Table 1 – Ratios of male and female poets published (1990 figures)

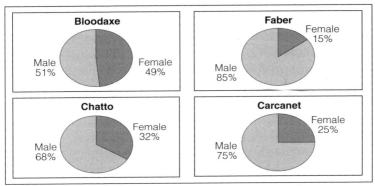

Table 2 – Ratios of male and female poets (2000 figures)

Of equal concern is the consistent under-representation of women poets in anthologies. O'Rourke also trawled through anthologies published in the 1970s and 1980s.[31] As my graph below illustrates, anthologies published in the 1990s show little change.

These later anthologies, published at the dawn of the new century, clearly stake their claims to be the authoritative record of twentieth-century poetry, so their selections are likely to determine future literary history.

It is true that today there *are* several high-profile women poets in Britain, but where is the discussion of their work? If the poetry of these women is so noticeable, what effects is it having? A look in published studies of contemporary poetry in the British Isles gives few answers; the questions are not even asked. Despite evident success in winning access to publication, even in the arguable achievement of becoming big names, if women's poetry is to survive, the work needs to be discussed. Literary criticism shapes canons. Academics and teachers play a large part in determining

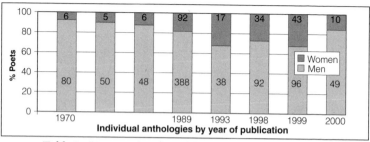

Table 3 – Ratios of male and female poets in anthologies

what gets read and taught, hence what secures a place in literary history. The lack of accessible secondary material acts as a major disincentive for teachers who would like to use particular poems or poets in classroom. If women poets do not get included in the 'general' analyses, overviews, and anthologies used in schools and universities, they will slip out of sight, and be forgotten until the next wave of female anger gathers and launches another period of recovery work. Currently women poets' writing merits a separate chapter, an easily accommodated tributary, while the main river flows on undisturbed. The lack of published criticism has a further damaging effect: it prevents the emergence of contexts within which the broader resonances of their work might emerge. Only when we have developed such a context will it be possible to identify the existence of subtle dialogues or intertextual references between these poets, so long the decisive feature of critically successful poetry.

This study of contemporary poetry includes both male and female poets. Until recently, the assumption has persisted that gender only matters to *women*; that it only makes a difference to *women's writing*. As thinkers like Luce Irigaray have demonstrated, this happens because western culture is gender blind: there is no recognition of sexual difference.[32] In Britain, the dominant view is still that 'genuine' poetry transcends gender, but there is growing recognition of differences between the way men and women conceive the role of the poet. Don Paterson acknowledges that the myths that sustain him are quintessentially male, and suggests that those that nurture women poets are different but, disappointingly, he shies away from attempting to define them.[33] Selima Hill hazards the generalisation that men poets are more concerned with 'some kind of agenda' than their female counterparts.[34] 'Poets needs must be / Or men or women—more's the pity,' as Elizabeth Barrett Browning's young poet Aurora Leigh asserts in the course of her spirited assertion of her right to aspire to be one.[35] Yet her view is out of step with the current climate, probably because of a combination of the continuing dominance of liberal humanist approaches and the assumption that, if a poet defines herself as a *woman* poet, her sex will delineate her subject matter in a constricting manner. Gender plays a role in *all* poetry, regardless of the sex of its author, and regardless of its content. This is because of the *process of reading poetry*: what happens as a reader interacts with a poem, and the part gender plays in this (see pp.31–5 and pp.45–8 for a full discussion of this).

GENDER AND POETRY: THE DEBATES SO FAR

There has been far less feminist work on poetry than on prose fiction, drama, life-writing or, indeed, any other literary genre, and North American academics have produced most of what exists. Initial activity centred on recovery work: the 1970s saw the compilation of many anthologies which attempted to uncover a female tradition in poetry. Four years after Bernikow's publication, *The Penguin Book of Women Poets*[36] attempted what now seems a foolhardy enterprise, seeking to represent women poets from across the world, from the earliest known written texts through to present-day writers. There was a spate of translations, as well as a number of politically motivated collections of contemporary work, prioritising polemical writing by feminists.

Paralleling this activity, scholars began to produce critiques of previously neglected women poets. Cora Kaplan's *Salt and Bitter and Good* appeared in 1975; Sandra Gilbert and Susan Gubar published *Shakespeare's Sisters* in 1979.[37] In 1976, *Naked and Fiery Forms*, Suzanne Juhasz's innovative delineation of what she named 'a new tradition—one that speaks in the voice of women, rather than in a pseudo-male or neuter voice'—appeared.[38] Chapters were devoted to Emily Dickinson, Marianne Moore, Denise Levertov, Sylvia Plath, Anne Sexton, Gwendolyn Brooks,

Nikki Giovanni, Alta and Adrienne Rich. Juhasz identified the situation of the woman poet as 'a double-bind...of conflict and strain. For the words "woman" and 'poet' denote opposite and contradictory qualities and roles.' (p.1) Alicia Suskin Ostriker's 1986 publication, *Stealing the Language: The Emergence of Women's Poetry in America*, concentrated on poetry since 1960, adopting a thematic focus that foregrounded the content of the poems. She argued that recent women's poetry subverted the masculine tradition. Emphasising women's cultural marginality, and drawing on the ideas of feminist philosophers, psychologists and sexologists, Ostriker's approach espoused a binary, oppositional model; she claimed that 'a gynocentric poetics is necessarily adversarial.'[39] Where, for example, the masculine tradition of love poetry depicts love as a conquest, she argues that women's love poetry enacts a woman-centred erotics that celebrates '[m]utuality, continuity, connection, identification, touch' (p.165); where patriarchal metaphysics privileges mind and spirit over the body, women poets accept no such hierarchy; their 'revisionist mythmaking' transforms classical stories, challenging the values they have been supposed to embody, rejecting the public/private distinction they espouse, and displaying an irreverent, questioning attitude to these hallowed sources.

Both studies were extremely influential; many more followed.[40] And in stark contrast to the situation in Britain, several important poets figured amongst the most high-profile members of the women's movement: Audre Lorde, Adrienne Rich, Judy Grahn, Marge Piercy, Alice Walker, Maya Angelou. Commenting on the contrast with Britain, where feminist interventions in poetry had much less impact, Claire Buck has suggested that the Vietnam War protests and the Civil Rights movements had already prepared the way for politicised poetry in America:

> There is an identifiable mainstream tradition of poetry allied to democratic ideals in the United States that could underwrite the claim that poetry was the natural language of a radical politics.[41]

She also points out that African-American poets like June Jordan drew upon international examples of politically active poets, individuals like Pablo Neruda, Gabriela Mistral, Langston Hughes and Edward Brathwaite. With so many models available:

> The presence of an alternative democratic tradition meant that the assertion of a meaningful cultural role for poetry in the US women's movement did not need to be as qualified and hedged by the consciousness of its elitist, high-culture value, in the way that it did in Britain. (p.101)

As her comments imply, the situation was (as it remains) different in Britain. Perhaps the most striking evidence of this is the lack of innovative critical material to be published in the UK. While production of anthologies kept pace with that in the United States, much less 'home-grown' criticism appeared; instead, the 1980s saw the reprinting of American work in Britain.

One of the earliest pieces of research in Britain was a paper delivered by Cora Kaplan (herself an American) at a London conference on patriarchy in 1976. It was published ten years later, in a collection of her work, *Sea Changes: Culture and Feminism*.[42] Kaplan stressed poetry's status as an elite discourse and, as such, one of those areas of language use like medicine and law, to which access was strictly guarded—and even prohibited to women. She used Lacan's theory of the mirror phase to explain how women discover themselves excluded from such high discourse, and then went on to consider how women poets' awareness of the insecurity and illegitimacy of their position marked their poetry in the Romantic period. In her use of psychoanalytic theory, her attentiveness to the vital importance of female subjectivity for the lyric poet and her emphasis on the intimate interconnections between culture and poetry, the article was well ahead of its time: 'We must re-understand poetry by introducing gender of the poet and the speaker as crucial categories which deny it a universalising suturing place in high culture' (p.92) Kaplan concludes; 27 years later, much of this still remains to be done.

Then, in 1987, Jan Montefiore's *Feminism and Poetry: Language, Experience, Identity in Women's Writing* was published.[43] As virtually the only book-length analysis of the area, it was enormously influential and was revised and reprinted in 1994, with a chapter added on feminism and postcolonial poetry. It has just been reissued again in a third edition. Montefiore adopts a longer historical perspective than her American counterparts; she includes discussion of Christina Rossetti and Edna St Vincent Millay and—in the revised 1994 edition—Mary Leapor and Phillis Wheatley. As will be clear from these names, she includes both British and American poets. Montefiore is less interested in the cultural contexts and work of poems, and more focused on *literary* tradition. She is critical of attempts to dismiss 'masculine thought and masculine tradition' (1994, p.4), a stance she associates with radical feminist critics. She cautions against assuming poetry to be the direct communication of experience: 'The question which such an assumption of the primacy of female experience in women's poems avoids asking is: What makes a poem different from autobiography, fictionalized or otherwise?' (1994, p.6) A lot of space is devoted to thorough, lucid theoretical expositions of the ideas of those who became known as 'the French feminists'—Kristeva, Irigaray and Cixous. There is a chapter on psychoanalysis and the love sonnet, and another that searches for evidence of Luce Irigaray's 'female Imaginary' in women poets. But there is a strange mismatch between Montefiore's aesthetic and critical framework—in which literary tradition is the central reference point—and these theoretical approaches. She sets out to find something completely different, 'purely female' (1994, p.178) in women's poetry, but discovers what she has stated at the outset: women poets have engaged with masculine poetic tradition. Thus she concludes that:

> A poetry of purely female identity is not…a really viable possibility….the examples of women's poetry which ought to correspond with Imaginary femaleness always turn out, when looked at closely, to be engaged with the same masculine language or symbolism which they are supposed to transcend. (1994, pp.178–9)

This is a methodological problem: Montefiore accepts the aesthetics of mainstream literary tradition, just as she asserts the unavoidable centrality of that tradition. With both firmly in place, she sets out to examine ways in which women's poetry is different: 'Defining a feminist poetics means, primarily, understanding the significance of women's poetry' she declares at the outset (1994, p.1), but that significance can only—according to her terms and approach—be understood *in relation to* the mainstream, masculine poetic tradition. To look for a women's tradition, or a purely female Imaginary, seems a strangely Utopian quest, since Irigaray herself (writing after 1970) suggests that we still lack a female Imaginary and urges women to create representations of mother/daughter relationships in an effort to alter this disabling absence. In the light of this, it seems odd to seek evidence of it in the work of women writers who predate Irigaray.[44]

Liz Yorke's book, *Impertinent Voices: Subversive Strategies in Contemporary Women's Poetry*, was published in 1991. Yorke's study reads Sylvia Plath, HD, Adrienne Rich and Audre Lorde through the ideas of Julia Kristeva, Hélène Cixous and Luce Irigaray. In these women's poems she finds evidence of their preoccupation with feminist revisionist myth-making, and an attempt to create a female Symbolic. Yorke tries to bring her concern for material and social reality alongside her interest in French poststructuralist theory, but the two sit uneasily together; as a result, the way she employs the term 'the female Symbolic' sometimes seems indistinguishable from the practice of women articulating previously unmentioned experiences. In her chapter on Plath, Yorke focuses on Plath's struggle to create an identity as female poet, and emphasises the vital importance of her relationship to her mother, placing this alongside psychoanalytic developmental theories that posit the fragmented, plural self as norm. Plath's writing 'continually works towards constructing a polyvalent identity, one which the poet herself knew to be radically traversed, multiform and fragmented'.[45] As this illustration suggests, the language of Yorke's study is highly specialised. Important for its ambitious attempt to show how these difficult philosophical ideas can be applied to twentieth-century women poets, the book does tend to take these ideas as unassailable truths.

While it is easy, in retrospect, to identify limitations in Montefiore and Yorke's approaches, it is important not to underestimate the inspiring impact of these books. *Feminism and Poetry*, in particular, appeared at a time when there was no discussion (in Britain) of the effects of feminist ideas on contemporary women poets; reprintings testify to its enduring importance.

TRICKY ENTANGLEMENTS: FEMINISM, WOMEN AND POETRY

Through the late 1980s and early 1990s publishers continued to commission new anthologies of poetry by women.[46] The visibility of women as poets provoked some strong reactions, often from well-established women poets who were unhappy at being associated with work they considered to be 'amateur' and poorly crafted.[47] Because it was aimed at female readers, this work was sometimes labelled feminist poetry, even though the anthologies themselves rarely used the phrase. One exception is the collection, *One Foot on the Mountain: An Anthology of British Feminist Poetry 1969–1979*, from the independent Onlywomen Press, which seemed to have a particularly powerful impact, judging by the vociferous objections that followed. The book's editor, Lillian Mohin, was unusual in the degree to which she fused her artistic and political commitments. The anthology's defiant introduction claims that feminists are creating a new kind of poetry: 'We have begun to do really new work, feminist work, with this form [poetry] and, by doing so, are redefining poetry as well.'[48] But many poets objected to what they experienced as a demand from feminists to produce feminist poetry. Eavan Boland rejected the 'powerful prescriptions' that feminism had begun to lay on writing by women, and urged women to resist 'separatist ideology' and 'the gradual emphasis on the appropriate subject matter and the correct feelings'.[49] A similar resistance to the assertion of a political agenda within the realm of literary creativity accounts for the cautious tones adopted by Fleur Adcock and Carol Rumens in their introductions to anthologies of women poets for Faber and Chatto respectively. Critic Sally Minogue published 'Prescriptions and Proscriptions', a lengthy rebuttal of the requirement for feminist poetry.[50] A few writers took a more relaxed attitude. Michèle Roberts spoke of her strategy of sending her angry poems to *Spare*

Rib and sneaking the soft lyrical ones off to *Country Living*.[51]

It is not at all clear from where these strictures were perceived as coming. It now seems as though the influence of *One Foot on the Mountain* and the few collections like it was vastly overestimated. Poet Sylvia Kantaris became so irritated by critics' derogatory references to what she labelled 'The Hysterical Women's Movement' that she wrote to *The Times Literary Supplement* challenging readers to come up with the names of some of these poets who were so often collectively condemned as what she termed 'post-Plath hysterics' and 'muscular harpies of the Adrienne Rich school'. In the debate that followed, no-one successfully refuted her claim that the phenomenon was a largely fictional invention.[52]

While few poets have ever been happy with the description, 'feminist poet', one or two critics have used the term 'feminist poetry'. Sara Mills conducted an experiment into readers' responses to what she called a 'feminist poem', basing her definition on her interpretation of the poem's subject matter and content (menstruation, and attitudes to pregnancy) (see pp.46–7 for further discussion of this essay). Jan Montefiore also applies the term because of content: she describes a poem by Alison Fell as 'feminist' ('however unobtrusively', 1994, p.18) because its account of a young girl making flower baskets employs floral imagery without invoking the traditional poetic associations between female sexuality and flowers, and because it 'represents itself as part of women's culture of making, sharing and enjoying, in which the process of creation is valued more than the artefact'. (1994, p.19) As this might suggest, definitions on the basis of individual interpretation are tricky, since not all readers will agree with this reading of the poem. Moreover, the usefulness of the terminology is questionable. Describing a poem as 'feminist' tends to fix its meaning. While there *are* many excellent poems whose purpose is to deliver a pithy, sharp, witty or angry political point, the 'aims' of feminism are clearcut in a way that the 'aims' of a poem rarely are.

'Women and poetry' is a more productive coupling than 'feminist poetry'. The *Kicking Daffodils: Women and Poetry* festival conferences of 1994 and 1997 used that clumsy subtitle in recognition of the complexity and potential variousness of the relationships between two such unwieldy generalised groups. Unless used within a specific context, 'women's poetry' implies a uniformity that is derogatory and inaccurate; it is as meaningless as the term 'men's poetry' would be. Thirty years ago, the neglect of women writers was so widespread that the phrase was politically useful, since it was a way of claiming visibility. But its shortcomings now outweigh its usefulness: not only does it collapse differences between women, it also encourages comparison of women poets with men poets, as though there is some fundamental opposition between them. In such a comparison, men emerge as standard, normal subjects against which women's 'difference' is measured. In the phrase 'women and poetry', that *and* keeps the terms independent of one another, but introduces the idea of a putative relationship. It is because there are such varied possible configurations, so many different kinds of women, and poem, that this openness is vital. The foregrounding of gender does not necessitate sameness between members of one biological sex.

Poets and critics alike have long recognised a fundamental conflict between the roles implied by the two terms 'woman' and 'poet'. This was Suzanne Juhasz' starting-point in her 1976 study, *Naked and Fiery Forms*, discussed above (p.13). Adrienne Rich identified the same dilemma in her celebrated essay 'When We Dead Awaken: Writing as Re-Vision', in which she described the clash experienced by a woman trying to be both. She argued that the 'energy of relation', central to womanhood, was in direct tension with the 'energy of creation'; where the former demanded continual attentiveness to the needs of others, the latter required the artist's complete attention and surrender.[53] Eavan Boland made a similar point, and claimed that this 'profound fracture between her sense of the obligations of her womanhood—to nourish the lives of others—and the shadowy, more self-involved demands of her gift' ultimately meant that women were far less likely to make the leap from saying, 'I write poetry' to the more confident, wholehearted commitment, 'I am a poet.'[54] Both Rich and Boland also suggested that poetry had neglected huge swathes of human experience that were rich in poetic potential: these experiences were of female lives. Most obviously, Boland referred to female experiences of childbirth and mothering, but, more subversively, the suggestion was there that perspectives are affected by gender; that the world—any and every aspect of it—may look and feel different through a woman's experience. Poetry had, thus far, grown almost exclusively out of male experiences. Rich declared that '[t]he creative energy of patriarchy is fast running out' (p.40); in characteristically less confrontational terms, Boland suggested that 'at this particular time [...] women have a destiny in the form'. (p.49) Where Rich focused, in keeping with 1970s' feminist concerns, on women's social roles and socialisation, Boland (in the mid-1980s) was more excited by her awareness of the discovery of vast realms of pristine experience available to her as poet.

In recent years, the anti-feminist backlash has had a startling effect on these questions of terminology. While a Masters course on W. B. Yeats, T. S. Eliot, W.H. Auden, Philip Larkin, Ted Hughes and Seamus Heaney would be considered perfectly acceptable as a comprehensive introduction to 'Twentieth Century Poetry', a course on 'Twentieth Century Women Poets' is assumed to be partial, partisan and 'feminist', simply by virtue of the fact that it focuses on women.[55] The phrase 'women poets' seems to have become synonymous with assumptions of feminism, which in turn is used as shorthand for 'partial, and ideologically-narrow'. Anne Stevenson dismisses 'any course or category that defines itself as Women's Poetry', continuing:

> How can a multiplicity of jostling, incongruous, historically produced texts be bundled up under a gendered and, especially in our time, emotively pressured appellation?[56]

It is the same assumption at work: that a course concentrating on women writers must be oversimplified and is bound to prioritise ideological concerns over and above those of literary history or style. The idea that a *focus* on women might bring about new perspectives from which to view literary tradition, might lead to recognition of the need to redefine certain time-honoured categories, might force review of the prevailing aesthetic, or version of literary periodisation, seems to have been lost. Rather than writing of 'feminist poetry' it is more productive and accurate to speak of a *feminist critical practice* (see pp.29–33 below).

GENDER AND POETIC FORM

Traditional poetic forms are back in fashion. This phenomenon appears to have followed on from male poets' virtuoso displays of formal skill, exemplified by Simon Armitage and Glyn Maxwell (see chapters 1 and 5 for further discussion of these poets). Women poets make an effort to distinguish themselves from what Rumens memorably described as the 'noisy amateurs',[57] by their mastery of sonnets and *villanelles*.[58] There is a widespread assumption that feminism demanded the abandonment of form in poetry. References are made to the feminists of the 1970s and 1980s who rejected poetic form as inherently oppressive. Poet Mimi Khalvati speaks of 'the seventies, when traditional forms were considered patriarchal';[59] critic Romana Huk refers to familiar 'old arguments' that assume 'traditional forms' enslavement to patriarchal poetry'.[60] But when the statements of earlier women poets are examined closely, it becomes clear that it was not poetic forms *per se* which they identified as problematic. In her account, Adrienne Rich described her gradual realisation that she could abandon the formal detachment of her early poems which, 'like asbestos gloves...allowed me to handle materials I couldn't pick up bare-handed'.[61] This is a question of tone—the legacy of Eliot's advocacy of impersonality—more than of form. Conventional forms had served their purpose; they had enabled her to remain distanced from difficult material; but she reached a point at which that very distance in itself became a handicap. As her confidence and skill grew, she found she was able to treat female experience more directly, without the shield of form; in so doing—and in breaking new ground for poetry—she also broke with the tighter, traditional forms of her earlier work. But Rich is not saying that poetic form prevented her from expressing what she wished to express; she is describing how difficult it was to reach a point at which female experience felt admissible in poetry. Eavan Boland recounts a similarly slow realisation that poetic tradition did not seem to validate or include women's lives, instead mythologising or objectifying women. Again, it was the use made of material, not poetic form, that she identified as the problem. The forms she inherited were not, of themselves, constraining, but they felt secondhand to her, while her taboo-breaking collection *In Her Own Image* employed free verse forms as part of their break with her past, and poetry's past.[62] Where Bernikow's parodic English professor insisted that women are biologically ill-equipped for the 'sharp, thrusting' motions of poetic art (see above, p.4), Lillian Mohin has claimed that it is the very form of poetry that makes women so ideally suited to the genre:

> Poetry, with its tradition of concentrated insights, its brevity of form, is an ideal vehicle for the kind of politics we propose....The nature of most women's lives...makes any written work more likely to come out in a short form, as we snatch moments from what we are supposed to be doing as mothers, as wives, as workers at the bottom of the heap. Poetry has traditionally been the place to state condensed and particular perceptions which elsewhere would be called mad or perhaps banal.[63]

So there is nothing inherently obstructive to women about conventional poetic forms. What may exert a problematic influence is the history of the uses to which such forms have been put: the examples of (almost invariably male) predecessors. Each form carries its own history, composed of the most successful examples of its use; this is part of what today's poets engage with when they use one of these established forms. But, as Marilyn Hacker's erotic lesbian sonnet sequence *Love, Death and the Changing of the Seasons* shows, poetic form is elastic, can be stretched to tackle whatever material the poet chooses.[64]

Some men poets' accounts of their attitudes raise intriguing possibilities about masculinity and poetic form. Tony Harrison has described his acquisition of formal virtuosity in terms that link it to expectations about his gender:

> The idea of becoming a master of something, of learning skills, was very important to me, and partly to show off to *them*....But also I wanted it to be real work—in the sense that my father's work was real work.[65]

Don Paterson suggests that he invokes the challenge of difficult forms when he feels inadequate or guilty about what he has written. He discusses the composition of 'Mooncalf', a short poem whose subject matter he calls 'guilt-inducing':

> When I wrote it down, I simply couldn't live with it or myself, so I recast it in four nine-line pentameter stanzas with the daftest rhyme scheme I could devise. Somehow the sheer labour and grief of trying to get it to sound natural had the effect of making me feel less guilty about the subject.[66]

It may well be that men poets—for reasons related to the ways in which masculinity is configured—respond enthusiastically to the cerebral and technical challenges of poetic form.

Rhythm and rhyme present less of an issue in relation to gender, although the terminology of 'masculine' and 'feminine' rhymes—the latter gentler and weaker—certainly carries gender ideology. These terms have now been replaced with the more neutral one- and two-syllable rhyme, although some (including Seamus Heaney) still use the old-fashioned terms.[67]

Punctuation, lineation and syntax would appear to be unconnected to gender, although David Brooks has suggested otherwise. During his work as a poetry editor in Australia, Brooks found that he could identify the sex of the poet from the text:

> [t]he poems... I could identify as having been written by a woman appeared to me to be more eccentric and disjunctive in style, less concerned to elaborate a distinct narrative or discursive line than to present the *Gestalt* of an experience or emotion in images that were, if not actually contradictory, often tangential to what I tried to identify as a central concern.[68]

His explanation for the popularity of this deliberately disruptive syntax amongst women poets is cultural rather than biological:

> If one gender seems more than the other to be the vehicle of semiotic eruption—if one more than the other seems to be the medium by which the language tries to right [write] itself—it may simply be because those who are so long denied a voice

become, ultimately, the repository not only of all that is not allowed to be voiced but of all proscribed ways of saying. (p.77)

His argument does not take account of the relevance of Modernist and post-modern influences, but it provides another illustration of a male writer who claims to detect a distinct difference between male and female poets' style, which is where this introduction began.

CHALLENGING THE DOMINANT AESTHETIC

While very few book-length studies of women and poetry have appeared in Britain, there has been plenty of related activity and much important recovery work has taken place.[69] The general enthusiasm for experimental or Language poetry has produced new critiques of neglected Modernist writers Mina Loy and Gertrude Stein. A volume of essays on Elizabeth Bishop is under preparation.[70] *Kicking Daffodils: Essays on Twentieth Century Women Poets* gives some sense of the variety of current approaches and emphases, and a special issue of the journal *Feminist Review*, in 1999, was devoted to contemporary women poets in Britain.[71] Countless PhDs are being completed, suggesting there is interesting work in the pipeline. Collections of interviews with women poets have been published, and poets feature significantly in the various creative-writing guidebooks that have appeared over the last few decades.[72] Most recently, *Contemporary Women's Poetry: Reading/Writing/Practice* offers an innovative mixture of critical essays and contributions from poets on aspects of their craft.[73]

Some of the most stimulating critical material is that produced by writers who are themselves poets, such as Vicki Feaver and Deryn Rees-Jones.[74] This helps to clarify the *process* of reading lyric poetry, and how gender participates in that process. University academics have been trained in the importance of objectivity and are reluctant to challenge the aesthetic and evaluative norms that underlie critical frameworks; futhermore, their work has tended to be more theoretically oriented over the last decades. To cite one example: Montefiore assumes, in a section of her book titled 'The question of bad poetry' that we all know, and agree, what a 'bad' poem looks like. She criticises the poetry in *Scars Upon My Heart* (a collection of poems by women written during the First World War) for its ideological chauvinism and its literary clichés—in other words, on both political and aesthetic grounds, but without differentiating between the two. The offensiveness of the patriotic sentiment expressed in these poems is portrayed as an aspect of their weakness. In just this way, aesthetic judgements often carry political import which remains hidden, just as each critical methodology prioritises particular characteristics of a literary text. This was recognised by Bernikow in her deliberately iconoclastic selection criteria for *The World Split Open* (see p.4), and by another American critic, Suzanne Juhasz, in an article published in 1977. Noting the general success of the attempt to 'remove criticism from the level of idiosyncratic impressionism', raising it to 'the status of an objective, even scientific discipline', Juhasz pointed out that the New Critical model of criticism valued 'generalization, objectification, and universalization' as hallmarks of greatness in literature.[75] If critics come across poetry that refuses to move in these directions, or that avoids literary sources or allusion, they tend to assume 'ignorance or lack of talent'.(p.117) But it may be that poets are deliberately rejecting these habits. Juhasz cites the example of a negative appraisal of Ann Sexton, written by Patricia Meyer Spacks, suggesting that because of the nature of Sexton's poems, it is difficult to 'expertly distinguish between the person revealed by the poems and poems that reveal her.' (p.121) Juhasz argues that what determines Spacks's harsh assessment is her dislike of the version of womanhood depicted in the poems:

> Spacks doesn't like Sexton; ....most of all, doesn't like having to be identified with them, just because she, too, is a woman. She wants everyone to realize that women don't have to be sloppy and emotional and self-indulgent and narcissistic and suicidal. (pp.120–1)

The strength of the critic's reaction testifies to the emotional impact of the poems—an *affect* that plays a crucial role in the critic's reaction, but nevertheless remains unacknowledged by her. What the critic must do is attempt to discover the terms the poem has set for itself; to do this, she must 'involve th[e] affect in her criticism'(p.119): allow herself to be affected by the poem, and then use her own reactions as part of her critique. Academic critics, because of our training, find this difficult. Perhaps poets are more willing to bring their own subjectivity into the discussion, examining their reactions to individual poems and relating those reactions to their own practice.[76]

More recently, critic Rebecca O'Rourke has expressed dissatisfaction with poetry critics' obsessive focus on hierarchies of excellence. She connects this to the poetry establishment's wish to maintain poetry as an élite preserve:

> Faced with questions of judgement, I don't rush out to fit the template of excellence over my poems and see how close the fit is. I ask who has drawn up these standards, and why? Will they include or exclude this poet—help to explain why they write as they do about this subject? Is there space for my pleasure as a reader?[77]

O'Rourke is unusual in voicing such misgivings; in Britain, there has been particularly strong reluctance to challenging received ideas about what constitutes 'good' poetry. Only one kind of poetry seems to be accepted as pure, or genuine; the rest is passed over in silence. There is no recognition of the idea that different poems might be written for very different purposes, occasions, and audiences. This has meant that criticism has shied away from work that makes maximum use of performance media (including film), and work that is overtly polemical or political in nature.

This entrenched conservatism affects women poets as well as critics. Most of the older, established women poets in Britain adhere to a liberal humanist aesthetic which insists on the apolitical, gender-neutral qualities of great art. Typical of this attitude is Anne Stevenson, who recently defended 'a real poem's universality, associated always with its music', and described poetry's 'essentially symbolical, apolitical nature'.[78] In a now-infamous anthology introduction, Carol Rumens insisted that she had not discriminated against poems about 'specifically female experiences, provided they are genuine poems'.[79] Because liberal humanist conceptions of the subject are masculine, there is no way in which female experience can be anything other than 'human'—which means, in practice, the same as men's.

In North America, perhaps partly because six centuries of poetic tradition do not cast their shadows over the present in the way that they do in Britain, liberal humanism is far less dominant, and poetry criticism is far more experimental. A recent collection of essays, *Feminist Measures: Soundings in Poetry and Theory*, exhibits a fascinating mixture of critical approaches. The editors welcome 'the broadening of the literary base' to include insights from related disciplines such as cultural studies, film theory and anthropology.[80] The volume includes some conventional literary critical essays that discuss poetry in terms of genre, but many others as well: some offer experimental combinations of autobiography and polemic, others mix poetry and criticism. The range of poetries covered is also far broader, attending to the work of specific ethnic groups, Language poets, etc. Rachel DuPlessis's latest work develops her determination to bring historical and cultural dimensions into the discussion of lyric poetry. She combines close reading and what she calls 'social philology'—'an application of the techniques of close reading to reveal social discourses, subjectivities negotiated, and ideological debates in a poetic text'.[81]

METHODOLOGY AND PREOCCUPATIONS

The poets discussed in this book are all published by mainstream presses.[82] I am particularly interested in the reading process: what happens between reader and poem. Eavan Boland's suggestion that 'A poem is not about an experience. A poem is an experience'[83] clarifies the extent to which the reader is having an experience when s/he reads (or hears) a poem. Poems draw attention to their language; rather than transparent communication, they demand thought and reflection. Reading a poem, the reader has to try to retrace chains of association operating at some level (conscious or unconscious) in the poet's mind. It is a peculiarly intimate process. There is little or no scene-setting, rarely much sense of location in time or place. The reader is plunged in a particularly intense way into the poem's experience.

An example of the methods of composition should make this clearer.

Poet Ruth Padel describes her habit of recording the odd phrases, ideas or pieces of information that come her way in a notebook:

> I suppose I vaguely assume that because all these different things feel important to me, they belong with each other somewhere and will cohere, in the end, in things I make, simply because it's me making it and my interest in them is what they have in common. There's a coherence it's not my business to see, though I'll have to work it out in action, for the movement of each poem. They work through images, these things.[84]

Where the poet works it out in the act of producing the poem, the reader works it out through the processes involved in reading. And this is a curiously paradoxical process. On the one hand, poetry offers more space for the reader's interpretation than other forms of writing. Reading a poem is rather like diving into a swimming pool, where reading prose is more like swimming lengths. Even the shape of lines on the page often implies this emphasis on verticality and depth. There is no lead-in, no temporal, spatial, semantic frame. Since the meanings of words derive in part from their context, in a poem the field is wide open. It is signalled by the space on the page: all that room, ambiguity, the openness of poetry, where language is freed from the constraints of grammatical or semantic meaning, where images can hang, can be brought alongside one another or not, as the reader determines. This indicates considerable freedom. But the process—whereby the reader is dropped into the poem's world, with no preparation—implies being in thrall to the poet's creation to a much more intense degree than is the case with prose writing. This process entails the meeting of three subjectivities: that of poet, poem and reader. Of course the poem is not the poet's 'whole' or 'real' subjectivity (if anything could be) but it is, as Padel indicates, the creation of that subjectivity.

This book explores work by men and women poets, picking up on a remark made by American poet Marge Piercy in 1987. In her introduction to an anthology, *Early Ripening: American Women's Poetry Now,* Piercy suggested it might be time to produce an anthology of poems by both men and women, in order to see how the formers' work was changed by the existence of the latter.[85] The

rationale behind this idea was, of course, to displace the centrality
of men's poetry, to do something that would dislodge masculinity
from its ostensibly gender-neutral occupation of 'universal' norms.
Where Piercy advocated 'an anthology that includes male poets in
that same landscape and looks at them in the perspective of the
exciting work that women are producing', this critique takes women
poets' work as its subject, and then considers male poets' work
against the backdrop of women's writing. In part this is an attempt
to avoid the tendency to view women's poetry as aberrant—'distinctively other' as Robinson has put it (see p.1). For, as other feminist
critics have noted, if we set out with the knowledge of women's
historical exclusion, and an expectation of their difference from
men, we are likely to find our expectations justified.

Gender does not unlock the meaning of all poems, male or
female-authored; but it is an important, and neglected, aspect of
the interaction. Poems offer evidence about masculine and feminine
subjectivities, and may attempt to interrogate or change such
constructions. Peter Middleton has argued for a similar thing in relation to men's writing produced during the Modernist period.
Defending the validity of literary texts as primary sources for
insights into knowledge and culture, he argues:

> Texts are not just symptoms, but proposed cures, prefigura-
> tive arguments as well as ideology....We can also read
> representations of consciousness, self-consciousness, articulacy
> and inarticulacy in men's texts as claims about men's subjec-
> tivity, and examine them for consequent aporias.'[86]

In tackling work by men and women, I have adopted Rachel
DuPlessis's argument for 'evenhandedness'. Aware of the 'asym-
metries of power' that exist in relation to access to production
and dissemination, DuPlessis argues that such evenhandedness is
necessary nonetheless because, '[i]f we do not use the same tools
to discuss writing by both genders, we still secretly "universal-
ize" male writing or uncritically overvalue writing by women.'[87]
One asymmetry is apparent even in terminology: while 'women
poets' sounds quite normal, 'men poets' sounds distinctly odd,
presumably because, on some level, it is understood as tautologi-

cal. In her study of metaphor, Helen Haste cites Lakoff's demonstration that we signal prototypes by our use of qualifying
terminology. Thus the need for the participle in the phrase 'working mother' indicates that mothers do not customarily 'work'.[88] I
suggest the construction 'woman poet' indicates that the term 'poet'
is implicitly sexed male. Prompted by Jane Gallop's example, I have
used the phrase 'men poets' in this book as a political strategy,
intended to discomfort readers who believe it is unnecessary. Gallop
uses 'he' and 'she' interchangeably throughout her study, *Reading
Lacan*, in an attempt to re-sex 'he':

> Lacan has said 'the phallus can play its role only when veiled.'
> The supposed universality of the pronoun 'he' depends on its
> not connoting the penis, on the veiling of its sexual attributes.
> When any possible pronoun for the epistemological subject
> cannot help but connote sexual difference, then the phallic
> authority of universal man will have more difficulty pronounc-
> ing itself.[89]

An interest in the process of reading lyric poetry leads to a focus
on what happens between text and critic/reader. But just as there
are different kinds of poem, and different intentions behind them,
so too there are different reasons for reading poems. Some people
enjoy poetry for the intellectual exercise it demands: a kind of
riddle-solving. Others might admire the virtuoso manipulations
of specific forms like the sestina, or appreciate witty allusions to
predecessors, or in-jokes. Perhaps more widespread—certainly
more accessible—is the appreciation of poetry for its ability to give
shape and articulation to incoherent, paradoxical states of emotion
and experience, or for the wisdom and insights that may be
expressed therein. Anne Stevenson has described poetic language
as 'essentially oxymoronic, a coinage stamped on two sides with
logically irreconcilable messages'.[90] Such a recognition of the
ambivalence latent within much poetry is important, since it
further emphasises how much interpretative scope lies with the
reader or critic.

Just as readers read for different reasons, so also academics hold
different ideas about the role of criticism. Montefiore stressed the

importance of attending to poems as artefacts: 'A poem is always a pattern of words, creating its particular meaning from the relation between the material reality of language—sounds, breathing, letters on a page—and the images and ideas which they signify.'[91] Her approach assumes the existence of one 'particular meaning', the critic's task being to illuminate this. The critic is thus a kind of translator or interpreter, and yet of a form of words that is as it is because it has to be thus to communicate what its author wishes to convey—that is, by its nature, untranslatable. In this model, the critic paraphrases, inelegantly. Others suggest the critic's role is one of clarification, or exegesis, giving readers pertinent information. But Jane Gallop, in the introduction to *Reading Lacan,* offers an idea that is rather more provocative. She cites Julia Kristeva's claim that 'interpretation necessarily represents appropriation, and thus an act of desire and murder.' She offers an analogy between the literary critic and the psychoanalyst (the text is the critic's 'client'), and claims that the heart of the interpretive act is in the transference between analyst and client (or critic and text). Hence, 'the power in analysis is not the analyst's power, but something very powerful that happens *between subjects.*' (my italics). In other words, it is not the critic's knowledge that results in interpretation, but the interaction between critic and text. Gallop comments on how disconcerting this feels for the critic:

> In the relation of transference, the critic is no longer analyst but patient. The position of patient can be terrifying in that it represents, to the critic who in her transference believes in the analyst's mastery, a position of non-mastery.[92]

It is this same idea—that interpretation is the outcome of something that happens *between* critic and poem—that underlies the readings that follow in this book.

Poets seem more ready to espouse this kind of reading model than academic critics. In a recent lecture on Emily Dickinson, Paul Muldoon began by saying that, as a reader, he was 'trying to put myself in the position of the poem's first reader' who, he went on to suggest, was also its author, 'the conduit through whom the poem gets written'.[93] In the course of the lecture, he drew on a variety of 'sources' as he created a tissue of suggestive contexts through which Dickinson's poems might be read. These included biographical information about her home situation (the installation of a new Franklin stove having the effect of radically altering the family dynamic); the ideas of thinkers known to have been read, and admired, by Dickinson; the recurrence of the same words or phrases in the poems immediately before or after the ones in question, and references to other poems that employ similar imagery. What he demonstrated in the lecture was both the opacity of poetry, and the tremendous interpretative scope available to its readers.

Muldoon spoke of the way in which the reader makes himself in the writer's image, and the writer in the reader's. Muldoon's critical practice, like that of T. S. Eliot, resembles his own poetic practice, described by Sean O'Brien as 'sidelong, at times hallucinatory, driven by long-distance association of ideas, poems and resemblances'.[94] As critics, we cannot rid ourselves of our own subjectivities; we end up—to some extent—recreating the text in our own image. And once this is acknowledged, the relevance of gender to poetry critique becomes incontrovertible.

One or two men poets have begun to acknowledge the part played by gender in poetry. Tom Paulin, in relation to Emily Dickinson, argues that her poetry depends for its fullest understanding on the reader acknowledging its specificity to female experience.[95] In his recent study of contemporary poets, Sean O'Brien makes the following observation about Jo Shapcott's work:

> The reader—perhaps especially the male reader—has to learn that the poems' excursions are not dependent on reference back to a place of interpretative safety.[96]

And discussing Selima Hill's preoccupation with 'psychic realities' he suggests that it:

> may help to account for the feelings of disorientation and irritation initially experienced by some male readers who find themselves turning back at the border to face the possibility that their vocabulary is simply not equipped for the job of reading the resulting poems. (p.257)

None of these men goes as far as to acknowledge their own responses to the poems under discussion, preferring to take refuge in a generalised, hypothetical male reader. John Lennard, author of *The Poetry Handbook*, which is aimed at sixth-form students, is more radical, declaring that 'the way forward for the gender-conscious study of poetry is the inclusion within practical critical responses of the *critic's* gender.'[97] But while he makes the claim, he does not put it into practice. The challenge to a male critic is considerable since it not only requires him to divest himself of the impersonal voice but also of the supposition of genderless 'humanity'. Men (especially white men) are used to writing and living as men without the specificity of their sex being noted. As Middleton puts it:

> Women writers know there are men writers, and black writers know there are white writers but we white men writers (I want to include myself for a moment very clearly) often don't see our own condition....Reflexivity works imperfectly for men because they don't see what they are seeing when they see themselves.[98]

In the readings that follow in this book, the relevance of my own sex is foregrounded. My approach emphasises the reception and interpretation of poetry, rather than examining the putative existence of innate differences within the poems themselves. One aspect of this which I do not consider in the chapters that follow is the degree to which readers' responses are affected by their knowledge of the poet's sex. This is, of course, impossible to measure.[99] A recent survey investigating how the sex of the author affected readers of prose fiction concluded that even a hint, in title or cover design, that a book was intended for women is sufficient to dissuade men from reading it. Some 72 per cent of male respondents said that they preferred books written by men; 56 per cent of female respondents said they preferred books written by women. The researchers explain:

> Designation of a female read is not only based upon the gender of the author, but also on the colour and general look of the cover (e.g. pastels/pink, floral scenes, etc.), the title (e.g. use of the word love) and then the description of the subject matter (e.g. love stories, relationships/feeling).[100]

To what extent do men read women poets, and vice versa? In keeping with the prevalent view that gender does not figure in poetry, the covers of poetry collections uniformly avoid any overt references to femininity or masculinity, opting instead for line drawings or abstract designs. Titles tend to be similarly opaque, and the cover-blurb descriptions likewise. In any case, since poetry is assumed, by the general public, to imply some connection to the emotions, the idea that 'relationships/feeling' are associated with 'a female read' is unsustainable.

POETRY AND THE 'POETIC'

Poetry, or more precisely *the poetic* occupies an interesting place within poststructuralist thought. Influential individuals like Roland Barthes, Julia Kristeva, Hélène Cixous and Luce Irigaray have all implied that poetic language is more radical and subversive than prose, claiming it has the potential to escape the Symbolic Order. In this schema, poetry is allied with 'the repressed feminine, maternal, and preoedipal', while narrative and prose are associated with 'the repressive masculine, paternal, and oedipal.'[101] Cixous describes poetry as the enemy of dictators, a genre that bears witness, and subverts fixity and truth claims.[102] Jane Gallop views poetry, like hieroglyphics, as akin to the riddle:

> A 'solved' riddle is the reduction of heterogeneous material to logic, to the homogeneity of logical thought, which produces a blind spot, the inability to see the otherness that gets lost in the reduction. Only the unsolved riddle, the process of riddle-work before its final completion, is a confrontation with otherness.[103]

In Elizabeth Hirsch's interpretation, Irigaray 'implicitly links what she calls a female *genre* or genealogy...and the poetic, the kind of linguistic expression that Irigaray describes as calling up, calling to or *addressing* its subject, rather than *speaking about* it (as object) in the ostensibly neutral or objective manner of narrative and discursive genres.'[104]

In more general usage, 'poetic prose' implies prose that flouts grammatical and compositional/rhetorical rules regarding syntax, sentence length, and so on. Gayatri Chakravorti Spivak suggests that prose-poetry is able to evoke 'power of indeterminate suggestion rather than determinate reference'.[105] Frequently 'poetic' becomes a synonym for non-literal, imaginative, metaphoric writing—invariably carrying connotations of freer, more radical insight.

In all these formulations, the poetic is associated with fluidity, plurality, dialogue, heterogeneity, openness, difference: all terms positively inflected in contemporary poststructuralist discourse. Leaving aside the interesting return of the dualism prose/poetry, all these suggestions owe a lot to Kristeva's claims about poetry in *Revolution in Poetic Language*.[106] Kristeva argued that through rhythms, beats or pulsions, the repressed semiotic successfully emerges, rupturing the tyrannical symbolic order; she suggests that, as a mode of writing less in thrall to the strictures of logic, grammar and rationality, poetry is better equipped to 'catch' this repressed matter. Her illustrations—avant-garde (male) modernists who eschewed narrative and mimetic representation—may not be poets, but their writing fits the looser descriptive term 'poetic'. The poetic is contrasted to phallogocentrist discourse, with its intolerance of difference. The implication of these ideas is that poetry, as a genre, is more radical, potentially freer from the rules and repressions of the symbolic order.

If this is the case, it seems strange that those who have been marginalised by the Symbolic Order and by British traditions of patriarchy and imperialism—women, the working class, minority ethnic communities, gays and lesbians—should not be more strongly represented in poetry from the British Isles. There is plenty of evidence to suggest that members of these groups *do* turn to poetry,[107] and the popularity of poetry competitions enables countless poetry magazines with minute circulation lists to survive on the proceeds of an annual competition with a modest entrance fee. But this work tends to be highly conventional, and derivative. To suggest that amateur poets are subverting the Symbolic Order and giving vent to the repressed semiotic in their poetry seems somewhat far-fetched. But poetry might provide those who rarely feel themselves to have access to a public voice with a temporary sense of their own agency. Critic Helen Carr has suggested that:

Precisely because in our culture poetry is associated with the private and the personal, it is a form which women can feel they have a right to use, even though elsewhere the social conventions they observe and the discourses they use may discount the subjectivity validated in their poetry....writing a poem is a statement that, within those lines at least, the poet is a speaking subject whose subjectivity is taken seriously. (p.78)

The stronger socialist materialist traditions of British scholarship make many uncomfortable with theoretical work like that of Kristeva. In 1989 Sara Mills applied Kristeva's ideas to a reading of a poem by Gertrude Stein; while Stein's style lends itself well to this kind of analysis, Mills was nevertheless dissatisfied with the result. She concluded that Kristeva's lack of interest in social and material contexts meant that her theories could only be of limited use to a feminist critique: 'whilst the destabilizing which goes on in experimental texts is important, a more truly political writing is that which impels action or which changes consciousness.'[108]

All these arguments about the liberatory potential of the *genre* of poetry imply a false separation between the text and its creator and readers, as if through poetry we could somehow escape social and political contexts. Interestingly, not long after completing her essay Mills turned her attention to the *reception* of texts, and analysis of readers' responses, perhaps suspecting that the real obstacles facing women were to be found outside the text. It is to this area—to gender relations in the real world—that I shall now turn for the last section of this introduction.

POETRY OFF THE PAGE: POWER, PATRONAGE AND NETWORKS IN THE POETRY WORLD

In the contemporary British poetry scene, there is no pretence that poets spring, like fully formed geniuses, from their mother's bellies; a poet is made, not born. Like an athlete, a poet's talent has to be honed and developed through the discipline of regular practice. In the 1950s, when such apprenticeships developed more informally within a far smaller, more relaxed university community, the groups tended to be composed of male tutor/patrician/poet, and male disciples. Homosocial or homosexual relations were integral. But a woman's position as trainee or apprentice to a man poet is likely to be complicated by sexuality in a more disruptive way. This is so whether she is lesbian or heterosexual (though its impact may be radically reduced if the man poet is himself gay). This sexual dynamic will affect not only the kind and degree of attention each poet secures, but will also then exert an influence over the sorts of writing s/he is encouraged (by his or her mentor) to pursue. Of course, sexual dynamics exist between all of us, regardless of our sex, or sexual orientation, and are likely to exert an effect over relations between an aspiring man poet and his male 'tutor'. But the combination of influential (therefore powerful) heterosexual man poet with female, heterosexual would-be-poet is by far the most common configuration in which aspiring women poets find themselves.

Today, a number of national writing centres nurture aspiring poets; most famous of these (and the first) is the Arvon Foundation. With centres in Scotland, Yorkshire, Shropshire and Devon, Arvon organises five-day writing workshops, hosted by professional writers (while they now offer courses on screenwriting and drama, the emphasis was originally on poetry). More recently, the London-based Poetry School has established a number of longer courses (the long poem; writing metrics, etc.) along similar lines. Across the country, local education authorities and Workers Educational Associations run creative writing workshops. As Debbie Taylor has noted, women make up the majority of students on such courses. The more experienced poet-students are well aware that making a good impression on the tutor can lead to valuable contacts and recommendations.

Far more powerful than a position as writing tutor is that of commissioning editor at one of the poetry publishing houses. There are only a few of them; none are women.[109] Of the poetry journals and magazines, almost none have female editors in positions of power (in other words, selecting the material that gets published). We can only ponder whether Jeni Couzyn's 1985 claim remains true: 'it has always been for the *content,* and not the style or form of their work that men have disliked women's poetry.'[110] The work

of many of the women poets who have had first collections
published in the last ten years does—sometimes obviously—reflect
their editor's tastes.[111] Is this simply the influence of the market:
editors responding to a perceived market for a particular kind of
women's writing?

It is usually the patronage of an established poet which provides
the break for new aspirants. Yet there seem to be few signs of
women poets in such influential positions. Nor do any of the better-
known women poets seem to have built up circles of apprentices
around them. Do they themselves lack access to the kind of influence that counts? Or is critic Jane Dowson correct in her suggestion
that the female affiliation complex 'prescribes women an *essential
ambivalence*' towards female literary foremothers, and this explains
why today's younger women poets seem so reluctant to acknowledge their immediate predecessors as influential?[112] Do women
poets still *feel* their position within the establishment is tenuous and
insecure, regardless of whether or not it is, and thus hold back
from using their influence to promote their protegées?

Of course, this is a complicated issue, since we cannot assume
that women will look more favourably on other women writers'
work than their male colleagues. Indeed, there is evidence to suggest
that women are harsher judges of their sisters, especially those
poets who write about specifically female experiences like pregnancy, childbirth or motherhood. Patricia Craig's review of the
anthology *Sixty Women Poets* criticised it fiercely for including
too much of such material; Sheenagh Pugh's reviews are similiar in
tone.[113] Such reactions seem reminiscent of Spacks's dislike of
Sexton's work, and Rumens's anxiety about the 'noisy amateurs':
a fear of pollution by association which itself says much about the
insecurity of women's position as poets. Several younger women
poets speak privately of their wish to avoid being labelled one of
the 'women's poetry' ghetto, which is dismissively identified with
weak poetry and 'strident' politics.

As the theory of the female affiliation complex indicates, relations between generations of women writers involve their own
gender-specific tensions. Betsy Erkkila's study of precisely such relationships between a number of American women poets, *The Wicked
Sisters: Women Poets, Literary History, and Discord*,[114] finds

evidence of the kind of intricate and contradictory emotions also identified by object relations psychologists Susie Orbach and Luise Eichenbaum in their studies of female psychology: in particular, women experiencing difficulties distinguishing between empathy and identification.[115] Harold Bloom's model of the 'anxiety of influence', which interpreted intergenerational relations between male poets as an ongoing struggle between fathers and sons, now seems intransigently gendered; it might be an interesting exercise to attempt to outline a theory for relations between women poets.[116]

Then there is the effect of traditional views of the poet as a man apart, spokesman for his community. The conventional poetry reading still evokes a religious, reverential atmosphere, with the audience quietly awaiting the dispensation of wisdom and perception distilled by the skill of the wordsmith. How do women poets create the necessary authority for their own voices within this public context, when there is such entrenched resistance to the acceptance of a female voice as transcending its sex-specificity? Sarah Maguire believes this presents inescapable difficulties:

> Despite the advantages women have achieved as poets, despite the fact that women can be the subjects of our own poetry, our work is still inflected (and infected) by inequalities and by our objectified subjectivity...We are not yet fully human.'[117]

Men can choose from a variety of roles for their public performance. If they do not feel comfortable as sages, there is always the lovable but dangerous rogue epitomised by Lord Byron, or more recently by Lachlan MacKinnon and Neil Rollinson. A woman poet has to confront the implications of being a female on public display, with the connotations of sexual objectification, in a context that traditionally disregards the body. This may be why many of today's women poets have been most successful as performers of their work: the theatricality of the event is upfront, thus releasing the body from the stasis of a conventional reading. The performers can *use* their bodies and their sexuality, avoiding the passivity of objectification. Performance also enables an integrated presentation of poetry as coming out of, delivered through the body, in place of the cerebral emphases of Western poetic tradition. It also pays heed to the audience: part of the skill is involving the listeners in the performance.[118]

Many have observed that women poets tend to publish their first collections much later in life than their male counterparts; a more worrying trend is how many women poets fall silent after a couple of collections. Michèle Roberts is celebrated as a novelist, but has published no book of poetry since her *Selected Poems* appeared in 1995. Grace Nichols has published only children's material since 1989. And there are many more: Deborah Randall, Suniti Namjoshi, Wendy Cope, Vicki Feaver, Fiona Pitt-Kethley. Is this silence a reflection of the pressures of women's lives; or are they finding it harder to get their work accepted? Or are there other explanations? There are certainly other questions: why, for example, are lesbian poets in Britain discreet about their sexuality in their writing? Lesbian poetry seems to have few advocates in Britain, unlike gay poetry which has benefited from the talent and knowledge of informed commentators such as Gregory Woods (himself also a poet).[119] Is this discretion their choice, determined by temperament, or the belief that a person's sexuality or lifestyle is a private matter? Or does the lack of recognition of lesbian existence—both in reality and in poetic tradition—make writing overtly about it too difficult? Why are there are so few Black or Asian women poets in Britain, and does it matter that the majority are primarily identified with the more popular sphere of poetry in performance?

What follows are ideas borrowed from a wide range of thinkers: poets, theorists, psychologists, reader-response critics, experts in linguistics and philosophers. There is no intention to disguise the subjective origins of my interpretations, but rather an attempt to broaden these responses through their dialogue with the ideas of others. This methodology is deliberately eclectic; it is one way of demonstrating my conviction that poetry participates in the same debates and trends that influence political discourse, philosophical inquiry and popular culture.

1.
FIRST IMPRESSIONS
GENDERING THE READING PROCESS

In the introduction what is specific about the reading process in relation to lyric poetry, and the encounter between lyric poem and reader was outlined. Here, the implications of that specificity will be fleshed out, as they relate to gender: of both poet and reader. Three key terms can be identified in relation to this process—reception, authority and metaphor.

'Reception' is the way the poem is received by its reader: his or her reaction, and the kind of meaning s/he ascribes to it. 'Authority' alludes to the crepuscular position of lyric poetry, on the boundary between personal and public discourse: presenting the voice of an individual, yet moving this voice into a public position, one which the lyric tradition invests with authority and for which it claims, ideally, universality. While this bardic Romantic voice— what Helen Kidd has called 'the great male writing "I"'[1]—is currently out of favour, because of its patriarchal, imperialistic connotations, its more recent manifestations are equally intransigently gendered and resistant to female speakers. A poem's voice may be fictive, rather than identical to that of the poet who produces it; it is not the poet's own voice, nor does it necessarily share the poet's sex. (See chapter 2 for discussion of poems in which the persona 'crosses gender'.) However (except in dramatic monologues, where the poet openly adopts a voice distinct from his or her own), there is usually a connection between the lyric poem's voice and the poet's subjectivity. Why else do literary critics draw on biographical information when writing about poets' work? Part of the reason is due to the opacity of much poetry: many of its references and associations issue so closely from the poet's unconscious as to be unrecoverable by readers. Of course, we do not need to 'decode' such material; the point of it is its effect as an integral part of the poem, not the recovery of its origins. But the fact that this opacity is a common feature of poetry indicates the intimacy of its entanglement with its creator. Lyric poetry is not, as Eavan Boland insists, autobiography;[2] it does not tell a life story. It transforms, imagines, and reshapes material from wherever the poet finds inspiration. Nevertheless, the work is intricately linked to the life, and its journey from private thought to public art (to Sutherland's 'published privacies' see p.6.) may render that link inscrutable, but does not dissolve it. Because poems move from personal origins into the public arena, poets have to find a voice capable of effecting this movement. Here, gender plays a crucial role. The voice is usually sexed—whether explicitly or not—and, in addition to the way in which the poem positions its reader, and the kind of reader (or auditor) it anticipates, this plays a vital part in the reader's response.

'Metaphor' is one of the key aspects of a poem to call upon the reader, requiring active involvement in its dynamic movement, its work of transferring associations. Like the issue of the poem's voice, poetic metaphor has a problematic history so far as women practitioners are concerned, since women have traditionally appeared as metaphorised, rather than themselves creators of metaphors. The significance of gender in relation to metaphor is discussed towards the end of this chapter. These three key terms form the basis for the readings that follow, the aim of which is to demonstrate the gendering of the reading process.

THE VOICE OR PERSONA

Cora Kaplan first suggested that poetry's expectation of a first-person lyric 'I' was problematic for women. Writing about the Romantic period, she argued that the idea of writing in a confident, assertive, public voice would have been overwhelmingly daunting during a period in which public speech was an entirely male prerogative:

The power of that individual voice was identified with the free-dom and transcendence of the individual and, in its most radical formulation, with the liberation of humanity.[3]

Fiction was more hospitable terrain for women because its struc-ture enabled the woman author to distance her own speech:

One might say that the narrative discourse itself provides a sort of third term for the woman author by locating (even, and perhaps especially, in a first person narrative) the loss or absence of power anywhere but in her own voice. (pp.82-3)

Writing 23 years later, poet Sarah Maguire echoes this theme:

The American critic, Helen Vendler defines lyric poetry as 'the self's concentration of itself into words'; and James Joyce said that it is 'the form wherein the artist presents his image in immediate relation to himself'. Although of course this self presented in the lyric is a fictional construction, it is a fiction which manifests itself in the fiction of a desiring subject, an 'I' that wants, that is in control (even if only to create the fiction of being without desire or loss of control). Women, of course, are not traditionally able to take the place of desiring subjects in a patriarchal society: we are the desired objects. And lyric poetry, of course, is the very form in which our status as desired objects has been most fully and most poignantly articulated.[4]

There are some women poets who have developed this kind of strong public lyric voice: Gillian Clarke and Eavan Boland, for example. Both have unapologetically asserted the centrality of female (and largely domestic) experience to their poetic terrain. In pieces like 'The Journey' and its accompanying 'Envoi', Boland imitates the heightened register of the male bard, with its intima-tions of religious discourse, in an attempt to lay claim to the authority of a public voice.[5]

But it is perhaps no coincidence that, in successfully establishing a first-person presence in the lyric tradition, both poets have done so by delineating a specifically female sphere: the neglected matter of women's domestic lives, past and present. So, while readers are asked to accept their authority as public spokeswomen, they do not venture beyond the confines of female-gendered experience. They are not attempting to present themselves as spokeswomen on ostensibly ungendered matters, like politics or religion.

The pre-eminent position of the lyric 'I', and the poem's movement from the private to a public sphere, are related to certain characteristics of the lyric mode, which is the most egotistical creative genre. In writing it, you describe the world through your own eyes, you cover everything with your words, your mark.[6] Poets have to summon considerable authority in order to manage this feat. The reader has to yield far more radically to the poem's authority. Reading prose or, at least, realist prose that obeys orthodox grammatical rules and depicts a recognisable reality—there is more space between the author's eye/I and the reader's: that space is the fictional world created by the author. The reader can form an attitude to the various characters, and to the narrator; s/he can assess characters' motivation and behaviour and compare his or her conclusions with those offered by the narrator; s/he can read descriptions of places and atmospheres, and test out their accuracy against his or her own knowledge and experience. In short, there is greater distance for the reader to negotiate their relationship with the text. While the reader's sense of influence and participation may—in a literal sense—be illusory, since it does not affect the text, it nevertheless exists as part of the reading experience. Reading poetry, there is nothing between the poem and the reader. You have no option, at first anyway, but to go with the poet's words and therefore their vision of things. It involves a far greater surrender. The reader is required to take the voice on trust, to work at the poem, pondering its tropes and metaphors, alert to the resonances that emerge. Poetry provides pleasures to compensate: the skilful deployment of sound patterning and rhythms, words chosen with precision and care, the elegance of language arranged formally, in what Don Paterson, referring to the sonnet form, calls a box for poet's dreams.[7] Nevertheless, these are big demands to make of readers: welcome to my world, work it out! There is a paradox here: poetry is a genre that expects the highest degree of submission from its readers, because of the lack of space for come-back or response, or of room to develop one's own angle on the story. Yet there is more scope for the reader's interpretation than is ever the case with realist prose: those few words open up to a greater number of readings. Paul Muldoon's suggestion (discussed in chapter 1, p.33) that poet and reader create their own mirror version of one another (the reader makes herself in the writer's image, and vice versa) indicates just how creative a part is played by the reader.

If lyric poetry places its reader in such an interestingly contradictory position, it should be revealing to study just what happens during the reading process. Sara Mills has compared the reactions of male and female readers to a poem that she chose for its unorthodoxy.[8] With the opening lines 'When the moon swings round / And I bleed my woman's blood', there is no ambiguity about the sex of the persona. She goes on to express serious misgivings about pregnancy; while celebrating her body's 'invincible power', she dreams of a baby 'shaped like shackles and chains'. Careful to avoid a simplistic notion of identification, Mills investigates instead whether readers can identify a dominant subject position being proposed by the poem. The results indicated that most could do this, but that female readers found it easier. Mills concludes this may be because male readers had a struggle to find a position from which to read *as males*. Responding to a question about whether or not they enjoyed the poem, female readers' answers focused on the degree to which they shared or disputed the speaker's ambivalent feelings. Male readers opted for more detached reasons, commenting on the language or the unusual nature of the poem's subject matter. Mills comments: 'Male readers seemed in a more difficult position, where their pleasure in the poem was not related to their recognition of subject positions.' (p.39)

What Mills calls difficulty could equally well be called detachment, and suggests a less involved response: hardly surprising, considering the explicit nature of the poem's discussion of an issue only directly available to women.[9] What emerges from her investigation is that female readers feel themselves directly addressed by a poem like this, one that employs a female voice and tackles an issue potentially relevant to all women. Male readers have to work harder; denied the opportunity of adopting the

poem's subject position (to do so would require cross-gender i
tification, which is of course feasible, but perhaps a more unusual
experience for men) they had to find other reasons for their
responses. This does not mean female readers are at an advantage;
in fact, the dangers of over-identification with the speaker may
well mislead them in constructing an interpretation. But it does
suggest that, in cases where the sexing of the poem's speaker is
explicit, readers are inevitably conscious of it, and that this becomes
a consideration in their response to the poem.[10]

Mills notes the methodological shortcomings of this kind of
research: quite apart from difficulties selecting respondents, you can
never be sure that those you do choose are not being led by the very
questions asked, nor can you assess whether they are providing
accurate accounts of the complex processes at work during what feels
like the natural 'common sense' activity of reading.[11] Furthermore,
the methodology is essentialist. It is more effective to work in terms
of positionality—'reading as/like a woman'—thus avoiding the
suggestion such a reading is only available to biological females.
More seriously, many variable constituents of identity are eclipsed
by the stark binary of male and female readers, which leaves no room
for considerations such as ethnicity, age, class and political viewpoint.

My own experiments with readers' responses have proved similarly tricky. After distributing the same questionnaire and poem to
each year's intake of students on a poetry course over a period of
four years, no useful conclusions can be drawn. However one
consistent finding was that, when asked to sex the speaker of a
poem, readers use word choice, and the gender associations that
accompany individual words or phrases, as evidence for their
answer. The poem used was Jo Shapcott's 'Muse', which leaves the
sex of its addressee ambiguous; and in the course of it, the speaker
compares him/her/it to a dog. Readers who concluded the addressee
must be male explained the decision on the grounds that dogs, like
men, were 'athletic', independent', 'greedy', 'selfish'. Those who
thought the muse was female selected other words that can be associated with dogs' temperaments, such as 'faithful' and 'obedient'.

The results of my reader-response questionnaires reveal some
20 different explanations for each detail. Such a variety of possibilities is not unusual. The art of learning to read poetry is about

close reading, and the marshalling of evidence to support your interpretation. Rather than being a case of right and wrong, it is up to
the reader to justify their interpretation by drawing on evidence—
from the poem, other phrases or sound arrangements that reinforce
it; or evidence from the poet's other work, or biography; or from
life experience. So, while expected to take the poem on, with no
pointers or help, to immerse oneself in the poet's world view, ultimately the reader makes the poem his or her own by the extent of
their investment in the process of making meaning from it. Of
course, the degree to which this process draws on a reader's subjectivity depends on the reader, although some have suggested there is
evidence of a clear difference between male and female readers (see
note 9 above). An intense meeting of subjectivities is at stake—and
while 'power' may seem a term too linked to real, material issues,
the negotiations between poet, poem and reader will bear the marks
of social and cultural practice.

FIRST IMPRESSIONS

Here is a close reading of the opening poem in six collections of
poetry, three by men and three by women. All are first collections:
as such the opening poem may be said to carry even greater import,
as an initial declaration—of personality, intent and preoccupations.[12] These are chosen from collections published between 1988
and 1999 in the hope that some change in focus or self-presentation might be evident. Particular attention should be paid to the
aspects outlined above: the kind of persona or voice employed,
how each poem addresses or positions its reader, and the effect of
its figurative language. The readings focus on the gendering of
interdiegetic and implied reader positions, rather than considering
possibilities for resistant readings. Michael Donaghy's 'Machines'
is the opening poem from his first collection, *Shibboleth* (1988).

> Dearest, note how these two are alike:
> This harpsichord pavane by Purcell
> And the racer's twelve-speed bike.
>
> The machinery of grace is always simple.

This chrome trapezoid, one wheel connected
To another of concentric gears,
Which Ptolemy dreamt of and Schwinn perfected,
Is gone. The cyclist, not the cycle, steers.
And in the playing, Purcell's chords are played away.

So this talk, or touch if I were there,
Should work its effortless gadgetry of love,
Like Dante's heaven, and melt into the air.

If it doesn't, of course, I've fallen. So much is chance,
So much agility, desire and feverish care,
As bicyclists and harpsichordists prove

Who only by moving can balance,
Only by balancing move.[13]

The poem's opening appeal to a quaintly named 'dearest' makes
its addressee unambiguous; while the addressee is not explicitly
sexed, the poem announces itself as a modern contribution to the
metaphysical tradition in which male speakers addressed female
lovers: hence it seems reasonable to assume this poem is spoken by
a male voice to a female object. While 'dearest' is not in itself
gendered, this tradition is, so in selecting both form and style, the
poet engages with the traditions associated with both, and these
traditions become an essential part of the new poem. Donaghy's
speaker is characterised slightly satirically; he seems a little pedan-
tic in the use of that precise directive, 'note'. As the poem progresses,
his absorption in the 'gadgetry of love' implies an obsession with
'the machinery of grace' that has blotted out the possibility of any
more sophisticated grasp of human nature which might alert him
to the fact that women cannot be wooed with the predictability of
concentric gears. This gentle mockery at his expense undercuts the
pomposity, and disarms criticism, making it possible to admire his
skill as well as finding his attitude faintly absurd. His elaborate
conceit—developed in order to show the unlikely similarities
between a racing bike and a piece of harpsichord music—owes
much of its technique to the Metaphysical poets. Donaghy's poem

also gestures to the metaphysical tradition in the way that his female addressee functions as an excuse for this opportunity of impressing male friends and patrons (note also, the lynchpin 'so', on which the analogy turns: another staple of metaphysical poetry).

It seems at first as though the poem's whole rationale is to seduce the lover ('this talk...Should work its effortless gadgetry of love'). The poem itself is presented as so insignificant that the poet hopes it will vanish once the seduction is accomplished. But it gradually becomes apparent that the poem's real intent is the display of its author's skill. There are crucial differences between the original two creations and the third (the poem) with which they are compared. The basis for comparison is that the intricately constructed artefact—in itself a feat, marvel of engineering, technical knowledge and imagination—is only a means to an end. If it works successfully, you do not notice it. The bicycle carries the cyclist, but it is the cyclist who steers. The power in Purcell's musical notes comes from their combination, the flow and rhythm, contrasts and motifs; even though the notes are individually intricate, they are not the point—the point is 'the playing', whereby a mood is created and a dance danced. By analogy then, this poem is designed to transport its addressee, the lover; to move her, and presumably seduce her, by its spell, but to do this without drawing attention to itself. But while the cyclist steers his bike, and the harpsichordist makes music from Purcell's pavane, what does the woman do? If the poem works, then it will work its magic *on* her. She will not do or become anything as a result; she has no agency. Where the cyclist steers, and the musician plays, she is simply the pretext for the whole ambitious exercise. It is the poet/speaker who, as architect of this graceful machinery, will benefit from it.

The poem gives this away, in admitting that it is he who will 'fall' if it fails: fall in both the senses that have already been invoked: from 'grace', and lose his balance. That the speaker takes centre-stage is apparent from some confusion in the last three lines: bicyclists and harpsichordists are the ones who use the clever machine. We might expect, according to the analogy, that it would be the lover, recipient of the poem, who would be in a parallel position. Yet it is actually the speaker who holds this position; he confesses it. The woman's role is to observe, admire and be seduced.

Furthermore, what the speaker proposes as a consequence of his elaborate conceit is, itself, impossible. If it effectively works its spell, the poem will vanish. Yet it is the poem that remains, and the woman who vanishes.

While the speaker is being mocked for his zealous, premeditated wooing strategy, the poem invites its readers to appreciate his craft. The intricate rhyme scheme, which repeatedly folds back on itself, then steps elegantly forwards (aba cdedef ghg ijk ik), enacts the closing chiasmus: a forward movement followed by a balancing pause. The speaker's authority stems from the confidence with which he takes on a metaphysical conceit, employing a subtle blend of registers: informal, technical and literary. Its force is apparent from the casual suggestion that this 'talk' is as powerfully affecting as his touch would be. While the ostensible addressee is his 'dearest', in fact her peripheral position is less significant than that of an informed, admiring audience, witness to his virtuoso performance of technical accomplishment. If the reader/lover is to accept the poet's ambitious attempt to prove the similarity between racing bike, a harpsichord and his own poem, s/he has to acquiesce in the speaker's cleverness. Donaghy is knowingly mocking the self-regarding tendencies of much Metaphysical poetry, but he has it both ways, because at the same time his ostentatious display of talent is there, on the page, for all to see.

The opening poem in Armitage's first collection is 'Snow Joke':

> Heard the one about the guy from Heaton Mersey?
> Wife at home, lover in Hyde, mistress
> in Newton-le-Willows and two pretty girls
> in the top grade at Werneth prep. Well,
>
> he was late and he had a good car so he snubbed
> the police warning-light and tried to finesse
> the last six miles of moorland blizzard,
> and the story goes he was stuck within minutes.
>
> So he sat there thinking about life and things;
> what the dog does when it catches its tail
> and about the snake that ate itself to death.

And he watched the windscreen filling up
with snow, and it felt good, and the whisky
from his hip-flask was warm and smooth.
And of course, there isn't a punchline
but the ending goes something like this.

They found him slumped against the steering wheel
With VOLVO printed backwards in his frozen brow.
And they fought in the pub over hot toddies
as to who was to take the most credit.

Him who took the aerial to be a hawthorn twig?
Him who figured out the contour of his car?
Or him who said he heard the horn, moaning
softly like an alarm clock under an eiderdown? [14]

Where the effect of Donaghy's opening poem is to present the poet as a cultured, urbane, self-mocking wordsmith, who knows his foibles as well as his craft, Armitage constructs a different persona in this debut. This is the poet as a man of the people, a bloke like any other. The poem is in syllabics, but part of its effectiveness lies in the unobtrusiveness of the form. It is the colloquial language that is obvious: the repetition of conjunctions which is a feature of casual speech ('and he had a good car', 'and about the snake that ate itself', 'And of course', 'And they fought'); sloppy constructions ('life and things'); casual fillers like 'well' and 'so', and the poem's anecdotal quality. There is nothing to sex the speaker or the audience, but from the way in which the protagonist is presented—the guy who has it all, smart car, abundant supply of mistresses and girlfriends all over town—it seems reasonable to assume a male speaker addressing a male audience. The story has the qualities of urban myth; it is dramatic, unlikely and yet plausible. As the pun in its title indicates ('Snow Joke' — 'it's no joke'), the poem turns on whether or not the tale is funny—which depends on your perspective. If you are wife, lover or mistress it is likely to be less amusing. The audience are primed to expect a light-hearted gag but, just as things unexpectedly take a deadly turn for the protagonist, so too the audience's own confident expectations are pulled up short as the story turns tragic. But by engaging this central uncertainty as to whether or not *the speaker* thinks it is funny, the poem evades both emotion and morality, avoiding any opinion about the man's adultery and/or about his fate. Perhaps unintentionally, it is an example of male reluctance to pass judgement on other men's behaviour. The guy who has everything (too much?) receives his come uppance, and there is more than a hint of *schadenfreude* to the tale. The heroes who gather in the pub afterwards compete over whose actions were most impressive, as if to suggest the circuit of male rivalry is unending: once the top dog's been toppled, competition for his successor begins. But there is still ambiguity. Is the man dead? His brow is frozen, but if he was dead, why would those men who found him be squabbling over who got the credit, since they had been too late to save him? Maybe that is the point: in this scenario what is really being played out is a vying for status amongst men. Women function as trophies, cited briefly as the man's appendage—wife, lover, mistress. The pleasure in the anecdote—for both teller and listener—lies in witnessing the downfall of this enviable dude, caught out by his own arrogance. The poem positions its reader as part of this audience, which is most likely a group of mates in the pub. And while women are not barred from such a scenario, there are plenty of clues that this story, in its retelling here, is both about, and for, men. While the interdiegetic audience is male, there is nothing to stop female readers enjoying the wit, particularly since the distinction between our narrator and the Volvo driver signals the importance of class intersecting gender.

There are no metaphors in Simon Armitage's 'Snow Joke': the poem presents itself as familiar anecdote and employs colloquial language. The only significant use of figure comes in the last two lines, in which the car horn is likened to the 'moaning' of 'an alarm clock under an eiderdown'. The simile's effect is to heighten poignancy, thus introducing a new note to the poem. It also functions as a reminder of the man's married home life and domestic routines—now yearned for as a place of safety. After the envy and bravado, the poem ends with the muted implication that if the adventurous adulterer had stayed at home, he would still be safe. But this is a fleeting suggestion perfectly designed for the close, because the poem's energy and zest stem from the man's high-risk lifestyle. The closing simile forms the sensible but dull moral of the story, appended as an afterthought. The clock's 'moaning' is not entirely desirable either, triggering memories of the wife's grumbling complaints (or perhaps her grieving).

Armitage's poem possesses a similarly forceful rhetoric to Donaghy's, in spite of the one using a self-consciously poetic regis- ter, and the other colloquial language. Both poems close with formal skill, underlining a firm tone, which brooks no disagreement (chias- mus in Donaghy; parallelisms in Armitage). Despite the way in which both poems make a direct appeal to an auditor ('Dearest', 'Heard the one...?'), it is striking that both appeals are ultimately only rhetorical; neither actually requires or even allows a response. Neither poet sexes his speaker, though it seems both are male. By placing himself within a tradition of metaphysical love poetry, Donaghy both signals his fitness as inheritor of such a tradition and demonstrates his contemporary nouse by sending up the tempta- tions for over-elaboration which that tradition courts. Armitage draws his public authority from a far less elevated sphere: pub talk, a predominantly masculine sphere. Both poets make use of modes of interlocution whose masculine histories make them particularly impenetrable to female listeners.

Neil Rollinson's 'Like the Blowing of Birds' Eggs' is taken from his first collection, *A Spillage of Mercury*, published in 1996:

> I crack the shell
> on the bedstead and open it
> over your stomach. It runs
> to your navel and settles there
> like the stone of a Sharon fruit.
>
> You ask me to gather it up
> and pour it over your breast
> without breaking the membrane.
>
> It swims in my palm, drools
> from the gaps in my fingers, fragrant,
> spotted with blood.

It slips down your chest,
moves on your skin like a woman
hurrying in her yellow dress, the long
transparent train dragging behind.

It slides down your belly and into your
pubic hair where you burst
the yolk with a tap of your finger.

It covers your cunt in a shock
of gold. You tell me to eat,
to feel the sticky glair on my tongue.

I lick the folds of your sex, the coarse
damp hairs, the slopes of your arse
until you're clean, and tense as a clock spring.

I touch your spot and something inside you
explodes like the blowing of birds' eggs.[15]

Once again, this poem appeals to a specific addressee, but the
mode of address is different; instead of public discourse, this poem
describes intimate love making. The speaker is not sexed but certain
characteristics suggest it is actually a male speaker (until the word
'cunt', the lover could be male too.) And while the poem is ostensibly addressed to the lover, its presence as the first piece in a
published collection problematises the nature of that private address.
The narrator provides an intricately detailed, wholly visual description of the egg on the lover's body, in a way that risks accusations
of a pornographic representation. To counter such a criticism, the
speaker emphasises his role as obedient accomplice: he simply does
as she first asks and then—more commandingly—tells him to do.
He presents himself as entirely subordinate to her pleasure, concentrating on the beloved during love making. It is the egg (yolk and
albumen) which is endowed with the power of agency: it runs,
settles, swims, drools, slips, moves and slides over her, as if it has
a life of its own. It is even described at one point, in an elaborate
simile, as being 'like a woman / hurrying in her yellow dress, the

long / transparent train dragging behind'. But while the syntax attribute this power to the egg, and the simile disarmingly hints at its femininity (and, by inference, the woman-centred nature of this scene), the egg actually enacts the speaker's movements by proxy, literally travelling where he might (like to) go, as well as moving as a result of his actions. Because the speaker presents himself as simply following instructions, it seems as though he is powerless, and this helps deflect criticism that the poem reduces the woman to an object of spectacle. Here the woman undoubtedly *is* the spectacle; while the speaker seems preoccupied with describing the egg, this technique enhances the titillation by inviting the reader to imagine the surfaces on and into which it slides—a substitution which is a classic ingredient of pornography. So while it is, syntactically, the egg that 'drools / from the gaps in my fingers, fragrant, / spotted with blood', all three parts of this description can also apply to the woman herself and this is what happens: the associations transfer themselves on to her body evoking, by inference, her mucus, blood and smell. Tellingly, the narrator is only the subject of three verbs throughout: the action of the opening line and then, in quick succession, twice in the last two verses. Only at this climactic moment in the poem does the male speaker assert himself as agent, producing the woman's orgasm. And what of the simile that gives the poem its title? Tellingly, the verb's passive construction once again seeks to conceal the man's presence, as if to grant full power and control to the woman. Yet it is, as we have just seen, the man's actions that precipitate the orgasm, just as it is his language that has determined its public representation. The description of a moment that epitomises release of control inevitably exposes the woman, and the effect of this exposure is intensified by its presentation as a private, intimate address. The speaker's strange absence (what does he feel? Is he aroused? Willing? Marvelling? Jealous?) makes the representation all the more disturbing.

So once again, even though the poem is explicitly addressed to a woman, her part in it is as an object on display. The speaker preserves the inscrutable detachment of a scientific observer, his own self curiously absent while he reveals and exposes the woman lying before him.[16]

Most of the metaphors in Rollinson's poem describe the egg as it moves across the woman's skin; invested with animation it eventually covers her 'cunt in a shock / of gold.' In this metaphor, the speaker's reaction is subsumed into the egg, in a strategy that is consistent with the figurative presentation of the egg's movements. This enables the speaker to sustain his position as a detached observer, and it enhances the pornographic characteristics of the representation. The woman's buttocks are described as 'slopes', in harmony with a long tradition of metaphorical depictions of the female body as land. But it is two similes right at the end that do most of the poem's work: the woman is described as 'tense as a clock spring' before a sudden (and confusing) switch in figurative ground to the title's analogy of orgasm as 'like the blowing of birds' eggs'. The employment of similes rather than metaphors is appropriate to the speaker's distanced perspective outside the event he is describing, since similes are less assertive, being overt about their own status as tropes that only *suggest* resemblances rather than claiming that one idea or concept *actually is* another. (See p.70 below for fuller discussion of this difference.) But the simile of blown birds' eggs suggests pre-empted fertility, as well as a disconcerting sense of violent expenditure imposed on the woman by some spontaneous physiological function; its overall effect is aggressively anti-fertility. (See chapter 5 for further examples of this in men's poems.) As a woman reader, I have two options in relation to Rollinson's poem: to place myself in the position of the woman, and enjoy a fantasy with this Byronic individual, or to become a voyeur of private love making. John Sutherland's description of poetry as 'published privacies' could not be more appropriate.

To turn now to women. The opening poem from Fiona Pitt-Kethley's first collection is 'Sky Ray Lolly':

A toddler on a day out in Herne Bay,
on seeing an ancient, civil-servant-type,
I held my Sky Ray lolly—red, yellow
and green striped, pointed, dripping down between
my legs and walked bandy. My Ma and Pa,
(old-fashioned innocents like Rupert Bear's),
just didn't notice this and ambled on,

that is, until they saw the old man's face,
jaw dislocated in surprise. They grabbed
that Martian's willy from my little hand.
The world still sees me as a nasty kid
usurping maleness. A foul brat to be
smacked down by figures of authority.
All things most natural in men, in me
are vice—having no urge to cook or clean,
lacking maternal instincts.

And they would take my pride, my rocket
of ambition, amputate my fun and geld
my laughter, depriving me of colour.
And smirk to see my little lolly melt,
me left with a stick.[17]

Pitt-Kethley's anecdote is delivered in the first-person. Like 'Snow Joke', it is written in syllabics, but the poem's conversational tone disguises this formal shaping. Its speaker is explicitly sexed (female); there is no direct appeal to an addressee and its audience is unspecific; indeed, this is not just unspecific, the poem almost doubts it will have an audience. Because she rejects the identification 'woman', there is no attempt to appeal to a collective female constituency either; the speaker's voice reflects the lonely limbo of the outsider.

The poem is preoccupied with its speaker's unstable position between two genders; as a female who does not identify with the attributes of femininity, her only option seems to be to imitate maleness. But imitation is dangerous, provoking punitive reactions; the speaker fears her figurative castration. Her parents' authority seems benign beside the anonymous but apparently ubiquitous authority figures who have replaced them, and whose resentment and scorn for her behaviour provoke not just the accusation of immaturity ('kid', 'brat') but physical reprisal. The poem underlines the inescapable binary that regulates gender roles: if she is not feminine, she is guilty of 'usurping maleness'; there is no other position for her to assume. Threats of castration emphasise the irony that she is already (in the world's view) castrated; the fact that her detractors want to inflict such a punishment can be read as a blatant refutation of the psychoanalytic claim that females are biologically lacking. As a poem expressing anxiety about her own creative potency and authority, the fear of gelding is particularly significant, since it suggests the speaker equates potency with masculinity. This is the poem's controversial, and depressing core, and she does not seem to disagree with the assessment; her fearful, sad tone suggests she even shares it to some extent. The lolly metaphor works on several levels: it pokes deflationary fun at the phallus, but it also emphasises her need for a prosthesis, and the vulnerability of her bravado, open to attack by those who would love to see her apparent confidence and pride melt away. In the final stanza, the string of pronouns asserting selfhood ('me' or 'my', used seven times in five lines) seem like a feeble defence against the world's hostility, and the monosyllabic pathos of the last line enacts the very gelding she fears: it has only five syllables, whereas all the other lines (bar one) have ten or eleven.

The poem's central metaphor of the lolly is first literally enacted, as the little girl's flippant mockery, but by the end of the poem it has been revealed to be an uncannily accurate symbol of female cultural lack. Critic Alan Robinson has offered a different reading. He praises the poem for the wit with which it 'debunks…the signifier that epitomises the patriarchal Symbolic Order [the phallus] by reducing it to a garish iced lolly', but he dismisses the rest of the poem as 'rather preachily superfluous self-commentary'[18] and thereby misses its pathos. Perhaps distracted by Pitt-Kethley's reputation as a scurrilous, feisty individual prone to 'smutty' poetry, he does not seem to notice the tone of defeat. Or perhaps Pitt-Kethley's boldly insulting reference to the penis is overwhelming. The 'superfluous self-commentary' is precisely the point of the poem, which is about the difficulty a woman faces in laying claim to authority: what she mocked as a little girl is, she now recognises, the culture's symbol of her own lack. Two very different interpretations emerge, and their difference hinges on the metaphor, suggesting just how big a part the reader plays in shaping meanings.

The second poem is similar in that it too employs the first person, creating a persona closely associated with the poet herself. Sujata Bhatt's first collection opens with 'Sujata: The First Disciple of Buddha':

One morning, a tall lean man
stumbled towards me.
His large eyes: half closed
as if he were seasick
his thick black hair full of dead leaves and bumble-
bees
grew wild as weeds and fell way below his hips.
His beard swayed gently as an elephant's trunk.
'I'm hungry', he muttered.
I took him home, fed him fresh yoghurt and bread.
Then, I bathed him, shaved his face clean and smooth,
coconut oiled his skin soft again.
It took four hours
to wash and comb his long hair,
which he refused to cut.
For four hours he bent his head this way and that
while I ploughed through his hair
with coconut oil on my fingers.
'And how did you get this way?' I asked.
'I haven't slept for years,' he said.
'I've been thinking, just thinking.
I couldn't sleep or eat
Until I had finished thinking.'
After the last knot
had been pulled out of his hair, he slept,
still holding on to my sore fingers.
The next morning, before the sun rose,
before my father could stop me,
he led me to the wide-trunked, thick-leafed bodhi tree
to the shady spot where he had sat for years
and asked me to listen.[19]

Despite the extreme difference in terms of tone and approach, the
story Bhatt tells reveals anxieties similar to Pitt-Kethley's: anxieties
about the source of her authority as a poet. The poem clearly stands
as an introduction to the work that follows it—even using the poet's
first name in its title. It offers an account of how the poet was first
inspired to write: the poet is chosen, singled out as worthy recipient

of the hard-won wisdom of Buddha. As such, Bhatt implicitly claims that her words are not only insightful, but legitimated by the divine man himself (who can be interpreted as her muse, or the spirit of poetry). So the poem both asserts the poet's authenticity as a genuine, inspired poet, and at the same time, admits that it is the male master who possesses the authority to legitimise the woman's writing, or who himself actually produces it, she the scribe. This unevenness of tone—vacillating between assertive authority and meek submissiveness—is characteristic of Bhatt's work.[20] Told as a story (and, in its simple, unsurprised narrative and framing, reminiscent of a religious tale), the free-verse account repeatedly asserts the woman speaker's agency. She is the subject of almost all the verbs, but her actions are those of the solicitous handmaiden. She tends him with complete disregard for her own comfort, combing his hair until her fingers are sore. In keeping with a strictly patriarchal social order, she moves from her father's jurisdiction to that of another man but, doing this without her father's approval, she displays a confident rebelliousness that is at odds with the idea of absolute submission. Interestingly, her relationship with Buddha does not seem to be sexual. He seems slightly feminine, with his long hair, and surrenders himself into her care to be shaved and oiled. Bhatt's muse is a kind of god and, while this poem asserts her status as legitimate heir and inheritor, it also comes close to repeating the traditional schema within which woman functions as the vessel or channel through which divine knowledge is communicated. Her own role is subject to his will. It is a frank exposition of the tentative foundations of this woman poet's authority.

The central metaphor in Sujata Bhatt's poem concerns the idea of the poet as disciple. Its radicalism lies in a woman's calm assertion of her suitability as an acolyte to the great man and, consequently, her right to claim such supreme authority as the inspiration behind her poems. On the other hand, if read as a poem about the muse, its implications are rather different: this muse demands her absolute surrender to his service, and her rejection of all possible rival claims on his attention; she must tend to his needs, and listen to his thoughts, if she is to glean inspiration for her own art.[21]

The last and most recent opening poem from a first collection by a woman is Kate Clanchy's 'Men' from the 1995 volume, *Slattern*:

I like the simple sort, the soft white-collared ones
smelling of wash that someone else has done,
of apples, hard new wood. I like the thin-skinned,
outdoor, crinkled kind, the athletes, big-limbed,
who stoop to hear, the moneyed men, the unironic
leisured sort who balk at jokes and have to blink,
the men with houses, kids in cars, who own
the earth and love it, know themselves at home
here, and so don't know they're born, or why
born is hard, but snatch life smack from the sky,
a cricket ball caught clean that fills the hand.

I put them all at sea. They peer at my dark land
as if through sun on dazzling waves, and laugh.[22]

Clanchy's first-person speaker is far more assured. She is not
addressing anyone in particular, but this account sounds declara-
tory, at ease with its own public tone. It is more obviously crafted
than the first two examples, using rhyming couplets and iambic
pentameter; it is a truncated sonnet, missing its fourteenth line.
The speaker's affectionate, but slightly condescending attitude is
shown in the way she resorts to repeated colloquial shorthand
('sort', 'ones', 'kind') in place of the specific name, 'men', and by
the way she categorises such an intimidatingly catholic list of her
favourites. It is the gentle giants she goes for, and she implies that
they are innocents. That she is unbothered by the naïve, over privileged ones suggests her own self-assurance, as well as her superior
experience and familiarity with the ways in which life can be hard.
But the speaker's attitude towards these men is not critical of them;
rather it is celebratory. That comment about their naïvety is quickly
followed by the cricket-ball metaphor that takes pleasure in their
capacity for decisive and effective action. There seems to be some
similarity between their style and her own, suggested by the satisfaction with which the speaker controls language and sound
patterning so commandingly. It is as if this skill is somehow comparable to the men's more physical, but equally talented, activity.

It is the closing lines that make the poem, with their clever pun
simultaneously suggesting this sassy woman runs rings around a

choice array of suitors, and that she shoos them out of her way as unimportant distractions. Clanchy appropriates Freud's metaphor of women as the dark continent, in order to send it up, since her persona's position as the one who really calls the shots is suggested by the way in which the poem contradicts the situation it describes: the men are peering at her ineffectually, but she has already studied them all sufficiently to be able to sum them up in pithy phrases. The impression of her own cool savvy is enhanced by the ease with which she appropriates two metaphors commonly associated with men's experience and usage: 'hard new wood' with its light allusion to the slang for an erection, and that of the cricket ball, employed by Clanchy to show how inextricably a certain kind of masculine assurance is bound up with class.

Clanchy's poem offers a far more confident assertion of an authoritative female poetic voice than the other two examples. But its focus and subject is still men, and the need to attend to them. Unlike the men's poems, there is no expectation of a sex-specific audience: male readers are not excluded by this address, far from it. The closing lines could even be read as being deliberately aimed at them, since they offer the perhaps reassuring possibility that these men, who seem to have been subject to her whim, nevertheless retain some control; they can have the last laugh.

DOMINANT SUBJECT POSITIONING AND GENDER

Of the men's poems, two of the three contained an explicit address to a woman interlocutor: Donaghy's 'dearest' and Rollinson's lover, the 'you' to whom the poem is ostensibly spoken. What effect might these interdiegetic positions—clearly gendered—have on *actual* readers? It is difficult, as a woman, to find a position from which to read. This is the same problem Sara Mills identified in relation to the poem about reproductive potential. The feminist critic Judith Fetterley coined the term 'immasculation' to describe the process whereby women readers steeped in androcentric literature develop the instinct 'to think as men, to identify with a male point of view'.[23] They acquire the capacity to bifurcate their response, reading as both male and female simultaneously. At its most extreme, if women only have access to male-centred writings, Fetterley claimed the results were damaging, producing:

> not simply the powerlessness which derives from not seeing one's experience articulated, clarified, and legitimised in art, but more significantly, the powerlessness which results from the endless division of self against self, the consequence of the invocation to identify as male while being reminded that to be male—to be universal-...is to be *not female.* (p.xiii)

None of the women's poems made direct appeal to an addressee of either sex; all three were framed as first-person accounts, which might suggest that, even though the lyric 'I' represents particular challenges for women poets (as Kaplan and Maguire claim), they feel a need to work with it, in order to carve out an authoritative, public persona. Pitt-Kethley and Bhatt's poems acknowledge the anxieties that accompany this effort—this is, in large part, what they are about. Clanchy's 'I' is coolly assured, though clearly acutely conscious of the novelty of the assertive position she claims, since the poem is precisely about objectification, gender and desire.

THE TRANSITION FROM PRIVATE TO PUBLIC VOICE

The anxieties displayed by Pitt-Kethley and Bhatt hinge on this difficult transition, and stem from the paucity of public discourses that are habituated to a female voice. Male poets benefit from a greater choice of collective public discourses: familiar forms of public communication in which one person addresses several others. Pub talk, political debate, educational, legal and religious discourses are historically the preserve of male speakers. Women now participate in them, but they are newcomers.[24] As Kaplan has pointed out, every society guards those areas of discourse considered most prestigious, and in such protected spheres there are still prohibitions forbidding women's participation (the Roman Catholic Church's refusal to ordain women is an example). Where women do assume these roles, they claim a certain public authority, akin to the authority a poet seeks, but the ways in which men and women use authority, and the meanings invested in it, differ.

In the poems just examined, Donaghy and Rollinson draw on traditions of Metaphysical and Romantic poetry in order to amplify their own authority; Armitage substitutes a more popular mode of discourse, but one that is just as deeply gendered masculine: pub-talk. There are few modes of public discourse in which women can speak *as women*, and this is reflected in their poetry, where it is rare to find an explicit address to other women, a collective female discourse. Furthermore, most public discourse is not overtly sexed as the speech of men to men; as Luce Irigaray has argued, the use of 'he' as a generic pronoun effectively veils its sexual specificity, enabling what is in fact communication between men to pass as neutral, objective speech. (This shows in the way the men poets feel no need to be explicit about the sex of speaker or addressee—except when either is female. Conversely, in poems by women, considerable effort or anxiety goes into sexing both speaker and addressee.) This is in keeping with Irigaray's empirical research into differences in usage between male and female speakers:

> Women sexualise their discourse. Just as they often attribute their concrete qualities to things and to places, they address themselves to sexed interlocutors. Men don't do this but remain among themselves, between *they* (*ils*), or between *I-he/they* (*je-il[s]*), which is equivalent to making a non-conscious sexual choice.[25]

She argues that, in both men's and women's speech, the mediating third generic term is always masculine: *he/il*, and that this has serious implications for the viability of women's capacity to 'situate themselves as *I, I-she / they* (*je-elle[s]*), to represent themselves as subjects, and to talk to other women'. (p.33)

Irigaray gives an example: in the language experiments she conducted, she recorded some therapy sessions. Both men and women clients referred to their (female) interlocutor as female during the sessions. But when they were placed with another female interlocutor and asked to make sentences out of a selection of given words, all respondents constructed sentences that assumed the interlocutor was '*he/they / il(s)*'; they ignored her sex, imposing what Irigaray calls 'a pseudo-neutrality, tellingly reintroducing a masculine he (*il*) in place of a feminine you (*tu*)'.(p.34) As Elizabeth Hirsh concludes, in an article that identifies a parallel project underway in Adrienne Rich's 1973 poetry collection, *Diving into the Wreck*:

> Female self-representation requires the constitution of an autonomous, generic she as a mediating term that relates the (female) *I* to the (female) *you*, and the female *I* to the male *you* (which at present can only relate only to *he*'s).[26]

The continuing lack of this generic 'she' has far-reaching effects. Some are apparent from the rare examples of poems that do attempt to address a collective female 'we'. 'Marigolds', by Vicki Feaver, is framed as a specific address to women.[27] The poem opens with a list of the flowers 'men give women', setting up a contrast between such flowers and the far more precious, disturbing, powerful marigolds of the title. The delicate femininity of 'carnations / the shades of bridesmaids' dresses', and the stiffness of red roses represent the pale, tamed version of femininity which men take for real, whereas marigolds, with their slimy, fast-blackening leaves and 'tight, explosive buds' are presented as the flowers women really love, responding to them as symbols of female lust and violence. (Women are described as capable of tearing men's heads off, and as bringing the marigolds 'secretly and shamefully / into the house, stroking our arms and breasts and legs / with their hot orange fringes, / the smell of arousal.') The poem asks its readers to acquiesce in the implicit criticism of men's foolish ignorance, conned (or attracted) by this fake version of meek, marriageable femininity. More controversially, halfway through it shifts from being situated in the present to the classical past, while preserving the same collective pronoun, so that the contemporary women who scour their vases to get rid of the marigolds' slime are suddenly participants in a wild, ecstatic dance on 'the Thracian mountain'.

'Marigolds' attempts a bold revision of poetic tradition in the way it harnesses the conventional metaphoric association between female sexuality and flowers. Where flower symbolism has traditionally stood in as substitute for female sexuality (or sex organs), Feaver's marigolds are made something much more potent than symbols; they are an essential part of women's lives: adornment and potion, playing a part in female rituals as well as being used auto-erotically, in private, to caress and arouse. So the flowers are connected to sexual desire, but they involve much more than that, they 'remind us we are killers'. Feaver's marigolds do not stand in for real women; they are sacred objects in their own right. Signalling its opposition from the opening negative ('Not the flowers men give women') her poem reintegrates the tenor and vehicle (female sexuality and flower) of poetic convention, and in so doing it dispenses with the connotations of passivity and frailty that traditionally accompanied it. At the same time, the ephemeral beauty of the flower is transformed from a warning to women and men about the transience of female beauty, into proof of the impossibility of domesticating (and thus taming) women. In this way Feaver cancels out the misogyny of that rich repository of poetic prophecies about the quick passing of female beauty, replacing it with a much more empowering declaration of female power.

However, the poem's presentation of a collective, uniform trans-historical womanhood is in itself problematic. It is open to the accusation that it homogenises difference in the way that it assumes a continuity of experience between women.[28] On a more basic level, women readers often resist such invitations to collective female identification, objecting to any appeal to a clearly female audience because the appeal feels prescriptive, a demand for acquiescence and agreement. Even in cases where such poems are not directed at female readers, but simply testify to specifically female experience, they tend to arouse hostility from women critics.[29] It seems that the unavoidably marked nature of a female speaker often alienates women readers because they feel themselves somehow drawn into, and submerged within it, as if such an explicit treatment of womanhood forces them to identify themselves as specifically female in a way that removes their freedom.[30] In this regard, it is probably significant that Clanchy's poem, which was the one that had least difficulty asserting a public female voice, is determinedly individualistic. There is no room for other women in it; their existence is eclipsed by the choice of that flat, vague 'someone else' who does the men's washing. This tone is reminiscent of the marketable side of women's liberation: confident and sexually assertive.[31]

In relation to this issue about an explicit female address, there is an interesting mismatch between what happens in most contemporary poetry by women in Britain, and the theoretical models outlined by feminist critics. The critics emphasise the importance of readers' involvement in the reading process. For example, Patrocinio Schweickart outlines a dialectical relationship between text and reader in which the central issue is not, as it is for conventional reader-response theorists, one of control (who is controlling whom—text or reader?) but 'of managing the contradictory implications of the desire for relationship...and the desire for intimacy, up to and including a symbiotic merger with the other.'[32] Alice Templeton has suggested that Adrienne Rich's poems are carefully framed so as to provoke responses from readers, and to lead to dialogue; she claims that this is central to Rich's feminist aesthetic, and that it represents a challenge to conventional poetry's monologic status.[33] Lynne Pearce's study of feminist readers argues that the urge for *interaction* lies at the root of all reading practice.[34] Nicole Ward Jouve also claims that readers are motivated by a desire for recognition or identification.[35] But Vicki Feaver's 'Marigolds' is highly unusual in its direct appeal to a collective female audience; it seems that North American women poets are more ready to make these collective appeals than British women.[36]

METAPHOR: A DYNAMIC PROCESS OF READER INTERACTION

> *Discover a language that they, listening intently (you hope) for your words, will understand, take in, recreate, give back to you. So that conversation can begin....Send up metaphor flares which he will think are just decoration not urgent complex signals of desire, intent.*[37]

If women's poems tend to avoid such direct appeals to their reader, there is another aspect of the reading process in which the reader's involvement plays a crucial part: the reception of metaphor. In this respect, all poetry is dialogic. Chris Baldick defines metaphor as:

the most important and widespread figure of speech, in which one thing, idea or action is referred to by a word or expression normally denoting another thing, idea or action so as to suggest some common quality shared by the two.[38]

What this definition does not convey is the creative, subversive potential of metaphor to bring about change in the way human beings perceive the world. As theorists of metaphor like George Lakoff have stressed, we understand the world via analogy: 'much of what is real in a society or in the experience of an individual is structured and made sense of via conventional metaphor'.[39] He gives several examples of ways in which metaphor influences our perceptions: use of phrases like 'the nation's health' to refer to its economic state, not the physical health of its citizens, or the metaphor 'time is money', now so frequently enacted. Our language is saturated with metaphors that we do not notice, but that carry information about the attitudes and values that underpin our society. Yet, as Lakoff notes, 'The system of conventional conceptual metaphor is mostly unconscious, automatic, and used with no noticeable effect.' (p.245)

Feminists (and other groups opposed to the dominant ideology within a particular society) have long recognised the potential of metaphor as a tool in their struggle to change attitudes. Its concentrated language, its relative freedom from narrative causality and logic, and its use of figurative language make it well suited for innovation in conceptions of gender identities and other challenges to the status quo. In her 1993 study *The Sexual Metaphor* Helen Haste argues that western societies are trapped within dualistic metaphors, and only release from this oppositional framework will make any change in conceptions of gender possible: 'changing ideas also require changed metaphors; it is necessary to shed the old models and assumptions', she claims, urging us to question previously unexamined metaphors and work to restock the existing repertoire.[40] Mary Daly similarly views the creation of new metaphors as a way of both recovering hidden, forgotten knowledge, and of moving towards transformation:

> Metaphors evoke action, movement. They…evoke a shock, a clash with the 'going logic' and they introduce a new logic. Metaphors function to name change, and therefore they elicit change.[41]

If metaphors contain this potential in their ordinary use, it is even more powerful in poetry. In his study of stylistics, Richard Bradford notes that in realist prose and everyday usage, metaphors remain grounded; the surrounding context stabilises the relationship between the two parts of the metaphor (labelled by I. A. Richards as the tenor, which is the principal subject of the metaphor, and the vehicle, which is the analogue, the subject or idea carried over from another field of reference). But in poetry, there is often a deliberate disruption of the tenor, vehicle and context, so that it becomes impossible to disentangle one from another:

> It is *the language of the poem, as much as the reader's* a priori *knowledge*, which creates its perceived situation and context. It constructs its own ground, and metaphor becomes less a departure from contextual terms and conditions and more a device which appropriates and even establishes them.[42] [my italics]

As a result, poetry has greater potential for invention; it is capable of actually changing the way reality is perceived, bringing about what Bradford calls 'an unbalancing of perceptions of reality' (p.28), a transformation or appropriation of normal reality. But in order to do this, the reader has to accept the metaphor's terms.

Poets recognise the potential power metaphor provides to remake the world according to their own vision. Gwyneth Lewis has written of the way that metaphor signals trust in the individual's vision above all other forms of logic or truth, and she comments on the subversive nature of such potential.[43] Michèle Roberts claims that metaphor 'offers a way into the land of images that is the unconscious, both collective and personal'.[44]

In a similar vein, Paul Ricoeur's work on metaphor emphasises its status as fiction, not truth—but fiction with powerful influence over what we perceive as 'reality'. He describes metaphor as 'the rhetorical process by which discourse unleashes the power that certain fictions have to redescribe reality...linking fiction and redescription in this way'.[45] Metaphor, in his opinion, is not really about naming, so much as about characterising what has already been named; it deals in concepts and ideas, not objects; this makes its ideological potential greater. Ricoeur recognises that, while simpler figurations (like simile and metonymy) only require the reader to acknowledge an already recognised association between two objects, metaphor requires him or her to concur with the maker in recognising a conceptual relationship where none previously existed. This entails negotiation and is a matter of judgement. He points out:

> The 'place' of metaphor...is neither the name, nor the sentence, nor even discourse, but the copula of the verb 'to be'. The metaphorical 'is' at once signifies both 'is not' and 'is like'. (p.7)

During the 1970s and 1980s, many women voiced wariness over metaphor. Anthologies with titles like *No More Masks!* declared their determination to break with the euphemisms of figurative language, and 'tell it like it is'. But, as others pointed out, this was to assume that language could divest itself of its status as representation.[46] Women's suspicion arose from the androcentrism of literary tradition's metaphorical staples, created by male authors, in which women invariably served as the vehicle. To take one example, Eavan Boland complained that the trope of woman as land led to stylised and idealised depictions of Irish womanhood:

> The women in Irish male poems tended to be emblematic and passive, granted a purely ornamental status....Once the feminine image in their poems became fused with a national concept then both were simplified and reduced...it was the absence of women in the poetic tradition which allowed women in the poems to be simplified.[47]

To give another example: in an essay on birth poetry, Karin Voth Harman argues that poets should use metonymy rather than metaphor, because after hundreds of years of metaphors that figure artistic creativity as 'birth', the realities of childbirth remained undescribed in poetry.[48] Voth Harman understandably wants to read poems about birth in which the body is not made to vanish, but is centre stage. But these misgivings arose because the repeated use of woman as the *vehicle* of metaphors inevitably eclipsed woman as subject. The real discontent is not with metaphor itself, but with the inheritance of a tradition composed overwhelmingly of male-created metaphors. As Ward Jouve puts it:

> Male poets have, throughout the ages, made a glorious job of singing reality. I would not be without their song. But some of the propositions that they make don't leave me room. I need the other sides, as it were, the many repressed sides. Among these, for a more complete, a multiple world, one in which...there is contradiction and complementarity, a world in which there could be 'an abundance of the other', as Hélène Cixous puts it, I need the woman creator. And she is not so easy to imagine, because of the ways in which woman has been metaphorized as sea as Pythoness as screen as cave as mirror.[49]

Ward Jouve argues that there is nothing innately gendered about metaphor, although differences in male and female experience both produce different metaphors and highlight different aspects of human existence. Her examination of male and female writers' metaphorical treatments of the sea reveals how metaphors emerge out of actual experience. Because for centuries men have gone to sea, she finds the experience transmuted into their writing in the form of metaphors that depict processes of maturation and individuation in terms of sea voyages. From this it follows that the more limited experiential range of women would be reflected in their metaphors. However, contemporary women writers have opened up new areas of experience and invented new metaphors to describe their versions of reality.[50]

But there is an issue about the reception of such innovative perspectives. Who decides the success of a metaphor? The matter is inevitably subjective to a high degree: as a reader, you test the metaphor against your own imagination and experience, as Bradford's model suggests: 'the language of the poem as much as the reader's a priori knowledge'. As an acrimonious exchange between John Hartley Williams and Sheenagh Pugh about the efficacy of Mark Doty's metaphors illustrated, readers do not necessarily agree. Pugh praised Doty's figurative impressions; Williams attacked them for artificiality.[51] It may well be, then, that male readers are sometimes poorly equipped to recognised the verisimilitude or ingenuity of women poets' metaphors, and vice versa. Sean O'Brien certainly hints at this in his suggestion that male readers are likely to encounter difficulties reading Selima Hill and Jo Shapcott (see Introduction, p.34).

Comprehension, or taste, are certainly not *determined* by the sex of the reader. Sex may play a part, but women themselves often resist work which is explicitly gendered female. Kelly, the woman editor of an anthology of Irish poetry by women confesses to her discomfort with the more recent poems therein, which:

> are often self regarding, and too conscious of their female function....Women poets now dare to write explicitly about their bodies. A glut of this subject, too explicitly expressed, should lessen as female metaphor becomes innate rather than innovative. Female metaphor is still insecure. Female taboos still permeate the subconscious.[52]

Kelly conflates frank treatment of the body with innovative metaphor making, but what is interesting is her suggestion that female metaphor is 'insecure', and not yet 'innate'. It is hard to imagine how female metaphor will ever become acceptable as innate within a humanist world view, and it is unclear whose subconscious is still permeated with taboos against female subject matter: does Kelly intend this to refer to a collective subconscious, or perhaps to a collective gendered subconscious? The lack of clarity indicates the slippery subjectivity at work in the reception of any metaphor—a fact which is invariably dodged by poetry critics (see the Introduction). And do these taboos to which Kelly refers inhibit recognition in the minds of the poets themselves, or of their readers? It is likely that the disturbing quality of these innovative metaphors tells us something about their originality: they are disturbing precisely because they break new ground, exploiting the subversive potential of the trope.

So what of the metaphors in the six poems considered earlier? Donaghy's ambitious attempt to prove the congruence between racing bike, harpsichord music and poem suggests that in this poem he approaches metaphor as an intellectual puzzle. It is the poet's task to prove that the three things are comparable. The reader has no scope to decide one way or the other. To use Bradford's terminology, the poet sets out to establish his own, novel contextual terms and conditions; via the persuasive strategies of form and tradition, he seeks to assert the metaphorical relationship on which the poem turns. Armitage's metaphoric use of the alarm clock draws upon reactionary associations of domesticity and wifely complaint. On the whole, Rollinson employs similes rather than metaphors, although the woman's buttocks are described as 'slopes'. Similes are less radically transformative, in that they are overt about their status as tropes that only suggest resemblance, rather than claiming that one idea or concept actually *is* another.[53] Similes are more appropriate to Rollinson's persona, too, since they emphasise the distance between himself and the subject of his figurative inventiveness. Pitt-Kethley's metaphor is—judging by Robinson's reaction—more disturbing. Bhatt's conveys the ambivalence with which she approaches her own authority as a poet. Clanchy's poem appropriates and subverts Freudian theory. So in these examples, it is the women poets who are more likely to develop original metaphors—which is not surprising, since it is their voices that have been absent from past tradition.

Two readings of poems by women further illustrate the ways in which innovative metaphors may be deployed. Rita Ann Higgins's 'The Did-You-Come-Yets of the Western World', like Feaver's 'Marigolds', risks a direct appeal to a female audience:

> When he says to you:
> You look so beautiful
> you smell so nice—
> how I've missed you—
> and did you come yet?
>
> It means nothing,
> and he is smaller
> than a mouse's fart.
>
> Don't listen to him...
> Go down to Annaghdown Pier
> with your father's rod.
> Don't necessarily hold out
> for the biggest one;
> oftentimes the biggest ones
> are the smallest in the end.

Bring them all home,
but not together.
One by one is the trick;
avoid red herrings and scandal.

Maybe you could take two
on the shortest day of the year.
Time is the cheater here
not you, so don't worry.

Many will bite the usual bait;
they will talk their slippery way
through fine clothes and expensive perfume,
fishing up your independence.

These are
the did-you-come-yets of the western world,
the feather and fin rufflers.
Pity them for they have no wisdom.

Others will bite at any bait.
Maggot, suspender, or dead worm.
Throw them to the sharks.

In time one will crawl
out from under thigh-land.
Although drowning he will say,

'Woman I am terrified, why is this house
shaking?'

And you'll know he's the one.[54]

This poem exploits one of the rare examples of interlocutory traditions in which a woman speaks specifically to other women: that of advice from older woman to younger. This is one of the few arenas in which women are credited with special wisdom or insight, and Higgins uses it to proffer some invaluable guidance about how to find the right man. The appeal to a specifically female audience is explicit from the opening line, and the poem thus places men in the position of onlookers, perhaps happy to learn a thing or two as they listen, but specifically excluded from the address. Playing on the cliché of potential partners as fish in the sea, she recommends a trip to the pier 'with your father's rod'. The puns come thick and fast, characterising the speaker as wily and indomitable, but she is also endowed with a mock-serious religious stature. Avoid those who flatter, and those who woo, she counsels, urging her audience to pity them in unmistakeably biblical cadences, a sly gesture towards the tradition of the Irish bard. Her colourful talk reduces these would-be suitors with withering iconoclasm, rendering them tiny beside the woman whose capacity for orgasmic pleasure dwarfs their own fishing rods. Her advice—that you will know the right man by his awed humility at your *jouissance*[55]—is delightfully raunchy, an all-too-rare example of a modern-day *Wife of Bath*. Higgins's deployment of the fishing metaphor is sustained throughout the poem. Some suitors will try 'fishing up your independence'; others, who 'bite at any bait. / Maggot, suspender, or dead worm', should be thrown 'to the sharks'. Finally, the poem returns to its suggestion that men's stature should be measured according to their recognition of women's orgasmic potential, depicting the exhausted, overwhelmed successful suitor as crawling out from beneath his woman's capacious thighs. While it clearly alludes to Synge's *Playboy of the Western World*, the poem does not *depend* on a reader's familiarity with that play. Although Higgins, like many others, is answering back at literary tradition, that strategy can itself end up reinscribing the tradition's centrality. Because of this, it may be more radical to ignore the allusion and foreground other dimensions.

A second example of the deliberate reworking of traditional metaphor is evident in another poem by Sujata Bhatt, 'White Asparagus':

> Who speaks of the strong currents
> streaming through the legs, the breasts
> of a pregnant woman
> in her fourth month?

She's young, this is her first time,
she's slim and the nausea has gone.
Her belly's just starting to get rounder
her breasts itch all day,

and she's surprised that what she wants
is *him*
 inside her again.
Oh come like a horse, she wants to say,
move like a dog, a wolf,
    become a suckling lion-cub-

Come here, and here, and here—
but swim fast and don't stop.

Who speaks of the green coconut uterus
the muscles sliding, a deeper undertow
and the green coconut milk that seals
her well, yet flows so she is wet
from his softest touch?
Who understands the logic
 behind this desire?

Who speaks of the rushing tide
    that awakens
her slowly increasing blood—?
And the hunger
    raw obsessions beginning
with the shape of asparagus:
sun-deprived white and purple-shadow-veined,
she buys three kilos
of the fat ones, thicker than anyone's fingers,
she strokes the silky heads,
some are so jauntily capped....
    even the smell pulls her in—[56]

Bhatt's treatment of pregnancy is factually accurate as well as
precise, but there is a striking ambiguity about just who this poem

is addressed to. If it were written in the first person, it would be a love poem, describing very private details of a woman's fierce desire for her man. By making it into a series of general questions, Bhatt makes it non-exclusive, inviting all readers to consider the questions it poses. Certainly the poem is challenging because of its focus on an aspect of pregnancy that is not usually discussed publicly, but there is also a disconcerting focus on the woman's physical appearance. Is it necessary to know that she is 'slim' and 'young', or that 'this is her first time', a phrase with presumably deliberate overtones of the loss of virginity? Part of the poem seems concerned to reassure the male lover that, despite the miraculous processes her body is going through, he is still central to them; he is the catalyst that motivates or stimulates these changes. At the same time, there is plenty of information that clearly comes from inside the woman's body so, unlike Rollinson's poem, it is not as though the narrator is wholly outside events, looking on. Bhatt's metaphor of 'the green coconut uterus' manages both to validate the physiological function of the womb, rescuing it from poetic circumlocutions by using its medical name, as well as adding to it; her metaphor does not displace the organ itself. The poem's real triumph comes at its close, in the sustained metaphor asserting an analogy between penis and asparagus. While, on one level, this could seem insulting, what has preceded the comparison has made the desirability of the penis so clear that the woman's insatiable appetite, and her sensuous stroking of their 'silky heads', is erotic rather than disparaging. At the same time, the metaphor's revisionist intentions are unmistakable: instead of phallic towers, pens or monuments, we are offered 'sun-deprived white and purple-shadow-veined' asparagus. And the real skill of the figure lies in the fact that it *depends on* the woman's active, desiring presence; it is *her obsessive yearning* for both penis and asparagus that seals the comparison.

Both Higgins and Bhatt create metaphors out of specifically female experience. As such, they are not unavailable to male readers, but they only work in the voice of a female speaker; they insist on an active, female agent. Contemporary women poets' work provides many illustrations of this kind of innovative use of figure. Men poets seem to show less interest in the process.

2.

THROWN VOICES
DRAMATIC MONOLOGUES BY CAROL ANN DUFFY, JACKIE KAY AND JO SHAPCOTT

What are the alternatives to the lyric voice, with its accompanying expectations of personal exposure and veracity? In what follows the ways in which three women poets—Carol Ann Duffy, Jackie Kay and Jo Shapcott—deploy dramatic monologue are examined. While the popularity of this mode has been noted (especially in relation to Duffy) there has been limited exploration of its gendering.[1] Over the last thirty years it is overwhelmingly *women poets* who have made use of the versatility of voices enabled by the monologue, suggesting that the mode offers a way round some of the difficulties presented by the lyric tradition. The first part of this chapter will outline some of those difficulties, before explaining how what Duffy has called 'thrown voices' can provide solutions.

In his study of dramatic monologue, Alan Sinfield opts for a broad definition: 'simply a poem in the first person spoken by, or almost entirely by, someone who is indicated not to be the poet'.[2] Most frequently the mode is associated with Robert Browning, in whose skilful hands its potential for dramatic irony—dependent on the speaker's unwitting revelation of more than s/he intends—was exploited to the full. Our own age shares with the Victorians a certain unease with the lyric, though for very different reasons. They were the direct inheritors of a Romantic tradition that espoused the idea of the poet as a man of exceptional sensitivity and insight; the poet's pronouncements were endowed with quasi-religious reverence. Yet the effect of this was debilitating, since it trapped poets into writing in one tone. Sinfield puts it succinctly:

Romantic stress upon the figure of the poet, his visionary capacity, his integrity and sincerity, greatly limited the flexibility of the first person. The poet felt that when he said 'I' it should really be his true voice; anything else would be a betrayal of his lofty vocation. (p.59)

Our present-day unease (affecting both women and men poets) is partly a consequence of post-Structuralism's effective challenge to humanist versions of the self. These have made lyric poetry, with its apparent insistence on a unified self, seem an embarrassing anachronism from a more naive age. In addition, there are cultural reasons for the discomfort. The relative affluence of most western lives—in contrast to those of others in different parts of the world—may make the heightened tone associated with the lyric voice in the British tradition even more unappealing. There are also pragmatic explanations: the growth in poetry residencies and specific commissions requires a new practicality and versatility from poets, who need to be able to write about experiences quite remote from their own, and thus to be adept mimics, at home in several different voices. There is also the more troubling possibility that the recent popularity of dramatic monologues may be but the latest manifestation of a colonising impulse. If poets feel the traditional lyric terrain is worn out, they need new territory: what better than imaginatively appropriating the more dramatic, sensational experiences of others?[3]

In lots of ways, then, the dramatic monologue seems well-suited to these post-modern times. The mode deliberately harnesses readers' consciousness of the conventions within which reading takes place; it uses irony, disguise and play; it is preoccupied with identity, ideally suited for exploring the relativity of perspectives and truths. Postmodern 'play' is the outcome of such misgivings: poets positing personae that initially appear to be straight self-representations; as the poem progresses, the joke becomes apparent. Michael Donaghy 's early work and much of Don Paterson's exemplify the tendency to adopt these masks that dupe and tease, using shock or humour to do so. (See chapter 5 for fuller discussion of these two poets.) But boredom with the lyric 'I' may well affect the sex which has conventionally employed that 'I' more strongly than those who have only just begun to enjoy a speaking subjectivity: this may help account for the recent popularity of irony amongst male poets.[4] The kinds of games played by these poets depend on readers' initial credulity, and on our expectations of lyric consistency.

During the 1970s and 1980s, many women wrote poems in the voices of well-known classical or historical figures: Helen of Troy, Clytemnestra, Mary Magdalene.[5] The American critic Ostriker gave this sub-genre the title 'revisionist mythmaking'.[6] Invariably the writing involved some act of reparation: telling the story from the woman's perspective, giving a voice to the silent wife or mother, shifting the focus.

Perhaps surprisingly, feminist critics have been lukewarm towards such efforts to redress the gender balance in this way. Montefiore concluded that attempts to retell old stories were doomed to fail:

> Just because this material [myth and fairytale] is both traditional and powerful, it is resistant to recasting. Political interpretations can deflect but not alter its meanings, which either return to haunt the poem that overtly discards them, or vanish into witty analysis.[7]

Diane Purkiss criticised this kind of revisionist work for making appeals to 'a real, shared and timeless female nature, one based on the body and on the experience of maternity'.[8] She called instead for feminists to show their resistance to patriarchal systems of representation by a more radical strategy: debunking the hallowed status accorded classical mythology. She argued that this collection of stories is revered, treated as 'a buried truth of culture' (p.445) simply because of the influence of Freud and Jung.

Duffy's more recent example of the revisionist mode, *The World's Wife*, certainly does go some way towards this debunking, by mixing characters from high and popular culture: Mrs Kong alongside Queen Herod, Mrs Darwin and Mrs Midas, figures familiar from myths and history, cinema and fairy-tale.[9] But women poets' exploitation of personae goes far beyond these acts of revisionism. Countless women have used the dramatic monologue form: Ruth Padel, Selima Hill, Menna Elfyn, Patience Agbabi amongst them. Why should adopting a mask prove so attractive to today's women poets? Is it a way of avoiding those difficulties with the lyric voice discussed in chapter 1? Does the adoption of personae clearly differentiated from the poet serve the purpose of disguise? Does it perhaps enable her to explore or articulate hidden or submerged aspects of her own self? Does the use of multiple personae offer an escape from self, self-exposure and self-consciousness? Or does it satisfy a curiosity about other lives: the kind of intense empathy found in Sylvia Plath's writing, with its fascination with, and continual movement towards, otherness? Is the strategy motivated by a political agenda: the desire to give voices to those marginalized or silenced within mainstream culture? In order to answer these questions, it is useful first to examine briefly the reception of those women who have taken the alternative route, embracing a more conventional, consistent lyric 'I'.

Eavan Boland and Gillian Clarke are both fine examples of woman poets who have done this, producing poems in an unambiguously female voice. Boland's tone is resonant and authoritative, modelled on the bardic tradition, offering lofty pronouncements with Biblical cadence and elevated rhythms. She stated her intention of securing a place for a female subjectivity within the lyric tradition back in 1986 when she warned that the great danger of 'feminist ideology' was its encouragement to the woman poet 'to feminize her perceptions rather than humanize her femininity.'[10] But it appears that femininity can only be humanized to a degree; despite her fame, Boland's poetry is only ever read as a woman's poems about specifically female experiences and perspectives. How can femininity be 'humanized', when humanism is blind to gender difference, taking 'man' as its universal unsexed, unraced, unclassed subject? Surely this is the proof that what Boland advocated is impossible: femininity cannot be humanized—that is, it cannot transcend its particular, explicit sexing—because femininity encodes within it the concept of *difference from* masculinity. It seems impossible to get round the fact that a female voice will be received by readers (male and female) as uttering female, rather than human, truths.

Use of the first person 'I' also invites the kind of biographical interpretations that have dogged women poets over the centuries.[11] While Boland fiercely resists the suggestion that her work is autobiographical,[12] its frames of reference and content are obviously relevant to her own life: her experience of domesticity in southern Ireland, her interest in Irish women of the past. Because our culture is so resistant to accepting the female voice as representative of anything beyond itself, the temptation is to read Boland's work as merely her own meditations. Somehow, the transformation accorded the bard is not easily won by a contemporary woman; her voice sounds too thin, too individual. Either that, or the assumption of the generality 'womankind' is felt by other women to be presumptuous, appropriative or essentialist. (See chapter 1 for further discussion of this.) A final drawback is that identified in relation to the Victorians' frustration with the Romantic mode: the expectation that a poet will write in her 'own' voice brings with it certain constraints in terms of tone. Elaine Feinstein and Gillian Clarke, like Boland, also generally use the first person 'I' in their lyric poems. While all three poets have secured impressive reputations, their use of the mode means that they are all associated with a rather earnest, sombre, meditative—even, at times, didactic—tone.[13]

So there are limitations associated with female poets' espousal of the lyric 'I'. There is still general resistance to accepting a woman's voice as representative. A woman's voice cannot shake off its explicit sexing (where a male voice is readily interpreted as a neutral, objective commentary on the human situation). If it is even able to move beyond the specifically personal and individual, it is only allowed to become the voice of a *female* collectivity. It may be that by using a variety of personae, the poet can conceal the personal origins of some of her material, thus avoiding the pitfalls of female confession. (See chapter 4 for further discussion of this.) The use of another's voice creates the kind of space absent from the lyric 'I', thus making possible the distancing identified by Kaplan (and quoted in chapter 1) as one explanation for women's historical preference for the novel over poetry:

The narrative discourse itself provides a sort of third term for the woman author by locating (even, and perhaps especially, in a first person narrative) the loss or absence of power anywhere but in her own voice.[14]

But these are all negative explanations for the attractions of the dramatic monologue; there are some positive benefits too. The monologue enables a poet to explore potentially infinite perspectives, not even limited to human experience. It provides subversive opportunities to invert or challenge the status quo by bringing marginalised voices to the fore, a way of making what is conventionally seen as weak appear strong.[15]

In his study of the mode, Sinfield emphasises the 'teasingly paradoxical' status of dramatic monologue, suggesting that readers are simultaneously compelled by the verisimilitude of the poem's speaker and aware of the poet's controlling pressure behind the voice. The result causes readers to experience 'a divided consciousness…we are obliged to posit simultaneously the speaking "I" and the poet's "I".' (p.32) He quotes one of Browning's contemporaries describing him as 'never quite dramatic, for we never lose sight of the critical eye of the poet himself'. (p.31) This awareness of the poet's controlling mind may be more or less explicit. The dramatic monologue 'lurks provocatively' (p.24) between first- and third-person narration; Sinfield—borrowing from Kate Hamburger—describes it as a literary feint:

> Dramatic monologue feigns because it pretends to be something other than what it is: an invented speaker masquerades in the first person which customarily signals the poet's voice. (p.25)

This provides scope for a partial concealment: the poet can be both hidden and also gently remind the reader of her presence behind the scenes. In the readings that follow, I shall explore these characteristics, and the uses to which they are being put.

The three poets who form the subject of this chapter employ very different versions of dramatic monologue, for different reasons and to different ends. Nevertheless, it is worth noting that each of them also experiments with poems in the second-person singular, as well. Occasionally this 'you' is a specific addressee—a lover or the reader; more often, it functions as a further means of distancing poet from voice, a mode of self-address from outside the self.[16]

None of the three seems interested in creating psychologically authentic, rounded characters. Duffy's *dramatis personae* are strangely familiar. They are composite beings, created out of stock phrases; defined entirely by their language, they speak in recognisable—often stereotypical—registers. Kay's characters are often based on actual individuals, but her interest is in what they did, or what happened to them—in short, the political aspects of their lives. Shapcott concentrates on the physical aspects of transformation. Her personae are often non-human, and the poems frequently describe acts of miraculous metamorphosis.

CAROL ANN DUFFY

Duffy is the poet most commonly associated with dramatic monologue. Her first mature collection, *Standing Female Nude*,[17] contains a dazzling variety of voices: a dolphin, several schoolchildren, an English teacher, a disaffected unemployed youth, three generations of women, a man haunted by his debts, an elderly woman in an old people's Home. There are also several (mainly love) poems in a very personal voice, and what is striking is the sharp contrast in tone and style between these spare pieces and the others. Her second collection, *Selling Manhattan*, contains a similarly high number of monologues.[18]

The majority of these early monologues are spoken by male characters.[19] If this seems surprising, it is probably because of the popularity and widespread anthologising of two poems where the voice is a woman's: 'Standing Female Nude' and 'Warming Her Pearls'. But aside from these, the few female monologues tend to be *about being a woman*: 'Recognition', 'Whoever She Was' and 'Brink of Shrieks' all deal with self-alienation; 'A Clear Note' tells the stories of grandmother, mother and daughter. By contrast, the male monologues are far more varied. Their subjects are often criminals, or at least blokes who live on the wrong side of the law—conman, vandal, rapist, hitman ('Too Bad'; 'Stealing'; 'Psychopath'; 'Human Interest'; 'Education for Leisure'). Or they may be the displaced and dispossessed: immigrants or native Americans ('Yes Officer'; 'Deportation'; 'Selling Manhattan'). But they are not, on the whole, *about masculinity* at all; they are about anomie, exile, powerlessness and revenge.

Not surprisingly, critics began to identify Duffy with the mode. In a 1988 interview with Andrew McAllister, she is obviously irritated by the focus on this aspect of her work: 'I'm beginning to get so pissed off about it that maybe I won't write any more,'[20] though whether she's irritated by the critics' attention or by the fact that she keeps producing poems in this mode is tanatalisingly unclear. She insisted that it was simply 'an accident' (p.70), just the way the poems developed though, in the same 1988 interview, she also linked it to 'a combination of bearing witness to human experience...and being moved by that—wanting to get close to that person'.(p.70) This commitment to the idea of the poet as witness, speaking on behalf of others, articulating experiences that would not otherwise win attention, attests to a crucial political dimension to Duffy's work during this period, a dimension that was especially welcome to disaffected readers during the Thatcherite years. But it also leads us to ask why Duffy found herself drawn to ventriloquise such marginalised figures: what versions of identification or recognition were triggered for her by their experiences as disenfranchised, powerless individuals?

The fact that she so rarely ventriloquised women characters in these early collections is surely significant. She was obviously not attracted by the themes that dominated women's poetry in the years of her apprenticeship, nor even when she became famous:

> For quite a long time even into this decade we've been allowed certain areas of subject matter, like children, what bastards men are, looms: all these things that appear in late seventies, early eighties women's anthologies. But I haven't got any children and I don't define myself entirely as a woman; I'm not interested in weaving. (p.72)

This revelation is important: in 1988, Duffy does not define herself 'entirely as a woman' because 'woman' is equated with behaviours and situations she does not share. 'Woman' is not an identity sufficiently capacious or flexible to incorporate 'human' within itself; 'woman' refers to activities normally conducted solely by females. Hence, the female who is not living out the aspects of human experience explicitly or implicitly barred to men (motherhood; weaving) finds the identity too small, too limiting. As a writer, she craves unrestricted licence; she needs to be able to explore imaginatively any and all aspects of experience. Being female, to

Duffy, produces certain unhelpful expectations about a writer's subject matter and interests. Dramatic monologues provide a mode of disguise: she can enter any number of different minds, bodies and voices; she can also investigate emotions like jealousy, anger and love without being forced to do so from the perspective of a woman and in a woman's voice. So, in the early stages of her writing career, the dramatic monologue provided a way of expanding the terrain available to her as a woman poet.[21]

Duffy's choice and characterisation of male speakers has won her praise from several male critics. Ian Gregson applauds her recognition of male vulnerability, and the impact of class and ethnic distinctions; he contrasts her with Adrienne Rich whom he criticises for assuming all men are patriarchs.[22] He finds evidence of the 'divided consciousness' described by Sinfield in her monologues, arguing that readers are simultaneously aware of her male speakers and of the controlling mind of the female poet behind their words. He sees this as a feminist strategy, Duffy's critique of the way patriarchal attitudes infiltrate individual consciousness: 'much of the language we speak infiltrates us from outside.' (p.100) In his survey of twentieth-century poetry, R. P. Draper appreciates her understanding of the nuances and paradoxes of gender, and finds her without 'animosity' towards men.[23] In more humble mode, Alan Robinson finds her portrayal of a macho man in 'You Jane' both compelling and disturbing.[24]

As well as relief at Duffy's awareness of the intersectionality of class, ethnicity and social status with sex, these reactions promote the idea that she is interested in verisimilitude and realism. This seems unlikely to me. There is a second-hand quality to these male speakers; they are somehow too familiar right from the outset. They say what we expect them to say, often speaking in recognisable clichés. The subject of 'You Jane' is a particularly striking illustration.[25] He is a composite character, an amalgam of macho phrases ('It's all muscle.' 'Man of the house. Master in my own home.' 'Just feel those thighs.') and stereotypical aspirations ('Australia next year and bugger / the mother-in-law'). The poem's title signals its derivation from *fictional* representations of masculinity, at the same time underscoring the oppositional binary on which such representations pivot. Its position in the collection further suggests the piece's preoccupation with roles, language and representation rather than realism or essence. On the facing page is another monologue, this time spoken by a mother, expressing bewilderment at her frail, almost vacant sense of self. Where 'Tarzan' secures his place in the world by means of his physicality, the speaker of 'Whoever she was' is insubstantial; she does not know who she is now that her children have flown the nest. But however poignantly drawn, the character is not realistic; her props are borrowed from dated cinematic and literary representations of mothers. Reference to wooden clothes pegs and the 'shilling screen' evoke the 1950s; the speaker imagines her children:

> When they
> think of me I'm bending over them at night
> to kiss. Perfume. Rustle of silk. Sleep tight.[26]

   The allusions are to idealised depictions of aristocratic mother figures, familiar from films, not real life. Cinematic references, and the 1950s' setting recur in several poems ('A Clear Note', 'A Provincial Party 1956'); while others are set even further back in time, during the Second World War ('Shooting Stars', 'Woman Seated in the Underground, 1941'). Even the widely discussed title poem of her first collection, 'Standing Female Nude', spoken by an artist's model in a contemporary colloquial register ('Six hours like this for a few francs. / Belly nipple arse in the window light, / he drains the colour from me' p.46), is imbued with the atmosphere of Paris at the dawning of the twentieth century. It is as though Duffy's imagination is peopled with cultural images from the last hundred years: popular, literary, cinematic. The frequency with which snatches of song or catch phrases interrupt the speakers' monologues also implies the high interdependence between culture and character—or the degree to which culture actually shapes character, and language plays the role of articulating culture's mouldings. (This poststructuralist approach is developed by Deryn Rees-Jones in her 1999 study of Duffy.[27])

   The same is true of 'Psychopath', whose fairground-rapist speaker is another composite character, a collage of images taken from popular culture.[28] In the course of his narcissistic monologue, he coolly recounts killing a girl he had picked up that night. In this poem we

are given more background information, as though in an attempt
to deepen characterisation: we are told about his first (traumatic and
humiliating) sexual experience and about his parents' broken
marriage. But once again it is his familiarity that is most striking:

> My reflection sucks a sour Woodbine and buys me a
>   drink. Here's looking
> at you. Deep down I'm talented. She found out. Don't
>   mess
> with me angel, I'm no nutter. Over in the corner, a
> dead ringer
> for Ruth Ellis smears a farewell kiss on the lip of a
> gin-and-lime.
> The barman calls Time. Bang in the centre of my skull,
> there's a strange coolness. I could almost fly.
>   Tomorrow
> will find me elsewhere, with a loss of memory. Drink
>   up son,
> the world's your fucking oyster. Awopbopaloobop...
>   alopbimbam. (p.29)

This is a 1950s fairground, a seedy place, dangerous but irresistibly sexy. Images of *A Hard Day's Night* and *Brighton Rock* lurk
in the background; the reference to Ruth Ellis (the last woman to be
hanged in Britain, for a crime of passion) and the dance tag reinforce
the period feel. The barman—silent witness to the anti-hero's solil-
oquy—evokes memories of *Casablanca*, emphasised by the use of
Bogart's catch phrase, 'here's looking at you, kid'. The poem is a skilful collage of these disparate referents, whose prominent place within
it suggest the poet's real interest is not so much in an attempt to depict
a convincing psychopath, as in the images that populate a culture's
imagination, and thus help determine the way its inhabitants interpret their surroundings. The historical setting is one clue to this and
the character's preoccupation with his own image is another:

> I run my metal comb through the D. A. and pose
> my reflection between dummies in the window at Burton's.
> Lamp light. Jimmy Dean. (p.28)

It is as though the speaker is aware of his own second-hand identity. He is obsessed with his image, always looking at himself in mirrors and shop-windows. He has modelled himself on famous movie heroes epitomising tough, desirable masculinity: men like Marlon Brando and James Dean. Here it appears as though it is not the poet's irony intervening in the monologue, but the speaker's. Gregson interprets his preoccupation with his own visual representation as the deliberate signature of the female ventriloquist, teasingly reminding us of her presence behind this creation.[29] But to my mind what the over-familiar, derivative qualities of all these speakers implies is Duffy's belief that there is no authenticity outside cultural representation or, at least, that the struggle to be and behave in a manner not dictated by such representations—visual, but more corrosively for the poet, linguistic—is a tough one. Poems like 'Translating the English', 'Stealing', and 'Education for Leisure', which are invariably read as socio-political critiques, all testify to her fascination with the surfaces that language paints so compellingly.

Duffy's interest in poststructuralist issues has been noted by several critics.[30] But the difference between her style in these monologues and in those few poems written in a voice that appears close to the poet's own suggests that there is an element of compulsion in her ventriloquism. It is as though she inherits a cluttered world, where too many pre-determined speakers jostle for expression; a cacophony of voices intrude on her, and she has no option but to give voice to them. They are not 'real' individuals, but their ready-made, formulaic phrases dominate our everyday reality; writing them out is a way of clearing the ground so as to make a little space in which to articulate something more original, more authentic. This is why her love poems have the arresting quality of language at its purest and feel so hard-won. Because while intellectually conscious of the validity of post-Structuralist critique, she is also a lyric poet, and as such struggles to find ways of expressing the unique and particular, in a language cleansed of its stereotypical moulds.

The coexistence of these contradictory pressures is clearly visible in *Thrown Voices*, a pamphlet collection published in 1986. As its title indicates, the contents are almost entirely dramatic monologues; only the last poem, with its insistent italicised '*This is me speaking*' (p.28), contradicts the pattern. The opening poem, 'The Dummy', confronts the subject directly. Together with the frontispiece illustration, it suggests that ventriloquism may be related to Duffy's own position as a woman poet. Just as the lyric tradition posits a male speaker, so too does the tradition of ventriloquist and dummy.[31] In Duffy's poem, neither participant is sexed. The dummy addresses its operator in caustic tones, sceptical about her talent and resentful at its manipulation by such an inferior being. As the poem that paves the way for a whole series of 'ventriloquist' monologues, it is clearly also setting the scene, emphasising the theatricality of what is to come. MacAllister describes it as 'splendidly funny'[32] but there is an edge to its tone suggestive of a more serious confrontation being staged (reminiscent of the 1945 film *Dead of Night*), as if the dummy's resentment is on the point of transforming itself into outright threat, speaking back through clenched teeth:

You can do getter than that, can't you?[33]

On one level, Duffy is simply reminding readers of the fictionality of her speaking voices; as Sinfield writes of T. S. Eliot's monologues, 'He thrusts forward the controlling mind of the poet so that the relationship between author and speaker becomes a theme of the poem.'[34] But this does not account for the dummy's threatening behaviour, which introduces the suggestion that these voices assert *themselves*, compelling the poet to utter their words, using her as mouthpiece.

If this seems far-fetched, it is worth considering the visual frontispiece selected for the volume, drawn by Eileen Cooper. It is a giant close-up of a woman. Her mouth is covered by one of her hands, raised for this purpose, as if forbidding speech. Her other hand lies against one ear, cupped as if to emphasise the act of listening. One of the woman's eyes is the focal centre of the charcoal drawing, staring out to meet the viewer's gaze. Disembodied mouths—some open, some closed—float around her; these mouths are full fleshed with succulent lips. The image is strongly suggestive of prohibitions on female speech. If woman is not supposed to talk, she may still listen; the floating mouths that surround her figure suggest the woman will give voice to something, but their lack of connectedness to any bodies suggests that what she utters will be radically other to her, disconnected from her own body.

Other references to ventriloquism in Duffy's poems emphasise its status as trickery and disguise; in 'Talent Contest', for example, the speaker warns:

> Beware the ventriloquist,
> The dark horse whose thrown voice juggles the
> truth.[35]

For truth or authenticity occurs fleetingly, is ephemeral, a temporary state of union between mind and body. Duffy's most familiar state seems to be one of disembodiment. Several of her poems describe states of extreme physical dissociation. 'Small Female Skull' (one of the later pieces that is written in a first-person voice) describes the speaker finding her own skull. What starts out as a humorous take on an impossible scenario gradually becomes a profoundly unsettling account of self-estrangement.[36]

Duffy's monologues do not avail themselves of the ironic distance that characterises Browning's iconic versions. The experience of disembodiment and of becoming the mouthpiece for some other person are far more significant than the deployment of irony. But in her third and fourth collections, *The Other Country* and *Mean Time*,[37] there are far fewer dramatic monologues, and more poems in a first-person voice that could be identified with Duffy herself.[38] Along with this development comes an increase in the use of the second person, suggesting distance from the self, the ability to stand outside, self-division as a preferred option. There is a gender difference here: male powerlessness derives from social or legislative exclusion, whereas Duffy's female speakers' powerlessness is communicated through estrangement from their bodies.

Sinfield has suggested that poets may employ the dramatic monologue *en route* to carving out their own poetic voice, one flexible enough to avoid the fixity and biographical connection that makes the first person problematic:

> If the poet can cultivate a poetic 'I' which is sufficiently elusive
> and impersonal to suggests the mysterious and incalculable
> nature of the human psyche; which heads off the Romantic

assumption that the poet's self may be encapsulated, and truth with it, in a single language act; which possesses an ironical self-awareness but does not inhibit commitment; then he will no longer need dramatic monologue.[39]

Perhaps Duffy's strategy of tempering the first person with the second has provided her with her own solution to the dangers of the lyric mode. Her recent publication, *The World's Wife*, provides another kind of distancing framework: this time through the use of familiar myths. The effect of the known name, and story it evokes, works to produce resonance; the poet can then use the mould, filling it with her own experience, which gets transmuted into a richer, thicker, and more publicly accessible narrative by being displaced on to a legendary character. Of course this is how poets have always worked, harnessing myths and recognisable literary figures as vehicles for their own insights. But, as suggested in chapter 1, there are far fewer female figures who are familiar to a general contemporary audience, and such figures are essential in order to provide vehicles for a female-sexed public discourse.

There is a different quality to these later monologues; their speakers are more fully individuated; they don't speak in clichés. 'Little Red Cap' melds the tale of a woman poet's apprenticeship onto the fairy tale 'Little Red Riding Hood'; in so doing, Duffy creates an archetypal account (the first?) of a woman poet's apprenticeship.[40] Red Cap ventures into the woods to hear the wolf's poetry reading; afterwards she uses her youthful charms to catch his attention. She goes back to his lair because she knows he will lead her to what she needs to become a poet: experience. The sex just has to be undergone, so she can have free rein amidst his books while he sleeps. She stays in the woods for ten years during which time she outgrows her mentor and hones the ruthless curiosity that her chosen job necessitates. Eventually the wolf himself is sacrificed to her future: slicing him open, she finds 'the glistening, virgin white of my grandmother's bones' (p.4), which she replaces with stones. The suggestion is that the female poet can *use* these talismans that symbolise a female tradition; they are not dispensable like the mentor/lover who has served his purpose.

This retelling divests masculinity of the aura of omnipotence and danger that accompany the wolf's characterisation in the older story. In Duffy's portrait of the poet as a young girl, the wolf symbolises experience; he is not a terrifying rapacious beast, but rather a means to an end. Masculinity is thus put to the service of a broader figurative meaning—and it is precisely this that our figurative language (mirroring here our social and cultural practice) generally refuses to do. While all manner of things are compared to femininity (countries, cars, etc) masculinity tends to remain the *sine qua non*, the bottom line. Duffy thus displaces two central pillars of cultural tradition: virginity as 'loss' and masculinity as 'dangerous'. As Angela Carter observed, these are the myths that help shape our behaviour, the 'consolatory nonsenses' that keep us unfree.[41]

'Queen Herod' introduces a shocking new perspective on the murder of all boy babies, by shifting the poem's story to an account of the Queen's fierce love for her baby daughter.[42] The implication is that she has her own reasons for acquiescing in the slaughter of innocents: to keep her beloved safe from men's desires for as long as possible. In both these treatments the poet's own personal experience merges with the fabular, expanding its resonance and at the same time laying claim to a broader applicability: that these poems describe the experiences of many women. Describing the collection as the result of 'looking for missing or hidden or unspoken truths in old stories', she outlined the poems' evolution:

> It wouldn't have worked if you'd just gone through a list of favourite tales and revised them. You had to find something hard and truthful in the story. That's why it took so long to write. Each poem had to be personally honest, and have some kind of autobiographical element in it, whether it had happened to me or whether it was an emotional or intellectual truth.[43]

For the first time in Duffy's *oeuvre*, the specificity of life as a woman finds repeated expression. That she chooses to secrete such accounts within the staple stories of western culture suggests she recognises that the female lyric 'I' benefits from the bolstering provided by use of such familiar figures. They provide a way of both distancing and generalising individual experience; a solution for the lyric poet who wishes to avoid the self-aggrandising tones of the post-Romantic 'I'.

JACKIE KAY

Where Duffy is known as a poet of dramatic monologues, Kay's first collection, *The Adoption Papers*, contained the dramatic sequence that gave the book its title, and made her name.[44] As well as signalling her interest in the dramatic potential of poetry, the collection's structure also showed that she was a poet who exploited the potential patterns and relationships between individual poems. In both these ways, Kay is clearly moving right away from the lyric tradition, with its concentration on brief, self-contained poems and the poet's sole subjectivity. The 'Adoption Papers' sequence accounts for about half the book, but as Gabrielle Griffin has demonstrated, there are carefully orchestrated thematic parallels between it and the poems in Part Two.[45] As regards subjectivity, it is not that Kay avoids writing in the first person or using her experience; indeed there are poems in each of her books that seem to draw on personal experience with no sense of reticence or inhibition. But, regardless of the subject matter, individual experience is invariably set in a social context, recognisably part of public life; there is none of the intense insularity of lyric subjectivity. However intimate an event may be, its social ramifications are also made explicit in her poems: the personal is always inescapably political.

Where Duffy's speakers often feel like identikit characters, built out of stock phrases and idioms, Kay's seem designed deliberately to flout expectations. So the gay barber who speaks in 'Close Shave' is a father of two, and his lover is a miner: hardly the stereotypical gay couple.[46] And where Duffy's monologues frequently employ her trademark one-word sentences, Kay's have less consistency in terms of style. There is even less evidence of Sinfield's 'divided consciousness', the reader's awareness of the poet behind the persona. These speakers do not seem employed as disguised mouthpieces to articulate experiences or emotions transposed from Kay.

What is most striking about Kay's use of the dramatic monologue is the way she combines so many diverse voices within an intricately patterned structure. Her 1998 collection, *Off Colour*,[47] provides a particularly tight-knit illustration. The poems are bound together by their participation in the two central ideas behind the collection: that sickness is both intimately individual and at the same time literally and metaphorically social, and that language functions very like disease, operating by means of arbitrary shifts and transfers, living off its human hosts like a parasite. The poems illustrate these ideas by enacting them: a series of poems about viruses pick up phrases and lines from other poems; a variety of speakers describe sicknesses mental and physical: the plague, racism, depression. The same images recur throughout the collection, finding homes in different poems, casting different connotations in each. When there is irony, it functions not at the expense of the speaker, but to drive home whatever political points are being made. So the speaker of 'Crown and Country', inhabitant of a totalitarian regime whose subjects pride themselves on their perfect teeth, explains how people from neighbouring states have abscesses and unstopped fillings:

> We identify people by their bite.
> The lower class have most unusual bites.
> They are sick to the back teeth.[48]

This rejuvenated cliché finds its way into the poem as an echo of the opening piece, 'Where It Hurts', another monologue whose speaker catalogues her endless discomforts and ailments, declaring she is 'Sick to the back Scotch teeth'.[49] But another poem recounts a speaker's erotic pleasure in a trip to the dentist: she opens her mouth and listens as the dentist conveys information about her teeth to the dental assistant. This 'language of ivory' contains vital ingredients of the speaker's identity:

> my vowels, my consonants, my country.[50]

Juxtaposed with the sinister regime of state control, this intimacy feels dangerous. This dreamy speaker's innocent conflation of language and nationality with her teeth echoes the other poems that raise precisely the same issues only do so in order to demonstrate the excessive, intrusive power of the state. By means of this kind of collage, Kay builds up complex semantic interrelations between the poems themselves, even while their speakers remain a diverse group.

Like Duffy, Kay is not interested in providing much psychological depth to her characters; instead, these different voices enable her to anatomise the operation of social and national rules and structures. For example, her poems demonstrate how the body is at once unique, personal, intimate—and, at the same time, utterly subject to culture. It means nothing without culture's naming. In the opening monologue, 'Where It Hurts', the speaker's catalogue of physical complaints is described *through* her culture and surroundings. Her body *is* the Scottishness she has lived: her knees are filled with fluid ('You could cross the water; you could speed bonny boat'); her teeth rotten with all the shortbread, scones and currant loaf they've munched; 'poison, bacteria, culture' are interchangeable, shooting through her veins.[51] That this sickness is metaphorical, and that everyone is suffering it becomes almost a source of macabre celebration by the end: a kind of elated defiance in the face of death. Utterly subject to the body, life is struggle: 'The body is a bloody battlefield,' (p.9) but, as this metaphor suggests, it is always also a site of political contestation. Kay is interested in language and its extraordinary power: like a body, language possesses its own vitality, its morphic potential; it is subject to change, birth, decay, political usurpation, manipulation, entrapment. Like a virus, language travels, is parasitic, jumps from host to host with supreme indifference. Extraordinarily fertile, it is indiscriminate, yet its consequences are often lethal. For ideas are communicated in language, as the poem 'Race, Racist, Racism' describes: 'Say the words came first'.[52] The sheer energy of what one reviewer called Kay's Scots demotic[53] seems to erupt out of the endless, self-replicating language system itself: hence the ebullience, frequent puns and play with asterisks, alphabetical lists and the catalogue of idioms to describe illness that litter the opening of 'Where it hurts':

> Sick as a parrot, a gambler, a joke, a dog, a mind.
> Sick as a simile, sick (sic), a poet, a plant.
> Drooping, limp, languid, flaccid, fatigued. (p.11)

These lists enact a series of slight shifts in semantic or phonetic components, revealing how the language system works. So the line moves through nouns that collocate with sickness, and then switches to sound shifts: the 'l' of drooping, limp, languid, flaccid—then the 'a' and 'id' / 'ed', as though these words and sounds possess their own independent life.

In addition to their deployment within this poetry of ideas, Kay's monologues cover a number of current 'issues': domestic violence, sexual abuse, the historical presence of black people in Britain, contemporary racism. Just as Duffy's approach foregrounded roles rather than essences, Kay emphasises the *structures* that put people in powerless or vulnerable positions. So, during plague, white crosses on black doors signal the infected; in the country of perfect teeth, decay represents exclusion. And the very last poem in the book, 'Pride', harnesses echoes of the physiological differences that have peopled its pages in order to imply a reluctant rejection of belief in geographical or racial origins as a source of identity.[54] The speaker describes meeting a black man on a train journey, who recognises her as an Ibo like him. This ascription of their shared membership of the west African Ibo people is transformative: he names her nose and teeth 'Ibo'; as she looks at him he begins to resemble her brother.

What she identifies in this man gives the poem its title, 'pride, / a quality of being certain'.(p.63) She imagines herself visiting her originary village:

> I danced a dance I never knew I knew.
>
> .....
>
> My grandmother was like me exactly, only darker. (p.64)

But the poem ends with the black man's disappearance, the implication being that such a blissful moment of reunion is not to be—is, actually, as the poem has hinted in the extraordinary precision with which this man can trace parts of her body back to parts of Africa, a comforting fiction, but one that carries within it claims of superiority and sets in motion the chain of differences that produces enmity. He implies that the Ibo people are superior in every way.

But, however thrilling the momentary fantasy of belonging, the woman who died at the hands of the immigration service had 'perfect pearls' for teeth (p.15), and the brain- and mouth-washed subjects of the tooth-proud nation boasted 'pints of creamy gleaming teeth, / pouring out our white grins'. (p.14) Both those poems demonstrate the ease with which physiological features can be deployed as markers of either inclusion or exclusion. As the final poem, this one releases its full implications only by drawing on the others in the collection.

Kay thus achieves what many have considered impossible: she broadens the capacities of lyric poetry, both in terms of content and form. She makes lyric poetry politically responsive and engaged.[55] Instead of self-contained poems, she creates a collection of voices, each of which participates in the whole that they make; as such, the poems are no longer isolated individual utterances, but genuinely affect one another, constructing dialogue and enacting critique. In addition to this, she—like Duffy, only more so—broadens the range of voices represented within lyric tradition: those forgotten by history, representatives of the demotic, or those who have chosen to remain silent out of fear. There is virtually no irony in Kay's work; nor, as I have indicated, does she exploit the reader's simultaneous awareness of speaker and poet; as poet, she herself is entirely absent from the dramatic monologues, and they are stylistically versatile, making such distracting recognition even less likely.

JO SHAPCOTT

Unlike that of Duffy or Kay, Shapcott's poetry foregrounds the sex of its author. She is also the only one of the three who systematically exploits Sinfield's 'divided consciousness', whereby readers are urged to attend simultaneously to the speaking persona and to their awareness of the poet behind that persona. She makes deliberate use of the reader's knowledge that there is a woman behind the persona, regardless of the latter's sex. Shapcott frequently chooses to speak as animal or vegetable, rather than human. Where I noted a *stylistic* consistency in Duffy's monologues, Shapcott's are consistent in terms of their tone and theme. Although she may choose the persona of a lettuce in one poem, and a goat in the next, both lettuce and goat are fascinated by their own powerful desires: to be ingested, and to ingest, respectively. Both therefore testify to Shapcott's interest in physical sensation, and in the erotic potential of the fantasy of penetrating the lover's body. For these reasons, in a way quite unlike the monologues of Duffy or Kay, her use of the mode serves as a form of semi-transparent disguise. Michael Hofmann comments, 'There is about Shapcott's poetry a passionate reticence. Once in disguise, though, pressed into other skins and other perspectives, she howls and sings.'[56]

But why the desire for disguise? Rather than a need for concealment or discretion, Shapcott's shape-shifting liberates new possibilities for her restlessly roving persona. These disguises provide ways of enhancing the erotics that play such an important part in her poetry. Again unlike Duffy or Kay, she subscribes to a clear theory of sexual difference, which is articulated most explicitly in a series of sonnets about Robert and Elizabeth. According to these poems, woman—or, at least, the woman writer/narrator (who is both Elizabeth Hardwick and Elizabeth Barrett Browning)—is untroubled by the need for borders or definitions. As Elizabeth cooks, Shapcott imagines the stove's heat entering her body; she seems to relish the resulting sensory confusion.

Often unsure where one thing ends and another begins, she works by analogy and figure, where Robert feels more at home with the precise, rule-bound operations of parsing and crossword puzzles. He dislikes the Norfolk fens: 'acres of confusion between land and water'; (p.28) he is frustrated by the 'nebulous' quality of Elizabeth's speech, and the impossibility of pinning down her arguments. (p.27) He cannot get his head round the 'feminine science' of knitting (p.32), with its curious combination of space, tension and interrelations.

This gender differentiation implies that it will be females rather than males who relish the metamorphoses Shapcott's poems enact and, with one or two exceptions, this is indeed the case.[57] What Gregson describes as her interest in 'the boundaries of the self shifting, and…the themes of splits and transformations'[58] may initially seem similar to tendencies in Plath's work, but there are significant differences: where Plath's encounter with otherness entailed a risk to the self, and never actually produced a loss of self, Shapcott presents self-transformation as a slow, sexy, wholly pleasurable experience. Her focus remains fixed on how it feels, on every detail of the body's steady transformation. These poems could be described as examples of Irigaray's sensible transcendent: in them, the speaker overcomes the physical limits of her body and assumes the characteristics of an other.

In 'Thetis' Shapcott specifically equates metamorphosis with
female creativity: 'My name is Thetis Creatrix' its speaker declares,
detailing the sensuous thrill of her constant physical transformations, from lizard to oak tree to tigress.[59] The process is infinitely
subtle and never-ending; no sooner is she embodied as the lizard
than the scales on her back begin to harden. Thetis revels in her
art, and the pleasures are primarily physical:

> Watch as I stretch
> my limbs for the transformation, I'm laughing
> to feel the surge of other shapes beneath my skin. (p.87)

In classical mythology Thetis's capacity to shapeshift is her protec-
tion against unwanted suitors—until Peleus is taught how to
overcome her rapid metamorphoses by clinging on tight. But
Shapcott's Thetis presents herself first and foremost as an artist: her
mercurial transformations are not conducted for self-protection;
they are—her own body is—her work of art. This cleverly transforms the stubbornly consistent equation of woman with the
corporeal into a creative, artistic strength: in her body she discovers this irrepressible instinct, a delightful capacity. But, interestingly,
Shapcott shies away from the one mode of self-transformation or
bodily elasticity that is genuinely physiologically female: pregnancy.
In her version of the myth, Peleus's brutal courtship is presented
as the trigger that forces Thetis to 'bring forth War'. The birth and
life of Achilles are compressed within this Biblical euphemism.[60]

As the extract above illustrates, Thetis is well aware of an audience; at one point, she even calls the addressee a 'voyeur' and
counsels him to look 'a little closer'. While the observer is unsexed,
both the implications of the term voyeur and the courtship context
of the classical myth imply a male viewer. Indeed, a very high
proportion of Shapcott's monologues include this consciousness of
being observed, often making direct reference to it. One of the
effects is to dramatise the gender politics of representation, signalling
the poet's entry into a realm in which women have invariably served
as objects of the male gaze. Instead of protesting at this, Shapcott
plays along with it, making the gender dynamics overt. Several of
her (female) personae appear to revel in self-display; feisty and

direct, they are unfazed by their status as spectacle, using it to their advantage to dazzle or taunt the male spectator.

'My Life Asleep' provides an interesting example.[61] Attempting a different mode of self-transformation—this time, evacuation of the self—the poet imagines her sleeping body from the point of view of someone watching her. But halfway through the poem, this attempt gives way to a direct address to the watcher:

> You'll find the body and all the air it exhales
> Smellier than by day; (p.97)

The effect of this invitation is disturbing, especially since it comes after a worrying allusion to the impossibility of defending private living space against intruders. Suddenly, someone is in the room, bending low over the speaker's body and being encouraged to probe further:

> put a finger
> On the spot you think the dream is.

The tone of this kind of tease is difficult to pinpoint, and this kind of ambiguity is a characteristic feature of Shapcott's style. By this means she can woo readers male and female. A poem like 'Muse' can be read either as an erotic celebration of its speaker's muse-lover, or as a spirited critique of the sexism of patriarchal tradition's female muses.[62] This is where Shapcott's flirtatiousness kicks in, and it is interesting to wonder how big a part this might play in the very positive responses she has received from several male critics. (Michael Hofman's appreciation is quoted earlier. Sean O'Brien has also commented on how strangely 'hospitable' Shapcott's poems feel.[63])

However, if Shapcott can use her feminine wiles when she chooses, she is also well aware of the political dimensions to female (self)representation. 'I'm Contemplated by a Portrait of a Divine' incorporates the familiar dual presence of speaker and poet, since the 'I' in the title is not the same first-person speaker as the one that delivers the monologue. It is the lady in the portrait, depicted as a symbol of divinity, who speaks even though, paradoxically, she cannot speak.

The poem dramatises the double objectification of woman—as painted image, and as symbol, her vitality denied and repressed. It is, we are forced to remember, the poet's imagination that produces these words for this silenced icon. And, as is the case with all these monologues, consciousness of the poet's crucial role as puppeteer prompts the reader to consider the poet—not in order to probe her personality and emotions (the flirtatiousness is sufficient as a defence against this impulse, even if it arises), but in order to remind readers of the sex of the poet. In this way, Shapcott harnesses the femaleness that has conventionally been surplus to the lyric tradition and makes it work for her.

Readers' constant awareness of the poet herself behind the persona enhances the impression of a self-conscious performance.[65] But there is an interesting twist to this: where conventional representations make woman the objectified spectacle, in Shapcott's poems she provides a running commentary on her own physicality, thus insisting on her existence as subject. Furthermore, the focus on visuals is replaced with an emphasis on touch and motion, because it is the speaker's version of events that dominates, and she is preoccupied with the feel, not the look, of things.[66] In 'Goat' she describes her transformation into one of the herd, revelling in the release of an enormous, insatiable appetite that accompanies this new embodiment.

Because it is a human speaker who recounts—with precision and detail—the process of this transformation, and because the poem ends with the goat's vision of 'a tiny human figure'—the poem's speaker—the reader is simultaneously conscious of both. The metamorphosis is liberating, enabling the speaker to discover a wholly new forceful desire through her senses: smell, touch and taste.

The body in these poems is a source of surprise. Several of her personae experience an extreme loss of control over their movements: the mad cow, most obviously, whose weird staggers are her version of dancing; Tom the Walt Disney cartoon cat; even a description of two friends slipping and sliding about helplessly in the snow.[67] Tom, like Thetis, describes the euphoria of such abandonment:

the ecstasy in the body when you fling
yourself into such mayhem, open yourself
to any shape at all[68]

Sometimes the speaker is an explorer, bent on scrutinising every cranny of her lover's body, using her witty, miraculous shape-shiftings to bypass the gendered economy within which males explore and females are the object of the exploration. Examples of this include her spectacular travels as a speck of dust in 'Her Lover's Ear':

I leaned outwards on the bend like a biker[69]

The fantasy enacts an unusual kind of erotic foreplay, culminating in a sensual, unmistakably triumphant act of penetration. 'Leonardo and the Vortex' performs a similar feat. Its speaker claims to understand Leonardo's obsession with the vortex, but declares her lack of interest in how vortices operate in the natural world. However, as the poem unfolds, she discovers more intimate vortices, on and inside her lover's body. Initially she spots the curve of his sleeve and the pattern of black hairs on his arm; then the poem enacts its own theme formally, as she imagines her lover's blood, veins and arteries.

Fantasies of incorporation or penetration are imbued with eroticism. The wilting lettuce that delivers the monologue 'Vegetable Love' comforts herself with a fantasy of being finally eaten by the man she desires. From her cold home at the bottom of the 'fridge, she defends herself against the ice crystals forming on her leaves by imagining:

another lovely version
of curl, then shrivel, then open again to desire.[70]

It is no coincidence that it is for poems expressing heterosexual desire that Shapcott makes fullest use of these inventive dramatis personae, for it is, of course, on the tradition of the love poem that the dominance of male poets' objectifications of women has left its deepest impression. Neither Duffy nor Kay venture on to this fraught terrain. Shapcott deliberately deploys stereotyped characteristics of femininity as a way of turning what at first sight seem to be the disadvantages of that position into positive benefits. After centuries of male poets using their poems to seduce, flirt or woo, Shapcott uses her poems to do the same.

3.
CARIBBEAN COMPARISONS
GRACE NICHOLS AND DAVID DABYDEEN

In the Introduction Marge Piercy is quoted as suggesting that it would be a useful exercise to consider a male poet from within a context that centred women's poetry as the norm (see p.30); now that context is established, it is time to take up her challenge. This chapter discusses a male and a female poet in order to see what kinds of differences emerge.

David Dabydeen and Grace Nichols, both born and raised in Guyana, have been resident in Britain since 1969 and 1977 respectively, and have both been categorised as 'Caribbean British' or 'Black British' poets.[1] Dabydeen's preoccupations are both cerebral and sexual; he is interested in high culture and in eroticism. Nichols's poems are frequently sensual, often humorous, and democratic in their accessibility. Where Dabydeen draws extensively on western cultural artefacts (especially books and paintings), there is barely an allusion to such material in Nichols's poetry.[2] Where Dabydeen draws a stark opposition between Creole and standard English, Nichols enacts a synthesis of the two.[3] It is tempting to explain such differences in terms of their gender positions. However, there are other equally valid explanations. Nichols is from African roots; Dabydeen is descended from East Indians who went to Guyana as indentured labourers. Given the history of ethnic divisions and tensions in the country, these differences are crucially important. Dabydeen had an extraordinary childhood, coming to England as a 14-year-old boy and spending several years in care, in London, before winning a place at Cambridge University; his experiences of the metropolitan colonial centre were thus more extreme, both in terms of deprivation, shock and witnessing of privilege, than Nichols's who studied at the University of Guyana, worked as a journalist there and came to Britain as an adult. Then there are the differences in personality, temperament and literary style that make any such comparison seem foolhardy. Nevertheless, this strategy is intended to foreground some of the problems inherent in my methodology, as well as offering observations on the differences between these two poets who share, at least, their position as Guyanese immigrant writers with a particular relationship to English poetic tradition. What emerges is a sense of how profoundly the legacy of colonisation and the experience of emigration are gendered.

The Anglophone Caribbean literary tradition—like that of all traditions which have recently struggled to win national independence—has tended to use women symbolically, as metaphors for the land.[4] In her study of West Indian literature, Nana Wilson-Tagoe admits that male writers' female characters have tended to be like this, rather than three-dimensional and fully realised. She cites Edward Kamau Brathwaite and Derek Walcott as examples of the idealising tendency that is related to this.[5] Writer Beryl Gilroy makes a similar point, commenting that the tradition of placing the Caribbean mother on a pedestal prevents Caribbean men from seeing the political issues that face women.[6] With the publication of more work by women writers, Wilson-Tagoe sees challenges to such idealisations emerging; women are exploring 'submerged and inarticulate variables of history'; literature is beginning to change as 'sexual politics is intertwined with the wider politics of history and transformation as women writers consistently deconstruct the divisions between domestic and public domains.' (p.251) An awareness of the extent to which colonialism entailed the entanglement of sexual with racial politics now informs much postcolonial research,[7] although this is a relatively recent development.

David Dabydeen is unusual amongst male writers for his interest in sexual politics and his preoccupation with what he has called 'the erotic energies of the colonial experience';[8] this makes him a particularly interesting candidate for comparison with a woman poet whose work shows a similar commitment to examining the legacies of colonial history in women's lives. Where Nichols fits Wilson-Tagoe's description of a writer deconstructing the divisions between domestic and public domains, Dabydeen's themes suggest initially, anyway, that a similar concern might be found in his poetry.

Both Nichols's and Dabydeen's first publications were long sequence poems: *i is a long memoried woman* and *Slave Song*, published in 1983 and 1984 respectively. Both were well received: Nichols was awarded the Commonwealth Poetry Prize; Dabydeen won the same prize the following year, as well as the Cambridge University Quiller-Couch Prize. Before turning to these poems it is worth noting that, when they were published, both poets had already been living outside Guyana for some time. Both books were published by European publishers—Karnak House, based in London (dedicated to publishing Caribbean literature); and Dangaroo, in Mundelstrup, Denmark (concentrating on literature from post-colonial countries). These facts raise important questions about readership: who were the poets writing for? Who were they writing to? Guyana had won independence in 1966, but tension between the Indo-Guyanese community (comprising about 50 per cent of the population) and the Afro-Guyanese (comprising about 43 per cent), which had been endemic during the lead up to independence, continued thereafter, producing severe economic and political instability, circumstances hardly conducive to the emergence of a sufficiently secure or prosperous country to make for a buoyant Guyanese readership. Guyana had already produced two internationally respected writers, Wilson Harris and Martin Carter, but the bulk of their readership came from outside the country. This situation is common across the Caribbean archipelago, and also in most African countries, where poverty and hardship make the leisured activity of reading a minority pursuit. The resulting scenario, in which Western publishing companies select authors, means that writers are encouraged to write in standard English, to secure a readership; indeed, some have described it as another form of neo-colonialism.[9] Dabydeen's volume includes translations of the poems (they are written in Creole), as well as an extensive commentary that provides information about Guyanese, and specifically Indo-Guyanese culture, suggesting he was expecting his readers to be unfamiliar with both language and location. Nichols's poem employs a softer version of

Creole, and it is probably fair to say that Karnak House was a more politically radical publishing house than the more academic Dangaroo and therefore commanded a wider readership. The tone of both Nichols's *i is a long memoried woman* and Dabydeen's *Slave Song* strongly indicate both poets' absorption in Caribbean history and its continuing impact over the inhabitants of these lands. However, it is worth noting that today, some twenty years later, neither text is taught in Guyanese schools.[10]

i is a long memoried woman is a sequence of poems testifying to the resilience of women under slavery. Most of the poems use the first-person singular; others use the first-person plural. Overall, the effect is the eschewal of an individual voice for a collective collage of trans-historical female experience. Nichols herself has described their speaker as 'something of a mythic figure'.[11] The collection's title immediately signals the importance of inter-generational memory, a key ingredient in much African and Amerindian mythology. The women draw support from one another, and from their dead ancestors, from sorcery and prayer. In the emphasis it places on sisterly solidarity, the poem concurs with Laura Niesen de Abruna's claim that Anglophone Caribbean women writers' concern with 'relational interaction' between women is a characteristic theme.[12] The poems do not shy away from recording women's maltreatment at the hands of their own people. They also confront a subject that dominates Dabydeen's first two collections: sexual relations between blacks and whites. 'Love Act', set during slavery, is a coolly dispassionate account of a slave woman who is forced to become mistress and nanny to the overseer. She is described as his 'fuel': the overseer, his wife and children 'take to her breasts / like leeches'. (p.49)

Finding herself pregnant, the woman wants to get rid of the child. She pleads with the mother goddess, eventually receiving comfort, solace and the strength to realise that the child is a benison, no sin; thus reassured, the mother blesses her new baby:

> my bastard fruit
> my seedling
> my sea grape
> my strange mulatto
> my little bloodling (p.57)

Nichols does not pretend that such an ability to rise above her own violation is either common or easy, although an earlier poem in the sequence describes the punishment meted out to Ala, who killed her child rather than let it be enslaved; she is tied up and smeared in molasses, left to be eaten alive by red ants.[13]

Nichols's poem was repeatedly turned down by distinguished publishers, on the grounds that the same thing had already been done by Edward Kamau Brathwaite.[14] Brathwaite's trilogy, *The Arrivants*,[15] is also a (far longer) sequence; it tells the story of the hero's journey back to Africa, in search of his roots after enforced exile and repatriation. The poem is founded on a classical epic model: it begins with invocations to (African) gods and goddesses as the warriors beat their drums and prepare for war. It moves through a dazzling variety of registers, from cricket commentaries to chants, lists of the genealogical credentials of African kings and religious invocations. The poem depicts a masculine world, a world of patrilineal ancestry, fierce fighting and glorified suffering of the hero, who is cast as a new, wandering Odysseus. Women appear only as victims, their sorry plight inflaming the men on to acts of greater bravado:

> I hear
> the whips of the slavers,
> see the tears
> of my daughters:
>
> over glad
> of their shattered
> cries, feet
>
> bleeding, I walk
> through the talk
> of the market. (p.132)

It seems surprising that publishers did not notice that Nichols's poem is framed as a female-centred response to Brathwaite's account. Her opening poem places a birth centre stage, in the midst of the appalling conditions of the Middle Passage crossing from Africa to the New World, a journey which is usually represented as a place of death. The men's battle cry is replaced with the cry of a woman in labour: 'her belly cry sounding the wind'; the elevated rhetoric of the opening line is interrupted by the abrupt intrusion of the woman's physical effort ('Child of the middle passage womb / push / daughter of a vengeful Chi') (both quotes p.6). This revisionism is accompanied by an equally radical transformation of Christian tradition. The poem employs Biblical cadences, declaring that this terrible time is actually 'the Black Beginning' (p.7)—a rewriting of Genesis. The women of Nichols's sequence carry their sense of origins with them; where Brathwaite depicts the urgent need to retrace steps geographically in order to recover this connection, Nichols represents it as a *psychic* inheritance, an innate spiritual legacy shared by the women. In a further act of deliberate revision, the individualist glory of the hero in *The Arrivants* is replaced in *long memoried woman* by the blurring of individuality: it is not clear whether mother or daughter speaks, because the speaker functions as a composite memorial to the forgotten women who survived the Middle Passage, and struggled to keep life going for their children.[16]

Nichols's poem was not well received by post-colonial critics, because they objected to its construction of a trans-historical, heroic depiction of Black womanhood. The poem was criticised by Dabydeen and Wilson-Tagoe for being 'little removed from the "earth mother" image' of women in Caribbean literature.[17] Coinciding with the height of anti-essentialism, and acute anxieties from Western critics over generalisations about human experience, this is not surprising. It is an example of the way in which these attitudes left no space for a spiritual, mythic presentation such as Nichols clearly had in mind. It is also worth emphasising the difference between the kind of idealisations of women invoked by Dabydeen and Wilson-Tagoe, and Nichols's more comprehensive, psychologically probing account. Trying to defend the poet, Patrick Williams pointed to evidence of some geographically and historically specific references, as proof of her desire to 'offset an idealising tendency within the poems, the feeling that an essential black femininity which persists regardless of circumstance is being posited'.[18] But in this, as in her approach to Creole language, Nichols was not in step with critical fashions, and her reputation has suffered as a result. *Long memoried woman* is a celebratory praise song that emphasises women's vital contribution not just to survival but to the struggles to overthrow the colonisers (reference is made to Toussaint L'Overture and Nanny of the Maroons). The poem does posit a commonality between its subjects, precisely because of the importance of such generational intactness. But this does not mean that Nichols believes in an essence of Blackness. Indeed, poems like 'Of course when they ask for poems about the "realities" of black women' make her opposition to such notions quite clear:

> I say I can write no poem big enough
> to hold the essence
>   of a black woman
>   or a white woman
>   or a green woman[19]

The switch in qualifying adjectives from black to white to green takes the reader through three stages of her argument: at first, it looks as though she is rejecting the idea that black women share an 'essence'; then she broadens that position, to make it clear she does not believe white women can be said to either. The ludicrous suggestion of a green woman underlines the absurdity of such categorising impulses.

There is a considerable difference between an intellectual refutation of essentialism and a poetic evocation of a spiritual and psychic bond. However, when it is placed alongside Dabydeen's brutally heightened realism in *Slave Song*, it does not seem so surprising that *long memoried woman* should have been attacked for its idealism.

The *Slave Song* sequence is a series of songs in the voices of workers on a sugar plantation. Dabydeen spent the first six-and-a-half years of his life on such a plantation, and in his introduction to the collection provides a vivid portrait of the harsh labour and squalid living conditions that continue to characterise workers' experiences in this industry. Alcoholism and domestic violence are ubiquitous, and the songs attempt an unflinching portrayal of these grim realities. Most are set during slavery and the indentured labour system that replaced it in 1838.[20] However, like *long memoried woman*, this poem also employs the idea of history as a continuum: some of the poems are set in the present and deal with Indo-Guyanese men's feelings about their womenfolk's preference for white European marriage partners.[21] The poems were written while Dabydeen was an undergraduate, studying English Literature at Cambridge; he returned to Guyana during one of his vacations and began the series there. They were published when he was only 21. The extreme contrast between his family's existence on a plantation and the privilege of Cambridge University probably accounts for some of the rage that fuels the collection, resulting in brilliantly succinct, vivid evocations of brutalised minds and perverted desires. Above all, the book is the work of a writer absorbed in—wrestling with—English literary tradition. In interviews and articles, he has described the inspirational impact of medieval alliterative verse, for its 'sheer naked energy and brutality of the language'.[22] He has compared his commentary to Eliot's 'Notes' to *The Waste Land*, describing it as 'an act of counterparody'.[23] Much of this is the mimicry of revenge. The critic Mark McWatt has suggested that the commentary serves a more subtle purpose, creating a layer or 'mask', in order to emphasise the complexity of West Indian identity.[24] While the commentary may contribute in all these ways, it offers *supplementary interpretation*, guiding readers' responses and imposing particular readings on poems which, in themselves, are both more subtle and more ambiguous. The collection has all the hallmarks of an urgent, polemical thesis.

Dabydeen's thesis is that the colonial plantation system resulted in the production of perverted sexual fantasies and desires on the part of both blacks and whites. The white male overseers were, he argues, 'bewitched' by the slave women, whose appearance and deportment were so different from their own stiffly decorous women.[25] Black men (it is predominantly black people and more specifically black men he is interested in) were similarly fascinated by, and obsessed with, white women—'except that this latter lust is an inverse to the former, describable in terms of inspiration, aspiration, assimilation into a superior scheme of things'. (p.10) Whiteness, for black men, represents the possibility of 'transfiguration'; so the black man's sexual fantasies about white women are depicted as inextricably tangled up in his desire for freedom and prosperity, spiritual and intellectual betterment. For example, 'Love Song' is, as its title suggests, a tender reverie in which the labourer, dirty and exhausted after a dangerous and physically gruelling day's work, consoles himself with dreams of the spotless, soft-skinned white woman:

> Leh yuh come wid milk in yuh breast an yuh white troat bare
> Wid bangle on yuh haan an bell rung yuh waiss
> Leh yuh come wid oil an perfume an lace.(p.31)

In the commentary, Dabydeen adds certain pieces of information: that the man is drunk, which explains his sentimental tone and why he starts yearning for a mother figure. But he does not explain why this mother figure should be a white woman, her breasts full of milk: presumably because, as a maudlin reverie, it epitomises the man's yearning for transformation.[26]

In an interview recorded in 1990 with Frank Birbalsingh, Dabydeen describes his approach in *Slave Song* as 'playful', and he says that 'the pure delight of writing in Creole about erotic experiences is a very sensuous pursuit'.[27] In the same interview Dabydeen suggests that this focus has enabled him to probe beneath the surface of Caribbean life and language in order to reveal what he calls 'the basest level of human emotions and actions...the energies that people exchange' (p.172). In the commentary to one of the slave songs he describes 'the meeting and interaction of the two cultures on the deepest and most equal level, the sexual level'.[28] But what is striking about these quotations is how utterly they erase any recognition of sexual inequalities, in terms of power. Dabydeen's preoccupation with the corrosive effects of slavery seems to leave him no room to consider that 'the sexual level' is not 'the most equal level' at all.

These poems are particularly brave in daring to write from within women's minds (both slave and coloniser women) and to represent their sexual desires. 'Song of the Creole Gang Women' depicts the labouring women as masochistic and obsessed with their overseer; as the commentary glosses their situation they experience the 'surreptitious savouring of their pain...fascinated and repelled by

his tyranny'.(p.44) Both slave and coloniser are depicted as fantasising about being raped. 'Nightmare' recounts a white woman's
night-time terror. She imagines a gang of 'sweat-stink niggas' breaking down the door and raping her, before dragging her to the canal
bank where they cut her throat. The poem's description of the
natural world's frighteningly sinister febrility and ruthlessness adds
a convincing sense of the woman's generalised fear and unease in
this alien world. But it saves its punch for the last line, which
describes how 'Wet she awake, cuss de daybreak!'(p.34) In other
words, in both these poems, Dabydeen presents women (slave and
coloniser women) sexually aroused by fantasising about painful,
violent sex. On the whole, the poems are less explicit about this
than the commentary: discussing 'Nightmare', the poet spells out
the point, by telling his readers that the woman awakens 'wet with
surreptitious sexual arousal and not with terror'.(p.61) 'The
Canecutters' Song' describes the slave men's collective fantasy of
raping the overseer's woman, bringing her down into the mud,
making her dirty and fearful like them. Again, the commentary
adds information that imposes a particular interpretation on the
poem, this time insisting that the woman herself wants this degradation too, dreaming of it and tempting the men with her loose frock
and flowing hair. It is in the commentary that the poet himself
speaks—which makes it difficult not to attribute these glosses to
Dabydeen himself.

The poems have been criticised by critic Benita Parry for using

> a discourse shared by the master's culture and beyond, one
> that represents rape as what woman wants. It could be antic-
> ipated that a poetry refusing colonialism's misconstructions
> would displace its premises.[29]

However, the poet needs to represent these disturbing desires, for
the sake of authenticity: recent assessments of slave psychology
have acknowledged the prevalence of self-mutilation and self-abase-
ment amongst slaves, and Dabydeen is explicit in describing the
legacy of the slave system as perverting sexual relations.[30] He might
be operating as Angela Carter's 'moral pornographer', a role she
defines as follows:

A moral pornographer might use pornography as a critique of current relations between the sexes. His business would be the total demystification of the flesh and the subsequent revelation, through the infinite modulations of the sexual act, of the real relations of man and his kind. Such a pornographer would not be the enemy of women, perhaps because he might begin to penetrate to the heart of the contempt for women that distorts our culture even as he entered the realms of true obscenity as he describes it.[31]

Ultimately, though, a number of factors mediate against this interpretation. The commentary shows no interest in exploring the women's psychological motivation, nor does it acknowledge that the poems' depiction of women 'gagging for it' replicates a misogynist tradition in which women are represented as desiring their own violent degradation. Nor is it clear whether the women in these poems are intended to be symbolic or real. In his commentary to another poem that is devoted to a black labourer's fantasy of fucking the overseer's wife ('yu caan stap me cack dippin in de honeypot', p.28), Dabydeen insists that this woman is 'only a symbol through which to express his desire for life'. (p.55) In a later article about the sequence, he described these sexual yearnings as containing an impulse towards beauty and romance, in terms that suggest a symbolic intent:

> I wanted to show in *Slave Song* the Creole mind struggling and straining after concepts of beauty and purity but held back by its physically crude vocabulary...So, to describe beauty [the canecutter] struggles to transform vulgar words and concepts into lyrical ones, the result being poignant and tragic.[32]

But, against this, in all the poems the quality of description is detailed and realistic, rather than symbolic. So it appears that the poems are operating on two, contradictory levels: on the one hand, the white woman is symbolic: of aspiration, betterment and transfiguration; but, on the other, she herself is a desiring woman who seems to want her own violation. If the women are supposed to be authentically drawn, why is there such a lack of attention to *their* psychology? And why is there no exploration of a phenomenon that would seem highly plausible: that some of the black women might view the overseer as representing an opportunity for their offsprings' escape—since the children of white men and black women were born legally free?[33] This would make such a liaison at least *imaginatively* desirable for the black women, in just the same way as for their menfolk, yet there is no suggestion of it.

There are several vivid depictions of women raped and murdered. In 'For Mala' two (male, though this is not stated) Creole voices describe the body of a young black girl who has been raped and dumped in the river.[34] They graphically imagine what the rapists did with a broken bottle and describe the bite-marks on her breasts. They view the tragedy in terms of its waste of this now 'ruined' young woman. Instead of her mature womb:

> full-flesh when you squash it open
> An all de ripe juice run dung yu finga, dung yu arm and troat.
> Now she hollow, now she float. (p.19)

One visualises the rapist running off, 'yolk a drip from e mout-kana' [corner of his mouth]. The men imagine her wholly in terms of her sexual and procreative capacity; her fate is lamented because it is a waste of her potential to give pleasure and children. The ironically titled 'Guyana Pastoral' describes the rotting corpse of another female victim as it lies amidst the fecund and indifferent natural world.[35] Doubtless the poet would claim that these are authentic representations of these men's attitudes to their womenfolk, and of the brutality of their lives; as he asserts several times in the commentary, their lives are harsh, and eating, killing and fucking are their main occupations. The commentary is again revealing. Dabydeen tells us that 'For Mala' is based on a real historical event, the bloody Wismar massacre of 1964, in which Negroes turned on Indians, raping and killing many. He notes that the racial conflict between the two groups was one of the main legacies of colonialism in Guyana. But his explanation of the event is troubling: he argues that the rapes were the result of 'the collective realisation of sexual fantasy on a frightening scale—the "savages" had become *real* savages and certainly not noble'.(p.46) Rather than interpreting rape as an act of war, or accepting the feminist claim that rape is not about sexual desire but about power, Dabydeen emphasises and even prioritises the sexual component within this inter-racial conflict.

The boldness of Dabydeen's approach in these poems is evident from comments made in the introduction: 'Even the appetite for sadistic sexual possession is life-giving, the strange vivid fruit of racial conquest and racial hatred' he claims. (p.10) Much of it can be explained as the iconoclasm and fury of a young Guyanese man encountering the privileged world of literary Cambridge. Their sensational impact becomes even clearer when we consider their entry for—and securing of—a Cambridge University poetry prize! For the poems were written in reaction to what struck the young undergraduate as the elegant hypocrises and euphemisms of the English literary canon, its poets creating falsifying idealisations of colonial enterprise. In an article published a couple of years later, Dabydeen cited the eighteenth-century poet James Grainger, whose poem 'The Sugar Cane' substituted the phrase 'master-swain' for 'overseer' and 'Afric's sable progeny' for 'blacks'.[36] A few years later, he accused writers of the English canon of 'colonizing the experience of others for the gratification of their own literary sensibilities.'[37] Such (wholly justifiable) criticisms suggest the particular force of a young poet's struggle with his poetic forebears, when allied with the anger of a post-colonial writer reacting to the literary tradition of the colonisers.

As part of his fierce riposte to such genteel falsification, Dabydeen exaggerated the distinctions between what he continued to call 'Creole' and standard English.[38] In his schema, English is polite, abstract, soft, modulated, genteel and euphemistic; Creole is physical and broken—like, he suggests, its speakers:

The language is angry, crude, energetic. The canecutter chopping away at the crops bursts into a spate of obscene words, a natural gush from the gut, like fresh faeces. It is hard to put two words together in Creole without swearing. Words are spat out from the mouth like live squibs, not pronounced with elocution...If one has learnt and used Queen's English for a long time, the return into Creole is painful, almost nauseous, for the language is uncomfortably raw. One has to shed one's protective sheath of abstracts and let the tongue move freely and bleed again.[39]

His own descriptive language here is highly sexualised, and indeed the closeness of the link between sex and language is made explicit when he declares in a later article:

I cannot feel or write poetry like a white man, however, much less serve him. And to become mulattos, black people literally have to be fucked (and fucked up) first.[40]

This derogatory mention of mulattos brings us back to Nichols's poem about the child of a forced union between white overseer and black labourer. Where Nichols's speaker finds the courage to bless and welcome her child, as a symbol of survival and the triumph of human (specifically mother-) love in the face of absolute degradation, Dabydeen's aggressive absolutism effectively claims that any sexual liaison between black and white partners will reduce the black partner to the status of a passive victim (who has 'to be fucked [and fucked up]'). Many postcolonial critics and writers follow this line, emphasising Creole's radical alterity as evidence of its (and its speakers') resistance to western colonial languages, and as proof of authenticity, although I am not aware of others who sexualise the matter in the way Dabydeen does.

Brathwaite's expansive celebratory approach to what he coined 'Nation language' has been overtaken. Dabydeen's declared intention is to 'adventure with the language and "pervert" it, which was opposite to Eddie Brathwaite's desire to purify it'.[41] He argues that the plantation workers' Creole is shaped out of the physical conditions in which its speakers live: their 'condition of squalor' produces 'crude diction';[42] or, as he puts it in the commentary to one of the slave songs, 'The savage imagination of the canecutters is the correlate to the physical savagery of their work.'[43] This is a popular view amongst cultural commentators, who construct a stark opposition between abstract, cerebral English, and the more immediately 'physical' Creole. Carolyn Cooper associates Creole with orality and the '"vulgar" body', delivering a radical challenge to 'the tightly-closed orifices of the Great Tradition'.[44] In his study of *Dub Poetry* Christian Habekost uses terms similar to Dabydeen's, establishing a contrast between the aggressive, confrontational polemic of dub and the polite, detached mode of 'traditional' lyric poetry.[45]

Denise DeCaires Narain has attempted to complicate this model, by pointing to examples of Caribbean writers who employ a more nuanced mixture of languages, like Jamaica Kincaid. Kincaid has repeatedly spoken about the problems she experiences with writing in Creole. She argues that, for her, Creole symbolises the colonial past and is associated with humiliation and barbarity.[46] In her view, this is not an appropriate language in which to forge a new consciousness. Grace Nichols appears to share her view. Her version of Creole is far gentler and much closer to standard English, if anything tending to the lyrical. She has spoken of her desire to 'fuse the two tongues because I come from a background where the two were constantly interacting'.[47]

Since *Slave Song* Dabydeen has made far less use of his radical full-blown Creole, perhaps because he now spends so little time in Guyana that the oral sources are less accessible to him, but perhaps also because the subjects of his enquiry have changed: no longer the plantation workers, but immigrants to Britain, and the repressed African or Indian 'other' so consistently relegated to the peripheries in English cultural representations. Nichols's later work also shifts its focus to the experience of immigrants in Britain and, since *The Fat Black Woman's Poems* were first published in 1984, I shall turn to this collection, and its successor, *Lazy Thoughts of a Lazy Woman* (1989), before I consider Dabydeen's second collection, *Coolie Odyssey*.

There is a discernible shift in focus between these two volumes. The dominant atmosphere in the first is nostalgic, the poems' subjects stirred by memories of 'back home', whereas *Lazy Thoughts* depicts characters who are more settled in England and more confident as a result; they enjoy a little light-hearted banter at the expense of their new neighbours, mocking their more bizarre habits and pinpointing English eccentricities with the outsider's acumen.

The central technique Nichols employs in *The Fat Black Woman's Poems* is one of sending up stereotypes by exaggeration. The eponymous heroine of the volume carries three negative markers. She flaunts her physical bulk, encompassing the familiar, controversial icons of Black womanhood: African matriarch, Mammy and sassy, insatiably rapacious lover. What have been markers of racist ideology are here acted out, only now the black woman is in control. In this way, the fearful imaginings of the colonisers seem to have been realised, although the woman herself is fully aware of her cultural history and is depicted as enjoying acting up to it. She is a performer, camping up the stereotypes as she sits in regal majesty, stubbornly refusing to budge despite the pleas and enticements offered by frustrated 'white robed chiefs'. Dismissing the efforts of these men, whose white robes make them symbols of both racial and patriarchal authority, the woman is defiant, revelling in her power and exploiting her matriarchal image to the full.[48] All we see of her are eyes, fingers and toes, in an ironic nod towards traditional representations' lingering descriptions of the corporeal.[49] Yet there is a sombre aspect to this poem as well; the 'fire of love' in her eyes is only barely held in check; the penetrative beady glare of her gaze and her laconic authority betray vestiges of a threatening power still smouldering beneath the patriarchal social order.

The humour of these poems distracts attention from the thorough critique they offer, and it may be that this partly explains the lack of serious critical attention given to her work.[50] So one poem, luxuriously titled 'Thoughts drifting through the fat black woman's head while having a full bubble bath', creates a refrain from one of the many linguistic coinages invented by the colonialists (and their accompanying anthropologists) to describe the native population:

> Steatopygous sky
> Steatopygous sea
> Steatopygous waves
> Steatopygous me[51]

'Steatopygia' derives from modern Latin for 'tallow' and 'rump', and was used to refer to what the *New Oxford Dictionary of English* defines as the 'accumulation of large amounts of fat on the buttocks, especially as a normal condition in the Khoikhoi and other peoples of arid parts of southern Africa'. The poem turns an offensive label into an insouciant chant, but its method is deceptively light hearted, and the implications unmistakable: anyone who consults a dictionary to discover the meaning of this unfamiliar word will receive a history lesson.[52]

Several of the poems celebrate this woman's voluptuousness. She has a healthy appetite for love and delights in her body's generous proportions, describing her thighs as 'twin seals' and her breasts as watermelons.[53] Nichols has said the woman is a symbol of a certain 'largeness of spirit' that is lacking in the West.[54] But she also makes a sharp contrast, once again, with Western capitalist countries' adulation for unnaturally skinny 'supermodels'.[55]

Nichols's critique is unobtrusive. The opening poem, 'Beauty' replaces the serene, impassive icon of white beauty with a carefree, self-absorbed, fat black woman frolicking in the waves.[56] Where the Western history of art is full of paintings that depict a motionless woman, invariably staring out to meet the viewer's gaze, this subject is too busy enjoying herself to be bothered who is looking at her. Effortlessly, she subverts centuries of androcentric representation, defying John Berger's famous statement that '[m]en look at women. Women watch themselves being looked at.'[57]

Nichols's third collection, *Lazy Thoughts*, continues the technique of picking up on stereotypes, only to undercut their traditional meanings. So indolence and laziness—both behaviours seen by colonialists as typical of the black population—are espoused enthusiastically by the poems' speakers. But, rather than simply attempting to subvert the stereotype by laying claim to it, the poems propound the superior capacities and advantages of this kind of behaviour, by juxtaposing it with examples of Western capitalist societies' extreme, almost pathological, intolerance of the body's natural properties, like sweat and hair. In 'On Poems and Crotches', Nichols flouts the cerebrality of literary tradition by flagrantly announcing that 'poems are born / in the bubbling soul of the crotch.'[58] The book's title does not prepare readers for the serious, considered poems it contains; it lulls us into assuming that 'liming knees' and 'idle toes' mean a laid-back brain, when in fact it contains some challenging, prescient critiques of globalisation. 'Always Potential' draws a sharp contrast between international big business and 'my raw underdeveloped country'; watching the lorries thunder past on the London North Circular Road, delivering their goods, the speaker notes their reliance on raw materials from Guyana; as the multinationals convert cheap raw materials into profit, it is not surprising that 'the back-home politician-drone / "We have a lot of potential / a lot of potential." // Always potential.'[59] The same kind of understated resistance characterises 'My Black Triangle', a celebration of its speaker's sex. The poem appropriates the tradition of using women's bodies to describe the land and exploits it to its own ends, so woman's sex is a rich, fertile 'Bermuda / of tiny atoms' which 'has spread beyond his story / beyond the dry fears of parch-ri-archy'.[60]

Where Dabydeen's approach insists on a rigid distinction between Creole and standard English, Nichols's work adopts a less programmatic style. 'Beverley's Saga' is an account of one woman's tolerant reaction to people who assume that, because she is black, she must be on holiday in Britain. Because it is written in Creole, her own assimilation is signalled by the ease with which English customs find accommodation within her language:

> But a have me lickle flat
> An a have me lickle key.
> You want to come in
> For a lickle cup-o-tea?[61]

'Dead Ya Fuh Tan'[62] harnesses Creole slang in order to make some sobering observations on racism beneath the guise of a humorous piece about white folks' obsession with getting a suntan. Its speaker expresses amazement at what—at first—seems to be whites' envy of black people's tans: 'People a dead ya fuh tan' ('they would kill for your suntan'). But by the end of the poem, more sinister connotations emerge, with the suggestion that 'Anyway dem can ketch a brown / People a dead ya fuh tan.', evoking the Ku Klux Klan and the indisputable claim that whites will kill someone because of their skin colour.

On the whole, though, the poems in *Lazy Thoughts* depict immigrants integrating themselves into British life, recognising the losses as well as the gains entailed. And rather than language being a weapon or the sign of difference and exclusion, Nichols opts for a more inclusive attitude. It is customs and manners that she hones in on, as the significant markers of 'Britishness' and, like Beverley, anyone can adopt such behaviours without changing their language. So the speaker of 'Wherever I Hang' describes her gradual assimilation through changes in her ways—learning to queue, no longer dropping in on friends without warning—not her speech.[63]

In keeping with this synthesising spirit, some of the poems make connections between the two, seemingly remote, countries, Guyana and Britain. In one poem the speaker is reminded of her childhood habit of collecting 'orange-coloured cockles', when she watches English schoolboys collecting conkers.[64] And 'Hurricane' uses the exceptionally strong winds that battered Britain in 1987 to move beyond national borders and differences in recognition that 'the earth is the earth is the earth.'[65]

For the most part, despite their overt celebration of sensuality and the body, Nichols's poems do not focus on sexual relations, unlike Dabydeen's. 'Configurations' is one of the few that does.[66] It explores the tensions that accompany a white man and a black woman's intimate relationship. Here Nichols literalises colonial metaphors, exploiting the tradition whereby heterosexual relations and colonisation share vocabularies ('conquests', 'the rape of the land'). These lovers, like Dabydeen's (as we shall see shortly), cannot escape history; they are portrayed as inescapably representative of their racial group, so the gifts they give to one another are symbols of the two races. He gives her 'concorde' and 'straight blond hairs'; she gives him 'black wool', 'her "Bantu buttocks"' and '[t]he darkness / of her twin fruits'. (p.31) Each gift carries its associations of exploitation, fetishisation, theft and violence, yet each is also a gesture of attempted intimacy. The poem plots the tentative 'movements' of a dance of sexual exploration, in which the fineness of the line between desire and appropriation is implicitly tested. Their exchanges are strangely muted, without the warmth or passionate absorption of lovers, as they feel their way across this sexual and racial minefield. The tension between marvelling appreciation and the desire to own and subjugate is perfected imaged in the analogy between sexual desire and colonisation. Until the final stanza, the woman is presented as instinctive, unreflecting; her gifts are the overdetermined symbols of the underdeveloped world. Only the last lines overturn this cliché, bringing the two levels of the poem together. The woman's legs encircle her white lover as she moves to intensify her own orgasm, no longer the passive catalyst for his pleasure but a seeker after her own:

> He does a Columbus
> falling on the shores of her tangled nappy orchard.
>
> She delivers up the whole Indies again
> But this time her wide legs close in
>   slowly
> Making a golden stool of the empire
> of his head.

He is the explorer, but this time his licence is checked; her generosity is tempered with foreknowledge. He is no pioneer; doing 'a Columbus' he finds himself re-enacting the coloniser's actions in a forced act of mimicry. She gives, but she also keeps control, making him her golden stool. That his head is described as an empire signals the poem's fine balance: he is still a descendant of the colonisers, but the metaphor also suggests both that he is now *her* empire, and that he is a valuable prize, a man worth having.

The lovers do manage to negotiate a way through the legacies of imperialism, many of which (as the references to 'uranium, platinum, aluminium' imply) continue to exert a severely detrimental effect over the developing world's political and economic situation, as well as over the way blacks and whites perceive one another. Such optimism is entirely absent from Dabydeen's *Coolie Odyssey*, a collection which, like *The Fat Black Woman's Poems* and *Lazy Thoughts,* is largely devoted to poems set in Britain, recounting the experiences of Caribbean immigrants.

Dabydeen's tone could not be more different. Life for immigrants in London is hard, and the English are not to be trusted. They like Harillal, who runs a cornershop, but only because he puts on an act for them, 'tropical smile, jolly small chat, credit';[67] he is known as 'the local Paki' although he comes from Guyana. His customers, who look like harmless pensioners, are described as 'muted claws of Empire'.(p.10) Emigration is portrayed as entailing loss rather than gain, and the characters depicted are embittered and scarred by their experiences. The London taxi driver who originates from Berbice whiles away the days venting his spleen on traffic lights and fantasising about 'some sweet bitch in some soap serial / How he'd like to mount and stuff her lipsticked mouth'.(p.26) Where his parents' generation struggled to overthrow their imperial rulers, his quest is less glorious:

> He grunts rebellion
> In back seat discount sex
> With the last night's last whore. (p.27)

These characters have only been able to find employment in menial jobs well below their ability. But these grim, realistic pieces form only a small part of the book; a larger part is devoted to one particular protagonist: highly educated, cultured and intelligent. The poems are written in the third person, and they describe his sexual encounters with a series of white women, in language whose formality imitates the style of sixteenth- and eighteenth-century poetry.

These sexual liaisons provoke trauma in the young, black immigrant. While the setting is present day, he exists in a psychological time warp because he has inherited the same fantasies about what white women represent as those that both tormented and comforted his forebears. Where Nichols's 'Configurations' described the tentative, difficult process of negotiation between the descendants of colonised and coloniser, the impasse between the lovers is far more extreme in Dabydeen's work. Clearly, these poems move the argument and themes of *Slave Song* into the present and illustrate the accuracy of Wilson Harris's summary of Dabydeen's theme as 'the pornography of empire that still rules the heart of coloniser and colonised.'[68] Sometimes there is no evidence that specifically locates a poem temporally, but the overall context suggests that, although they use the language of overseer and cane, this is done to reflect the way in which fear, and the distortions imposed by imperial rule, continue to reverberate today.

'Caliban' describes a man's memories of the first night of love-making with a white woman. He remembers how he succumbed to her appetite for his exotic tales, but in retrospect the act of sharing these stories of his childhood acquires a different resonance. He describes them '[f]oraging...like two tramps at a tip: // Finding riches among the rubble was your Romance.'[69] While, at the time, he relished feeling transformed by her enthusiasm, the gulf between them becomes clear in the sober morning. She is quite unaffected by what has passed between them, while its effect on him is dramatic; he craves the continuance of her transformative power, and recognition of it evokes in him the helplessness of his ancestors, in thrall to the magic of whiteness. The white woman has a God-like capacity to fashion him as she chooses: she is his 'womb of myth'

> Where, like a Hindu corpse I burn and shrink
> To be reborn to your desire! (p.34)

Despite the fact that these two young people meet as equals in a cosmopolitan setting, for him she embodies the investments and fantasies of plantation days, when white women symbolised aspiration, forbidden desire and the possibility of alchemical transformation. 'Water with Berries' describes another casual encounter, after which the woman departs, apparently contented, leaving the man in turmoil provoked by his brief blissful taste of the solace of 'her white spacious body'. The experience hurls him back into buried memories of the slave era; he wakes 'from sleep as from ship's bowel / Desperate to dream again'. (p.36) In another poem, the gesture of touching a white woman's breast for the first time triggers a series of imagined reprisals: 'coolieman skin' burning, dogs set upon him, slaves being thrown overboard.[70] The poem's title, 'Rebel Love', suggests it could be set during plantation times, but its place right in the middle of a series of others that are clearly contemporary makes this less certain and fuels the idea that it too deals with the *psychic aftermath* of slavery.

The aspect of this damage in which Dabydeen is interested is clearly the effect it has had over Caribbean manhood. 'Shame' is a word that appears repeatedly in conjunction with sexual desire, and the male speakers often feel themselves emasculated. Frequently they seem paralysed by what they imagine to be white women's expectations of them. One speaker, refusing sex, explains despairingly:

> I cannot come to you tonight
> With monstrous organ of delight
> I have no claw no appetite
> I am not Caliban but sprite.[71]

However, it is not only impotence that accounts for his refusal. This woman, whatever her real name, is—to him—Miranda, or Britannia; she is the colonial mistress, and her presence torments him, throwing him back on to the 'rack' of memories he cannot shake off. It is interesting that, despite the distress she causes him, and despite her role as one of the colonisers, the man is not quite able to hate her—presumably because he still carries internalised fantasies of white woman as the embodiment of aspiration and betterment. In another poem Miranda comes to him in a dream and tends his 'black bony peasant body / Stalk of blighted cane':

> She wiped him with the moist cloth of her tongue
> Like a new mother licking clean its calf
> And hugged milk from her breast to his cracked
> mouth. [72]

This is similar in tone and imagery to 'Love Song', from the earlier collection in which the plantation worker also imagines receiving succour at the white woman's hands. It is not until *Turner*, Dabydeen's third collection, that maternal images are wrested from their sole association with white women.

Of course these are fantasies; nevertheless they are confusing when placed alongside the poet's angry rejection of any kind of inter-course—sexual or cultural—with whites: 'to become mulattos, black people literally have to be fucked (and fucked up) first'.[73] This ambivalence—which shows in the caustic self critique of some of the poems in this collection—is explored in the long title poem, which also shows Dabydeen (like Brathwaite and Walcott) appro-priating classical mythology, since the poem makes its speaker a modern-day Odysseus.[74] He and the other Indo-Guyanese now living in London exist between two worlds. The poem opens with a caustic reference to the popularity of Tony Harrison and Seamus

Heaney, suggesting that English poetry has suddenly discovered a taste for humble folk material. Memories of his childhood, and accounts of his grandparents and cousins follow, as it becomes an explicit address to his recently deceased mother. But even as he tells these stories he is wondering about his motives. It is as though he, and other exiles, discover it is *they* who need such tales:

> In a winter of England's scorn
> We huddle together memories, hoard them from
> The opulence of our masters. (p.9)

He realises that his mother would not have understood his desire to write about their lives: the desire grows out of exile. But as well as imagining her scepticism he faces his own: who is he writing for? Is he himself guilty of a strange kind of 'plunder' of his own country, stealing these tales for the entertainment of 'congregations of the educated / Sipping wine, attentive between courses'? (p.13) Similarly uncomfortable questions are raised in 'Homecoming', in which the speaker addresses a street salesman, seeing him as the tourists see him ('perplexed your blessed sunshine country / Should breed such you-lice, shacks'), but also viewing the bold, naïve tourists with disdain.[75] This dual focus emphasises his own uneasy position as an outsider, but not a tourist. He becomes furious when the street-seller fails to deliver the 'old-time Indian talk' he wants in return for some rum; instead, the man just 'stutter Creole stupidness'. (p.43) But his extreme disappointment makes him realise how desperate he must be for this 'history', the familiar banter, the tales, the idioms he never hears in England. He sums himself up mercilessly, likening his behaviour towards the old man to that of the colonisers:

> As hungry as any white man for native gold,
> To plant flag and to map your mind. (p.43)

However, not all the criticism is directed internally. 'The New Poetry' describes a (presumably white) woman's impatience with her lover's obsessive interest in what she sees as a remote colonial history. In this 'modern' age, poetry concerns itself with nature and pastoral scenes; she cannot see the point of pouring over 'esoteric notes in a scholar's curious book'.[76] But she turns on the television to news coverage of:

> The bone-shaped plane of fat white men and foreign
>   aid
> Met by loud spears and women jigging waist. (p.28)

The legacies of colonialism live on, with the developing world forced, literally, to dance to the rich white man's tune. And while Dabydeen himself may feel uneasy about his own 'use' of his compatriots in poems that are consumed by a privileged white audience enjoying exotic tales of Caribbean life, it is worse when he realises that audience's appetite for this material stems from their own awareness of inhabiting a worn-out, moribund culture. In 'New World Words' the white woman is likened to a '[s]harp-beaked hummingbird / Drunk on the sweat of jungle flower'[77] as she tries to suck his words out of him in order to refresh and re-energise her 'dull plumage'. She is like a vampire sapping his life-force, and, as she sucks, she also steals his potency:

> He clamped his loins
> From her consumptive mouth
> …
> Curled away shyly
> To a finger of feeble ash. (p.37)

Words are sexualised, imbued with the potential for creation—the alchemical transformation which Dabydeen has said he yearns to bring about. Such remaking of history turns the poet into a kind of God, capable of such creation. 'The Sexual Word' describes a white woman's resistance to this attempt. The man yearns:

> To remake her from his famished rib
> To redeem her from the white world.[78]

But such a fantasy would entail the white woman's degradation, and, not surprisingly, she refuses to acquiesce in it. The poem ends bitterly:

She could not endure the repetition
Necessary for new beginning

Yet was ravished by the poetry. (p.32)

The black man needs to enact his fantasy—which involves raping the white woman, thus destroying the symbolic superiority of the colonisers, and all the connotations of whiteness and white femininity—in order to effect redemption for the sins perpetrated on his ancestors: out of this will grow a 'new beginning'. It is a controversial claim, particularly because it sits amidst a series of poems that focus on the intimate, private scenes of love-making. The effect of this is to demonstrate that no space is immune from the corrosive effects of colonial history. Redemption is tragic, when based on the desire for revenge through repetition, but the poems force us to consider what alternatives exist.[79]

Dabydeen's latest collection *Turner*, contains a long poem, 'Turner', alongside reprints from *Slave Song* and *Coolie Odyssey*. 'Turner' is based on J. M. W. Turner's famous painting, 'Slavers Throwing Overboard the Dead and Dying', which Dabydeen describes, in a preface, as the artist's 'finest painting in the sublime style'.[80] In this poem, as in much of his academic retrieval work, the poet reveals the racist ideology latent in such so-called masterpieces of English high culture. While critics at the time, and since, have praised the painter's technical accomplishment, none saw fit to comment on its terrible subject matter. In his poem, Dabydeen assumes the voice of one of those thrown overboard. Instead of decomposing, his hatred has kept him alive in an anguished limbo, '[l]ike cork, buoying me when I should have sunk'.[81] In his loneliness, he has tried to behave like Adam, bestowing new names on the creatures in the world around him. This is most likely a dry allusion to Derek Walcott's enthusiastic description of the opportunities available to Caribbean writers:

We were blest with a virginal, unpainted world
with Adam's task of giving things their names.[82]

For Dabydeen's 'Adam' is unaware of the extent to which his

perceptions and language are still in thrall to the colonisers. When a stillborn baby miraculously lands in the waters next to him, thrown overboard from a ship hundreds of years later, he seizes the opportunity to create a truly new world for the child, but one of his first acts is to give it a 'fresh name', 'Turner'—even though this is the very name he gives to all white men, the slavers.(p.1) Amidst the 'words of my own dreaming' lie 'those that Turner / Primed in my mouth' (p.14), and it is this indelible stain that becomes the real subject of the piece.[83]

For the first time Dabydeen chooses the metaphor of mothering as a suitable vehicle for what has been his consistent aim: that of transfiguration, or renewal, through writing.[84] The poem's protagonist has yearned for the opportunity represented by this baby: that of creating new stories and myths for his tribe. In so doing, he meets the prophet Manu's challenge (delivered just as the white men began to land amidst their community) that in order to survive, future generations would need to do precisely this:

> Each
> Will be barren of ancestral memory
> But each endowed richly with such emptiness
> From which to dream, surmise, invent, immortalise.[85]

The preface explains that the sea has 'transformed him— bleached him of colour and complicated his sense of gender'. (p.x) But the survivor's 'longed-for gift of motherhood' (p.1) does not bring the desired new beginnings. Instead, the child's presence triggers his own memories: of childhood pranks with his sisters, of the time he hit his head diving into a pool and was nursed by his mother; of earlier memories of being a baby strapped to her back as she worked in the fields. Metaphors of pregnancy and birth are appropriated as the speaker finds himself thrown back into his own past. As the baby is thrown into the ocean, it 'broke the waters and made the years / Stir'. (p.16) Rather than mothering the child, the protagonist nurtures him/herself:

> My breasts a woman's which I surrender
> To my child-mouth, feeding my own hurt

For the taste of sugared milk. (p.16)

In the poem, the colonisers are shown as having usurped two of the most fundamental ingredients of the tribe's continuity: the maternal role and the storyteller's. The speaker's most poignant memories are of his mother's loving care, but he also remembers Manu the teacher's version of nurture: delivering stories to the youngsters, to give them knowledge of their ancestry. Manu's instruction is depicted as a kind of feeding: the stories are compared to grains of wheat which nourish the children who gather at his knee. But the colonisers wiped out both. Turner tempted the children on to his ship and away from their people by bribing them with sweets and shada juice:

> Five of us hold his hand,
> Each takes a finger, like jenti cubs
> Clinging to their mother's teats. (p.8)

He thus ousts both mother and teacher, inculcating his own language in a way that makes this imitation of the maternal role even more explicit. Once again, Dabydeen connects language and sex, suggesting that Turner's enforcement of his own language goes hand-in-hand with his sexual abuse of the children:

> Turner crammed our boys' mouths too with riches,
> His tongue spurting strange potions upon ours
> Which left us dazed, which made us forget
> The very sound of our speech. (p.38)

The narrator hopes to be able to instil new tales in the sea-foundling, to repair this damage, but he discovers that the child itself has internalised the colonisers' rhetoric: it calls him 'nigger' in recognition (p.28; p.39), and resists his attempts to bring it back to life, wanting to be allowed to die, too eaten up with self-hatred to wish to survive. He has to admit defeat, the failure of his 'redemptive song':

> But the child would not bear the future

Nor its inventions, and my face was rooted
In the ground of memory. (p.39)

The implication of this bleak scenario is that it is simply not possible to transfigure history by writing, to write a way out of the
colonial past. Both child and narrator are trapped in the represen-
tational systems that have held sway over them and continue to do
so. Both unknowingly re-enact the past, which they cannot escape.

Some critics read the poem as being more positive than this.
Karen McIntyre argues that by calling multiple characters 'Turner',
the poet is deliberately unfixing notions of identity as stable, which,
following Homi Bhabha (the post-colonial critic and theorist), she
sees as an essential part of decolonisation, because colonial discourse
typically exaggerates differences between coloniser and colonised.
She finds evidence of what Wilson Harris has called an 'Infinite
Rehearsal' in the poem: 'a continuous repetition, with difference,
of the major strategies of a particular discursive practice in order
to disempower and subvert them'.[86] Only the leg of a drowning man
is visible in Turner's painting, while Dabydeen re-visions this as the
man's head; McIntyre interprets this as evidence of the poem's recu-
perative mode, overturning the hierarchy of importance signalled
by colonisers' representations of the past. While her sophisticated
article is quite convincing within its own terms, it does not seem
to address the pessimism of the poem itself, which depicts the
impossibility of escaping the suffocating shadows of history and
representation.

Of particular interest here is Dabydeen's use of maternity as a
metaphor. For, as his preface acknowledges, the stillborn child is
actually only a means to an end; it is 'an agent of self-recognition'
for the narrator, 'his unconscious and his origin'.(p.x) In other
words, this child has no real separate existence, but serves as an
extension of the narrator. This means that the attempted mothering that takes place is really narcissistic self-mothering, nothing to
do with the other at all. In the light of this, the way in which the
child's mother is dispensed with begins to seem rather disturbing.

Nor, despite the preface's claim that the sea has 'complicated' the
protagonist's sense of gender, is there any evidence of this in the

poem. The survivor yearns for a child—but men can yearn for children just as strongly as women. He/she also craves self-mothering, which leads to the ascription of metaphorical breasts (see p.16 quoted earlier)—but neither of these points seem adequate to validate a claim which appears unsubstantiated. An uncharitable reading might suggest that this is simply the poet's attempt to show that he is now working with more complicated notions of gender than was the case in his earlier work.[87]

There is one further troubling aspect to the poem and that is the way in which Turner is demonised. In his preface, Dabydeen explains that he has chosen to interpret certain aspects of the painter's personality—so, for example, his celebrated love of children becomes evidence of his paedophiliac inclinations, and his 'extreme prudence with money' is translated into the avaricious sea captain's mercantile brutality, trading people for money. Dabydeen argues that the artist's painting is so intensely realised that it can only be accounted for by his satisfaction at contemplating the imagined scene: in other words, that he took sadistic pleasure from the idea of black people being thrown overboard. McIntyre reads the poet's deployment of the painting as a daring act that is 'both necrophilial or appropriative...and uniquely creative'.(p.146) But what is the effect of this wholesale attack on the painter? It could be argued that it actually reduces the scale and severity of the slave trade, and colonialist exploitation, by personalising it to this degree. On the other hand, by calling all white men 'Turner', Dabydeen is making his reading of the painting clear, in that he thus aligns Turner with the slave industry, via the production of such a horrific scene as nothing other than fodder for European consumption and aesthetic appraisal. However, there is at least the possibility of interpreting Turner's painting as an *indictment* of what it represents, not a celebration of it. It is only as the viewer recognises the full horror of the scene that the 'sublime' aspect of the painting is fully activated. Consequently, the work becomes, itself, a critique of the sublime, and the way it pivots on the spectacle of death as an instance of awe-inspiring terror.[88]

Perhaps the most surprising contrast between these two poets concerns their personae. Where many women poets encounter difficulties in relation to asserting an authoritative public voice, Nichols's espousal of such a persona seems effortless. Poems like 'Always Potential' and 'There is No Centre of the Universe' are fine examples; in many others, she speaks for a public collective 'we', sometimes black women, sometimes black people.[89] On the other hand Dabydeen's personae are absorbed in internal, personal traumas, which themselves derive from the huge historical trauma of slavery. Wilson-Tagoe is quoted at the start of this chapter, suggesting that women writers were beginning to 'deconstruct the divisions between domestic and public domains' (see p.106). It does seem as though both Nichols's and Dabydeen's poems do effect such a deconstruction. Both do this by demonstrating that, for Caribbean immigrants, there is no such thing as a 'private' domain, unaffected by public discourses—whether historical or contemporary—about colonialism and racism.

There are clear explanations that account, in part, for these two poets' different attitudes to literary tradition. Dabydeen was educated at an English university, and during his ongoing career as an academic he has extended his post-colonial critique in several non-fictional studies of eighteenth-century British art and literature, painstakingly unpicking the racist ideologies latent in such productions. It may be too, that he is partly motivated by Oedipal rivalry, not just towards what Harold Bloom would call his 'strong' English predecessors, but also towards his Caribbean poetic forebears, Brathwaite and Walcott.[90] Derek Walcott has provocatively suggested that the urge for revenge is 'a filial impulse',[91] and in the course of this chapter are noted the occasions on which Dabydeen signals his distance from these older Caribbean poets. Walcott has argued that the New World poet must rise above history, rather than simply trying to tell the story from the victim's viewpoint. Remembering Nichols's 'black triangle' that 'has spread beyond his story / beyond the dry fears of parch-ri-archy', this could be taken as an accurate description of much of her work. But, as Stewart Brown notes, Walcott's assertion suggests it is possible for language itself to be 'somehow beyond the contamination of its own history'.[92] All Dabydeen's poetry is proof that he views this as an impossibility. Where the epilogue to Nichols's *long memoried woman* ('I have crossed an ocean / I have lost my tongue / From the root of the old one / A new one has sprung'[93] announces survival, Dabydeen finds there are insuperable impediments to such self-reinvention.

In her study of West Indian literature, Belinda Edmondson emphasises the ongoing influence of the English colonial legacy over the ways in which indigenous writers conceptualise the role of the writer. She suggests there is a significant gender dimension to this: Victorian models of the intellectual took for granted that such a figure would be a gentleman. As a result, male West Indian writers 'must re-vision what constitutes literary authority itself by rewriting the paradigm of the gentleman author'.[94] Edmondson argues that it is this pervasive legacy that helps account for these writers' preoccupation with Victorian sensibilities and themes, and with rewritings of English literary classics. Dabydeen's obsessive interest in earlier British cultural artefacts could well be a version of this absorption. Several other Caribbean writers have said they view such absorption as a trap: the novelist Caryl Phillips decided to follow poet Fred D'Aguiar's lead and learn Spanish precisely in order to break away from nineteenth-century English prose which is, he claims, not adequate for describing a culture as heterogeneous as that of the Caribbean.[95] Jamaica Kincaid described her move to the United States as enabling her to find a voice and an identity that were not available to her in England.[96]

Edmondson points out that, for women, there are no such inherited models of the literary mode and suggests this may be why West Indian women writers (far more than their brothers) have looked to their North American sisters as role models and influences. This is borne out by Nichols's oeuvre, with its gestures of solidarity towards Maya Angelou and Ntozake Shange.[97] It seems that, in this case, a woman's exclusion from literary tradition might be said to be advantageous.

4.

THE INTIMATE AUTHORITY OF TED HUGHES'S *BIRTHDAY LETTERS* *

Ted Hughes—icon of taciturn masculinity—did not seem likely, after years of silence, to speak out about his relationship with Sylvia Plath. Then, in January 1998, *Birthday Letters* appeared. The book received huge attention and—in Britain—almost unanimously positive reactions.[1] Reviewers were moved by the tenderness of these writings. The book won prizes: the Forward Prize for Poetry, the T. S. Eliot Prize, the South Bank Show Literary Award and the Whitbread Prize. Accepting one on behalf of her dead father, Frieda read from a letter Hughes had sent to a close friend. In it, he said that those 'letters' had released the story he had evaded in his earlier writing. He described publishing them as 'a kind of desperation' since he had believed them to be 'unpublishably raw and unguarded, simply too vulnerable.'[2]

Excerpts from private correspondence are usually accepted as more genuine; this letter, we may feel sure, was not written for publication. In it, Hughes testifies to the *Birthday Letters'* authenticity—'unpublishably raw and unguarded'. He also insists, interestingly, on their status as *letters*. By using the term 'story' to describe what is in them, Hughes acknowledges—most unusually—the inescapable entanglement of fiction, or versions of reality, in any account of 'what actually happened' in his relationship with Plath.

---

* *After reading this chapter, Faber & Faber/the Hughes Estate refused to allow or discuss the inclusion of illustrative quotations. For this reason, readers are directed to the relevant lines in Hughes's poetry publications.*

If the *Birthday Letters* really are *letters* does this mean they require a different kind of reading? They are all addressed to Plath herself (only one or two in the collection do not use the second-person mode of address); but they were written after her death, so there was never any possibility of Hughes receiving replies. Nor do the letters ask questions that might expect any answer, and they are remarkable in this respect. Then, of course, these 'letters' are not at all of the same genre as the letter quoted by Hughes's daughter. They are highly crafted; they employ poetic images and line breaks; they are allusive and literary in style. And, of course, Hughes chose to publish them, thereby instantly problematising their status as intimate, personal communications. Why does Hughes call them letters rather than poems? What effect does this have over their readers?

Almost all the book's reviewers agreed with Hughes that this material was intimate and revelatory. But Ian Sansom, writing in the *London Review of Books*, had a different analysis:

> This is no snatched glimpse at private correspondence; if anything, it's more like a mailshot, or a press release: coming out of the blue and serialised in the cut-price *Times*, it is explicit, unapologetic and unashamed. These are public poems: not Laureate art, like the poems in *Rain-Charm for the Duchy* (1992), but another kind of public art—indignant, accusatory, evangelical.[3]

In Sansom's view (which is not unsympathetic but is less in thrall to the emotional charge of the collection), the book 'has a clear and practical purpose—correcting distortions, setting the record straight'; it is addressed to the general public, or at least to those of the general public interested in the Plath and Hughes story.[4] Sansom concludes by suggesting that the late Poet Laureate may have had another motive at heart: paraphrasing Robert Frost, he wonders whether, in publishing the *Birthday Letters*, Hughes has actually 'satisfied the over-curious, and kept the secret places to himself'.

My interest is not in Hughes's intention, which may after all have been consciously benign and unconsciously vengeful at the same time. What I am interested in is how he reads Plath's writings, and what that reveals—not about the specifics of their relationship, but about the deployment of gendered roles in literary and mythic paradigms. What fascinates me about the *Birthday Letters* is the insights they give into Hughes's inability to read Plath's poetry, and the extent to which they seem stuck in an obsessive rewriting of her poems. Taken cumulatively, the *Birthday Letters* tell a familiar tragic story of the beautiful, but psychologically unhinged lady.[5] In addition, they reinscribe certain deep-seated anxieties about creative women: that their creativity is dangerous (to themselves and to those close to them), that it emerges out of their pathology, and that it is not quite *of* them, but a form of possession, a creative energy that passes *through* them, merely using the woman as a channel. In such misogynistic accounts, the female artist's agency and effort are denied. Finally, Hughes's book raises questions about the troublesome boundaries between life and art, and the ways in which gender is caught up in their shifting negotiation.

Plath's words came to assume terrifying authority over Hughes's life; their capacity to judge and sentence unrivalled, perhaps, in the history of English literature. Hughes may have been the first man to learn of the dreadful effect of having one's life transformed into art—an experience familiar to countless women who have functioned (unwittingly) as muses through the ages. Ironically, though, despite his sophistication as a reader and critic, Hughes has encouraged readers to read Plath through her biography, to make connections between her life and her art. His own notes to his edition of her *Collected Poems* are full of such cross references, even though they shed no light whatsoever on the poems. About 'Totem', the reader is informed that 'the bowl' refers to 'a pyrex bowl, used on different occasions both for her son's afterbirth and the cleaned body of a hare', and 'a counterfeit snake' is glossed with the description of 'an articulated toy snake of scorch-patterned bamboo joints'.[6] This is strange, not just because the biographical information is of no help, but more because Plath herself took care to work her poems up to a state in which they were released from any connection to her personal life; she often withheld poems from publication on the grounds that she felt they were too personal.

The extent of the *Birthday Letters*' intertextual entanglement with Plath's writings is only obvious to readers who are familiar with her work, and without this familiarity the book is a vividly compelling, tragic love story. But the *Birthday Letters* are highly referential; almost every episode used as the basis for one of Hughes's letters appears in one of Plath's poems—sometimes explicitly, sometimes as the hidden trigger behind the piece. Many even use exactly the same titles ('Ouija'; 'The Rabbit Catcher', 'Totem', 'Brasilia', 'Wuthering Heights'); others are close, or clearly allude to specific poems (Plath's 'Fever 103' becomes Hughes's 'Fever'; her 'The Lady and the Earthenware Head' becomes his 'The Earthenware Head'; her 'Child's Park Stones' becomes 'Child's Park'; her 'Ariel' is recast as 'Night-Ride on Ariel'; her 'Man in Black' becomes his 'Black Coat'). Still others make use of imagery familiar from her poems—images of bees, gods, arrows, volts, the moon, sometimes even quoting directly ('Crackling and dragging their blacks' from 'Night-Ride on Ariel'; 'Deaf to your pleas as the fixed stars / At the bottom of the well' from 'The Bee God'.)[7] Some of the letters are phrased as direct replies to her poems, as though he has just finished reading one and lifts his pen to respond. 'Black Coat' begins with its narrator recalling his walk on a beach; its use of the deictic 'there' clearly refers to Plath's setting of 'Man in Black'. In Plath's poem the speaker watches her lover stride out across the beach at low tide becoming, as he does so, the defining feature (the '[f]ixed vortex') of the vast panorama 'riveting' the whole scene together.[9]

Its emotional tone is ambiguous; it could be a love poem (in her journal, Plath describes it as such).[10] But Hughes's 'Black Coat' is clearly a biographical piece and recollects the specific moment transformed in Plath's poem, making it the critical moment in the drama that is their relationship. He describes unwittingly stepping into the path of 'the paparazzo sniper' in Plath's eye. (pp.102–3) Hughes's version not only personalises Plath's poem, by making it refer to him, and to her father, thus insisting on a biographical interpretation which the poem itself does not require or request; it also suggests that he feels himself somehow accused by 'Man in Black'.

It does seem as though most of the *Birthday Letters* contain something of this defensive quality. Plath's suicide meant, of course, a sudden and violent curtailment of communication; perhaps the *Birthday Letters* are Hughes's final rejoinder. The American poet

Louise Glück has drawn a useful distinction between 'inclusive' and 'exclusive' poems: those that invite the reader in, almost as a co-author, and those that impose a kind of passivity on their readers. Of the latter she writes:

> To overhear is to experience exclusion; reading [Wallace] Stevens, I felt myself superfluous, part of some marginal throng...The difficulty to the reader is a function of the poem's mode, its privacy: to be allowed to follow is not to be asked along.[11]

In many respects (not just the title), the *Birthday Letters* are generically unlike most poetry, which may discover its initial germ in an actual event or emotion, but which moves away from that 'fact', transforming or recreating it in the process of composition. A poem takes off from its origins; it has to, in order to make space for a reader; it goes somewhere quite else. This is the distinction Eavan Boland refers to when she claims that 'A poem is not *about* an experience; a poem *is* an experience.'[12] This is where the exhilaration comes from. In the process of its crafting what actually happened is no longer relevant. Poetry is not an elaborate coding of personal experience which the reader is invited to decipher. As so many writers testify, writing is itself a process of discovery, of transformation, a journey; the intention, at least, is to enable the reader to experience that process too.[13]

It is this transformation, this take-off from the personal that Hughes is not able to grant Plath's writing. But to read poetry as though it tells us about the poet who wrote it is to ignore the poetry itself, to attempt to tie it back up to the moorings it has deliberately detached itself from. And just as he cannot let Plath's poetry free of her life, nor can he allow the *Birthday Letters* such freedom; they are stubbornly moored to *their* origins—Plath's poems. Glück says she finds the poems that exclude her as a reader tempt her into futile efforts to rewrite them, resulting in 'dogged imitation'.[14] Could this be what happens to Hughes, frustratedly rewriting Plath's poems, reusing her images but producing only 'stillborn' poems? Ruth Padel's review of the book identified a kind of flatness in its technique; she complained that the letters were too wedded to giving explanations—'telling not showing'—and described them as 'poetically inert...[Hughes] has withdrawn his own active presence, sexually and poetically.'[15] It is this curious passivity—or, more accurately, absence—that seems to accompany male poets' writing when tackling explicitly personal material.[16]

In this, as well as in their intimate, emotional content, the *Birthday Letters* are unlike Hughes's other writing. Their style is looser, heavily adjectival, often close to prose; there is little attention to the sound of words or lines; their mode of address is invariably second person, 'I' and 'you' the only pronouns in their intense, even claustrophobic atmosphere. Hughes's characteristic tone was more compressed: short lines, a taut muscularity, employing few adverbs but punchy, active verbs and concrete nouns. Nevertheless, if the style is different, there are thematic continuities between Hughes's earlier work and this late volume. Three surprising preoccupations of his earliest work recur. The first is violence, especially that of war. The second is the impersonal, irresistible ruthless power of Mother Nature embodying and promoting the procreative instinct. The third is a close association between woman—as the bearer of children—and death. But however disturbing Hughes's earlier poems may have sometimes been, they possess none of the relentless exclusivity of the intimate *Letters*; there is always space for the reader to move, interpret or challenge.

If the *Birthday Letters* are so different, is it appropriate to describe them as confessional writing? After all, that letter Hughes sent to his friend described the sense of relief and release he felt on their publication, as if it were a form of catharsis. This raises once again the tricky question of who the confessor or priest might be. And what about gender: do men confess differently? Or does a man's public confession have a different impact because he is a man? Such questions need to be asked, particularly since the late 1990s saw the publication of a spate of confessional memoirs by men: for example Blake Morrison's *And When Did You Last See Your Father?*, Tim Lott's *The Scent of Dried Roses*, Tony Parsons's *Man and Boy*, Craig Raine's *A La Recherche du Temps Perdu*, Hugo Williams's *Billy's Rain*, Hanif Kureshi's *Intimacy*.

It is interesting that Hughes chose the same moment as these younger men to break his long silence and speak about his relationship with Plath. Suddenly, there was a vogue for male writers venturing into the territory of the domestic, laying aside the costume of machismo, revealing their 'feminine' side. In an article on Anne Sexton, poet/critic Deryn Rees-Jones suggests that confession is always gendered:

> Without in any way negating or trivializing the anguish or difficulties of the male confessional, or the powerfulness of the poetry, it seems fair to say that the male confessional is radical precisely because it can be seen to be exploring new territories of the male psyche; it breaks down patriarchal notions of masculinity while at the same time offering an extremity of experience as a testimony of suffering that equates with prophecy and 'strength', and yet may also be disclaimed.[17]

In other words, the impact of a man's confession stems from the way in which the act of confessing seems to contradict ideas about masculinity: it flouts the unspoken rules of stoicism, endurance and emotional control. But what is even more interesting about the *Birthday Letters* is certain characteristics of them *as* confession. For material that tells such an intimate story about a relationship, Hughes as *one half of that relationship* seems strangely uninvolved. He is the observer, usually on the sidelines, witnessing events, or reacting to Plath. It is almost as though he sees himself as detached all along and therefore somehow licensed to claim the objectivity to which the preponderance of factual statements in the *Letters* lay claim.

Nor—if for a moment we continue to think of the collection as confessional—is there much sense given of Hughes himself; the focus is on Plath throughout. Yet in his exposure of this private relationship, Hughes draws on pre-existing myths. As a result, real cultural contexts are replaced by literary and mythic ones. The *Letters* thus erase the real structural inequalities between Plath and Hughes because, with the exception of one or two references to the post-War climate and the 'newness' and glamour of America, they unfold in a timeless space. So there is no recognition of Plath's uneasy status as an American away from home, or of what it meant to be a (younger) wife in 1950s' Britain, nor of the fact that Hughes was already a relatively well-known, fêted poet, and she was unknown.[18]

Whether these are confessional or not, the *Letters* are acutely personal in the nature of the material they divulge—however highly crafted or 'literary'. During a period that has seen such dramatic challenges to nineteenth-century notions of the clear boundaries between the public and the private, this kind of writing occupies an uneasy position. The *Birthday Letters* are 'published privacies':[19] intimate material nevertheless offered up for public consumption. 'Prostitute words', as one of the poems in *Crow* puts it?[20]

Hughes is not able to read Plath's poetry—or, for that matter, her short stories and journals—as anything other than evidence about her feelings and experience. This is not surprising, given the terrible circumstances of her death. Add to this the way in which critics began to read Plath's poems as revealing insights into her relationship with Hughes, and it becomes almost inevitable.

But, while the particular circumstances of Plath's death (and, perhaps, her association with the confessional poets Robert Lowell and Anne Sexton) encouraged the tendency to read her poems biographically, it is something that often happens to writing by women. Critics notice biographical material more when reading women's writing; or they are reluctant to credit women with the capacity for transcending the personal, which stems from their own resistance to the notion of a female voice imbued with public authority. It is interesting, for example, that contemporary reviewers of Hughes's *Crow* made no mention of the biographical circumstances surrounding that volume's composition, despite the possibility that its macabre celebration of perversity, violence and misanthropy (misogyny, more accurately) may not be unconnected to the poet's experience of the suicides of two lovers (and the consequent death of a child). Crow's universe is a match for the perversity of suicide. Much of the fury in the collection is directed against female figures, especially the mother. God is an ineffectual bumbler, outclassed and inept, no fit target for rage; but the mother is gigantic, and inescapable. Female genitalia, rather than women, feature throughout. The womb stores rotting matter; it is a place of gore and decomposition. There are visions of vagina dentata and of female genitalia likened to the torn face of a heart.[21] Yet critic Neil Corcoran describes the volume as 'very much a poem of the moment of the Vietnam war', in its insistence on 'the way violence comes to us ready processed, already assimilated, in contemporary media'.[22] It is as though, in order for the poet to be a *proper* poet, to observe and comment on the surrounding *Zeitgeist*, he has to be quite detached from any smear of personal material. But how does Corcoran account for the acute sense of accusation that hangs over many of the *Crow* poems?[23] Are the allusions only to Vietnam?

In her study of suicide Alison Wertheimer calls the people close to a suicide 'survivors'.[24] She notes that the emotions of anger and guilt that are a normal part of the grieving process are intensified. Survivors have to make sense of an act that is perverse; just as the dead person is a victim, so too are those who are left behind. In *Birthday Letters* Hughes gives eloquent expression to this confusion. The letters are preoccupied with their search for the cause of the tragedy of Plath's death. Sometimes (but rarely) Plath is the perpetrator, as in the closing lines of 'Sam'. More often, she is the helpless victim of the nameless beast or demon spirit that stalks her. The last lines of 'The Inscription' demonstrate syntactically the way in which suicide inflicts violent damage on all those involved. The barrage of shifting pronouns represent the confused exchanges over who is giving or doing what to whom.[26] 'From him', 'from her hands', 'from nowhere': while the poem asserts Plath's self-destructiveness, repeating the idea that she has hurt herself, its assurance is belied by this uncertainty about the source of the damage. What is clear is that wherever it has come from, it goes right through both of them. This confusion, arguably characteristic of the effects of suicide, may be the reason the *Birthday Letters* offer so many different versions of malevolence. It is as though Hughes is trying to identify the origin or source of the violence, but cannot. In 'Trophies' it is impossible even to locate the panther that threatens both Plath and Hughes: in some lines it appears to be inhabiting Plath, looking out through her eyes while in others it is described springing over Plath to attack him.[27]

The *Birthday Letters* often detail gradations of difference between 'you' and 'I'. What is also striking is the theatricality evident in these oppositions, as if, in Hughes's recollection, both of them were role playing. This concern to identify differences is most obvious in the attribution of emotion to Plath: in most of the poems, she emotes, he observes, and the letters are full of visual descriptions of her: her blonde bangs, her scar, her long legs, her 'rubbery' face.[28] This stark, almost obsessive itemising of differences is related to what Ian Gregson has identified as a strict biologism underlying Hughes's conception of gender differences.[29] In most of his work prior to *Birthday Letters*, awe and terror characterise his attitude towards the feminine, which is allied to the earth and Mother Nature. Particular fear (and fascination) accompanies the representation of what is out of sight, under water or the earth: whatever is there is primeval and incohate, concealed by the murky depths, a sinister site of darkness and gestation. An early Hughes poem, 'To Paint a Water Lily', takes the flower as a metaphor for woman's duality and is disgusted by the sharp contrast it draws between the flower's delicate beauty, and the slimy depths of its root system. The pond is described as a war zone; ruthless nature busy at its ceaseless activity, with insects eating one another, and death inflicted on all sides.[30] But if what can be seen above the water is grim, how much worse is what is out of sight! The poem visualises semi-formed creatures that have lain on the pond bed, untouched by centuries of evolution, while the lily, with its long neck, retains its elegant composure, regardless of the foul things that lie close to its roots.

Femininity looks pretty, but has its roots in abject realms. 'Fragment of an Ancient Tablet' again juxtaposes visible and concealed aspects of woman. At its close, female genitalia are figured as a gash.[31]

Nicole Ward Jouve has suggested that the misogyny of much men's writing in the twentieth century can be linked to fear and rage at the self-sacrifice war demanded of men. War unmanned and feminised men. Ward notes 'the abundance of images that feminise the slaughter'[32]—part of a widespread impulse to turn impotent rage against female symbols—archaic mother, nature, woman:

How then, with such a tradition behind, all around one, how to resist the slippage from pitted earth and bloodied trench and grave and bodily wound to red maw to womb? From power, absolute and deadly, highly mechanized and haphazard, hierarchical and impersonal and petty all at once, to the once absolute power of the archaic mother? Where else to project one's anger at being wounded, but on the nurser of the wound? For in actuality, the division of parts that the war enforced (the women at home, the men enduring all sorts of dangers and abominations...) led to acute resentment. (p.95)

Hughes's early poems are preoccupied with war: his imagination is haunted by photographs of young soldiers killed, and his dreams peopled with visions of corpses, plane-crashes and dismembered bodies. Such scenes are exclusively male.[33] Hughes's father's experience in the Second World War, and his silence about that experience, haunted Hughes. One poem about his father describes this explicitly.[34] In another poem Hughes describes himself as his father's 'luckless double, / His memory's buried, immovable anchor'.[35] It seems plausible that this inherited mixture of impotence and trauma may have played a part in creating the violently dichotomised versions of femininity that feature in his poems. In his post-*Crow* work, Nature is admired for her intractable, single-minded force: invariably, males are hapless 'conscripts', called to carry out her bidding.[36] In 'Eclipse' the poet watches two spiders mating: the female's pincers are 'hideously dextrous', the ultimate in sophisticated weaponry. She is a ruthlessly efficient seductress and killer, the male a powerless, unwitting innocent.[37]

But any sense of a powerful, primitive female force is absent from the *Birthday Letters*. In every poem, Plath is presented as a figure of pathos: frail, highly strung, hypersensitive, endlessly weeping, crying, sobbing, while Hughes stands by, perplexed. However Hughes figures the destructive force that leads to Plath's death, it is always split off from Plath herself (just as, in his introduction to her *Journals*, her writing is figured as passing through her, being pulled out of her, bloody like a birth or a parasitic alien bursting forth, she the mere vessel through which this unstoppable creation travels).[38] It is a beast—panther, bull—or spirit-demon—Daddy. In frequent images, both Plath and Hughes are shot or wounded: hunted, pursued animals. But the rage, and the violence, are not integral to her. Plath is the victim—desperate, often hysterical, usually wracked with pain.

'Totem' is a good example of this soft, vulnerable feminine version of Plath, which the *Birthday Letters* promote so determinedly. In it, Hughes recalls how Plath would paint little hearts on her furniture before concluding regretfully that they had scant effect.[39] The hearts in question here are far removed from that metaphor of female genitalia as the torn face of a heart, and after this it comes as a shock to re-read Plath's own poem 'Totem'. It describes a speaker mired in the ubiquity of death, figured as an inexorable, impersonal force of destruction.[40]

Hughes's version domesticates the scale of this intense awareness of impending catastrophe. Another example of the way in which his *Letters* tend to tame or restrain Plath's ferocity is apparent in 'Trophies', in which Hughes picks up on the image of the panther employed in Plath's 'Pursuit'.[41] Her poem was written shortly after her first meeting with Hughes in 1956; it is a searing account of thrilled sexual arousal, in which the speaker is both terrified and irresistibly lured and mesmerised by the beast's steady tracking. She bolts the door, ostensibly to keep it out, but she has already thrown it her heart. In 'Trophies', Hughes transforms the panther into a large cat that drags her in its jaws; Plath is its helpless victim, crying, bleeding words and tears. He cannot admit, or see, her lust—which is also the source of her creativity. In her journal she wrote, 'I want to…confront that big panther, to make the daylight whittle him to lifesize,'[42]—an indication that she recognises this as a fantasy figure. Far from finding herself trampled underfoot by it, her poems record a taut mixture of desire and terror evoked by this gigantic ogre.[43] Plath is not in thrall to this figure; she is deliberately manipulating these emotions in a controlled, wry depiction of the force of such desire. In Hughes's imagination, this deliberateness, control and knowledge is erased, replaced by Plath the passive victim of the beast's ferocious attack.

Another example of this can be found in Hughes's version of Plath's short story, 'The Fifty-Ninth Bear'. It details a couple's camping trip and ends with the man being mauled to death by a bear.[44] Hughes's 'The 59th Bear' tells the apparently factual story of their own trip, and their encounter with a bear, but it interprets the close of her story as being the work of her death-wish: as though she were driven by this, as though the aesthetic decisions of her writing were the outcome of this violent pathological possession.[45]

Further stark misreadings are evident in Hughes's account of their honeymoon visit to Spain. He describes Plath, epitomising naïve safe American suburbia in bobby-sox, as being appalled by the primitive roughness of the land of bullfights, deformed street-beggars and machismo. Yet her poem 'The Goring' describes the bull's attack with heartfelt admiration, contrasting the animal's grace with the clumsy movements of the matador.[46] And 'The Beggars' is a cool, unflinching portrait of street life, not at all what you would expect from Hughes's sweet clean all-American girl. He cannot see her lust, cannot let it be part of her; instead it gets split off from her and transposed on to some external malevolent force (panther, Daddy, evil spirit).

So in the *Birthday Letters* Hughes seems to create a Plath devoid of lust, rage, purposeful energy or agency. It is as though she has to be the innocent, frail creature in this reactionary plot; otherwise how can he be cast as her would-be rescuer? As the book develops, its real focus gradually emerges. Plath fades to the margins of the drama, and the *real* confrontation takes centre-stage: the struggle between Hughes and Otto Plath, her father. Hughes tries on various mythic and literary masks—Theseus, Ferdinand, the dead soldier from Wilfred Owen's 'Strange Meeting'—all of which have the effect of displacing the interaction between Plath and himself, and substituting a male drama of rivalry, in which the woman—if she figures at all—is simply the possession fought over. In these borrowings Hughes seems to be seeking the reassurances of a familiar plot.[47]

In her Introduction to *Between Men*, Eve Kosofsky Sedgwick cites René Girard's study of erotic triangles in the European novel. She summarises Girard's conclusion that:

> In any erotic rivalry, the bond that links the two rivals is as intense and potent as the bond that links either of the rivals to the beloved: that the bonds of 'rivalry' and 'love,' differently as they are experienced, are equally powerful and in many senses equivalent.[48]

These triangular relationships usually feature two men in competition over a woman, a scenario that the *Birthday Letters* inscribes. Repeatedly Otto Plath is figured as Hughes's rival. In 'The Table'

Otto is described as a 'German cuckoo', the bird that steals into another's nest in order to lay its egg. Hughes imagines his father-in-law as an intruder in the marital bed, absconding with his bride.[49] Hughes thinks both he and his wife were covertly possessed by Otto, his 'two immense hands' insinuating themselves, like gloves, over their own.[50] And, if the *Birthday Letters* describe his beliefs, he believes Plath confused her husband and her late father.[51] In 'Fairy Tale' Plath is described like an enchanted maiden who flies off each night to rendezvous with her 'ogre lover'.[52]

In Hughes's interpretation, Plath's suicide was caused by her obsessive, incestuous desire for her dead father.[53] Could it be that this explanation enabled him to focus on the drama with which he was really preoccupied, that of war and rivalry with another man? What he describes is his own sense of emasculation as he is 'entered' by Otto; earlier in this piece he has been trying to strengthen his own physical boundaries, to be '[s]imply myself, with sharp edges.'[54]

In an article on *Birthday Letters*, Lynda K. Bundtzen recognises that one of the compelling motivations behind the collection seems to be Hughes's need to free himself from what he experienced as an enforced merger with Otto, created by Plath's poetry. Hughes needs, Bunddtzen says, 'to "tell" himself "apart" from Otto Plath'; 'Plath's poetic terms...deny Hughes an identity separate from her father'.[55]

The relationship between Hughes and Otto Plath becomes crucial in the *Letters*. 'A Picture of Otto' is a revealing piece: in it, Hughes adapts Wilfred Owen's famous staging of a meeting between two dead enemies, German and English. Owen's poem is about forgiveness, and the pointlessness of enmity. Bundtzen interprets the poem as though it is Sylvia Plath who is the dead German (she writes: 'like Owen "Sleeping with his German as if alone"', Plath too, sleeps with her German father', p.459). Yet in Hughes's version the meeting is *between the two men*; it is addressed throughout to Otto.

The hostility in his tone is startling, despite the poem's movement towards forgiveness (what is he forgiving his dead father-in-law for, we may ask?). At its close the focus is again on the two men, trapped together for ever in a ghastly irony. It is odd that Bundtzen chooses to see Plath as the German, since she is so clearly absent from the poem. Hughes's deployment of Owen's war poem is very revealing, since it implies that enmity between a woman's father and her husband is structurally inevitable (as it is inevitable that two soldiers on different sides during a war must be enemies), while also indicating that, were it not for this impediment (war/marriage), the two men would be comrades. Thus, it is *woman* who causes the rift between men.[57] This is strikingly close to Giraud's analysis of erotic triangles in the novel: the woman functions merely as a device to enable contest between the men.

Military terms and allusions form a muted undercurrent in many of the *Letters*. Occasionally they surface, as in 'Perfect Light', where a snapshot of Plath as Madonna, with newborn swaddled in her arms, is undermined by Hughes's consciousness of impending disaster, figured as territorial invasion. In the photograph Plath is perched on top of the remains of an ancient fort, and the future is described surreptitiously approaching, like a soldier moving slowly from no-man's land.[58]

As well as subduing the fierce eroticism and force of her poetry, and edging Plath herself to the margins of the story, Hughes misses the irony, humour and control that characterised Plath's treatment of the father figure. Hughes's 'Daddy' figure is a malevolent demon: like one of the undead, he rises up out of his coffin to repossess his daughter, he sneaks into the marital bed like an adulterer; he is 'your god' and a 'false god'.[59] He is intent on bringing death. Yet the most striking aspect of Plath's journals is the degree of insight they show about her feelings towards her father.[60] The same control is apparent in her poems. In 'The Colossus' the speaker is exasperated by the hulk before her, her tone calm and assured as she sets about her labour of cleaning and repairing.[61] Therapeutic, rather than confessional—part of, or a record of, the process of a woman working through the legacy of her father's early death and the effect on her feelings towards her mother—one thing that can be traced in Plath's poetry is the resolution reached over these feelings. But in Hughes's *Birthday Letters* it is Otto who is seen as impelling Plath to her death. Of course this enables Hughes, as protector/husband, to pit his strength against a figure he sets up as his rival. It is as though, at a certain point, he refused to enter into communication and exchange with Plath. There is a further irony to the dominant position held by 'Daddy' in *Birthday Letters*. In Plath's poetry it is dead *women* who haunt the speaker, exerting irresistible force over her, whether benign ('Point Shirley') or sinister ('Disquieting Muses';

'All the Dead Dears'). But these powerful female presences are replaced, in *Birthday Letters*, by Otto and Hughes himself.

In her important study of Plath, Jacqueline Rose insists that women writers' imaginations often reveal their entanglement in sexist or misogynist beliefs:

> It has never been part of feminism's argument that because an image of femininity can be identified as male fantasy, it is any the less intensely lived by women. Conversely, the fact that the woman discovers something as a component of her own self-imagining does not mean that it cannot also be the object, or even product, of the wildest male projection, repulsion or desire. Who owns what? Who gives what to whom?[62]

This sharp-eyed description of Plath's writings signals not only the existence of disturbingly patriarchal fantasies in them but also raises another essential issue: the extent to which Plath's poems conceal agency. *Who is doing what to whom?* is a question it is impossible to answer in much of her work. Rose shows how Plath's poems may, at the same time, act out internalised male fantasies with relish and offer those very fantasies up for critique. In this way, Rose argues, Plath interrogates oppositional terms—constructions of male and female, active and passive, masculine and feminine. By contrast, the *Birthday Letters* seem obsessed with identifying exactly who did what, when and to whom. The *Letters* seek to establish clear boundaries and distinctions between Plath and Hughes. (In this respect they contrast with Plath's early work, in which her interest was in probing the boundaries of selfhood.) Despite his faith in astrology, Hughes was fundamentally a literalist: a thing was either true, or it was not. Describing her clashes with the Plath Estate, Rose claims that Hughes and his sister Olwyn refused her permission to reprint an extract from Plath's journals on the grounds that 'it is not only "damaging" but "untrue"'.[63] But, of course, journals don't usually purport to tell 'the truth'; they are impressionistic and subjective. Rose comments: 'it appears that...there is only one version of reality, one version—their version—of the truth.' The *Birthday Letters* are packed with factual statements, just as they are preoccupied with registering distinctions between their two protagonists.

Hughes's conception of truth is allied to his experience of being accused. The court witness has to swear to tell 'the truth, the whole truth and nothing but the truth', again assuming that truth is factual, easily grasped. We need to turn to a writer like Sybille Bedford, one well aware of the tricky, elusive nature of truth, in order to find a more accurate understanding of its nature. The following exchange takes place early in her novel *A Compass Error*:

> For the second time that day, deliberately now, Flavia said, 'It takes two to tell the truth.'
> 'One for one side, one for the other?'
> 'That's not what I mean. I mean one to tell, one to hear. A speaker and a receiver. To tell the truth about any complex situation requires a certain attitude in the receiver.'
> 'What is required from the receiver?'
> 'I would say first of all a level of emotional intelligence.'
> 'Imagination?'
> 'Disciplined.'
> 'Sympathy? Attention?'
> 'And patience.'
> 'Detachment?'
> 'All of these. And a taste for the truth—an immense willingness to *see*.'[64]

Flavia's conception of truth is dialogic; truth takes two: 'one to tell, one to hear'. She places great emphasis on the receiver's role, because the communication of truth depends on their ability to hear it. Truth is thus something that emerges in relationship, in dialogue; it is not detachable, it does not pass from one to the other; it emerges in the act of telling, and depends as much on the listener as the teller. Truth does not reside in the writing or the telling; it is entangled in the reception too.

What does this mean, though, if the real addressee of Hughes's *Birthday Letters* is really the dead Plath? There is no possibility of the communication of 'truth', because she cannot hear him. If the real addressee is actually Plath's readers, or any of us interested in their 'story', then Flavia's conception of truth would require a far more active role from us than the *Letters* allow. For they make no space for a reader; the insistence of their tight second-person address to Plath, and their reliance on supposedly factual statements prohibits this, positioning the reader as little other than a voyeur.

Flavia's emphasis on the dialogic nature of truth is very much in keeping with Plath's conception of the entangled complexity of relationship; both are far from Hughes's angle on truth as locatable, if only he can get it in his huntsman's sights. This radical difference can be seen by comparing the two poems titled 'The Rabbit Catcher'. Hughes's version presents itself as a memoir, recalling precise details about the particular outing that he believes is being used in Plath's poem. He is the onlooker, like a fly on a glass window, watching the row.[65] Throughout his poem, he juxtaposes what he sees with what (he claims to know) she sees: this series of contrasts establishes a clear oppositional structure between the two protagonists. She is furious, he calm; she rants, he studies the map; she strides off, and he trails behind her. This opposition reaches its climax in relation to the rabbit traps: situating himself as descendant of rural peasants, he emphasises her position as outsider: sentimental and ignorant of country ways. Using many of the same words that appear in her poem ('simmering', 'hollow', 'gorse', 'snare'), Hughes makes some crucial alterations. Plath's lines:

> I felt hands round a tea mug, dull, blunt,
> Ringing the white china.[66]

are recast thus:

> You saw blunt fingers, blood in the cuticles,
> Clamped round a blue mug.(p.145)

Hughes's reliance on visual evidence and its interpretation is striking, and his letter attributes violence (blood spilled) to the trapper far more explicitly than Plath's poem, where what is arresting is the sense of impending, potential—rather than actual—violence. Hughes has a reason for altering hands to fingers; they reappear at the end of his poem, only this time they belong to Plath, in the guise of high priestess, coaxing poems from the rabbits' dead bodies. In her poem some lines have been interpreted, by

Rose, as accusing Hughes of sadism. The poem's addressee, with whom the speaker has had a relationship, is not explicitly equated with the rabbit catcher of the title, but the inference is there. Hughes now turns it against Plath: it is *she* who wants these corpses, cradling them 'like smoking entrails' and effecting their magical transformation (also clearly likened to bringing a man off) as they 'Came soft into your hands'.[67] Where Plath's persona describes the wind blowing her hair against her mouth like a gag, Hughes transforms the scene to Plath's private pathology, invoking the famous 'bell jar', and claiming her rage had nothing to do with concern for the rabbits. The claustrophobia that she attributes to their *situation*— the ghastly tension of a relationship that is falling apart—is thus placed firmly back on to *her* as another symptom of her illness. Her bad mood is nothing to do with him, or the effects of a failing relationship; it is the work of her wicked spirit, he claims, thus introducing the dead father's harmful evil spirit and removing Plath's agency even from her own bad mood. But he is still concerned, in keeping with the opposition that has governed the whole poem, to locate whatever it is Plath has seen in the traps: is it something in him, or in her? The weight of the four adjectives that accompany the second option make his answer to what pretends to be an open rhetorical question, clear: the sickness is in her. Lines 5–10 on p.146 are absolutely key to the poem. They express his determination to distance himself from any involvement (reiterated throughout with statements of his incomprehension in the face of her fury, as if her rage has nothing to do with his actions): quite striking when you consider how Plath's metaphor of the relationship as being like a trap implicates *both* of them.[68] This is how it works: the wires between them are tense, holding them at a claustrophobic distance from one another, locked into the relationship, however fiercely one or both of them might desire to break free of it. Her metaphor acknowledges mutual involvement. They have 'a mind' between the two of them.

But for Hughes the *Birthday Letters* are not about reciprocity or relationship; they are obsessed instead with evidence and truth. Nor are they about understanding. It is as though Hughes admits quite frankly that understanding was and is beyond him, but recording the facts, producing an account that makes sense, to him, in his terms, as he remembers events afterwards, becomes essential. He 'annotates' or rewrites Plath's poems because he can only see them as purporting to tell *her* truth about their life together, and the versions he finds in them are accusatory. But is that accusation in the poems? Or is it in him? As we saw earlier, 'Man in Black' is far less unambiguously accusatory than Hughes appears to find it.

Hughes was, tormentedly, his own accuser. He felt attacked by her words, but those words were also a form of possession: they robbed him of his freedom, they emasculated him, eroded his 'stark edges'. Perhaps this experience triggered reactions to his own father's impotence as conscripted war fodder—reactions that Hughes, as his father's 'memory's buried, immovable anchor', carried on into his own life. And he cannot surmount Plath's poems, in the sense of getting over them. They are, in Louise Glück's terms, 'exclusive', he finds he cannot get beyond them. His writing gets stuck in its efforts to do this, but they produce just what Glück describes: 'dogged imitation', 'dead products of fear and inhibition'.[69] They are far from dead emotionally, but in their tonal flatness, their endless recycling of second-hand images, their reliance on statement and assertion, and their fixed positioning of the reader, they do seem to be dead products.

'[P]oems belong to readers—just as houses belong to those who live in them,' Hughes wrote in a letter to his friend Keith Sagar.[70] But it seems the *Birthday Letters* belonged only to him. Three months before his death in October 1998, in another letter to Sagar, he speculated on whether 'an all-out attempt to complete a full account, in the manner of those *Birthday Letters*, of that part of my life would not have liberated me to deal with it on deeper, more creative levels'. He recognised that the collection was only at its first stage—a kind of clearing of the path, an exorcism, before the more creative work of writing real poems could get under way.

5.
IRON(IC) JOHN: MEN POETS ON MASCULINITY

MATTHEW SWEENEY, MICHAEL DONAGHY, ROBERT CRAWFORD, NEIL ROLLINSON, GLYN MAXWELL, DON PATERSON

Most studies of contemporary poetry ignore the work of women poets until their final chapter, when they bundle the women together and offer a cursory overview, with no clear rationale for so doing beyond a vague expectation those poets will have something in common. This study will end with a chapter devoted to men poets.

There is a serious rationale for this decision. In his study of gay literature, Gregory Woods mentions the effeminacy that often attaches to poetry: many, he claims, dismiss the genre as 'suited only to eggheads and sissies'.[1] Anxiety over the feasibility of reconciling heterosexual masculinity with the role of poet has been a theme in the work of several high-profile men poets—all of whom I assume (because of the lack of indication otherwise) to be heterosexual—of the twentieth century. In selecting six younger men poets the intention is to explore how masculinity is configured in their poetry.[2]

What follows builds on the invaluable work of critic Ian Gregson: his 1999 study, *The Male Image: Representations of Masculinity in Post-War Poetry*, focuses on a number of prominent men poets born in or around the 1930s, including Robert Lowell, Ted Hughes, Paul Muldoon and John Ashbery. Gregson suggests these poets contributed to a loosening of the 'rigid set of gender relations'[3] that held sway during the Modernist period, and, in a series of close analyses, he offer critiques of the gender ideologies that govern each poet's approach. Gregson's study is rare in acknowledging the relevance of gender to poetry by men, as well as women.

The poets looked at here are drawn from a younger generation, those born after 1950. The idea is to concentrate on men who would have grown up with an awareness of feminism and the critiques of masculinity associated with the Women's Liberation Movement and the rise of gay and queer politics. So, still just about qualifying as the 'younger generation', the poets discussed in this chapter are Matthew Sweeney, born in 1952; Michael Donaghy in 1954; Robert Crawford in 1959; Neil Rollinson in 1960; Glyn Maxwell and Don Paterson in 1963. For the most part, the focus is on a single volume in each case, in order to provide a series of 'snapshots' of particular moments in each poet's development. This is important since what emerges in every case is a preoccupation with the *performance* of masculinity in which emphasis is placed on the age or developmental status of the male subject: the process of ageing and concomitant anxiety about the successful realisation of masculine identity emerges as a common theme in these poets' work. With this in mind, the poets are discussed in order of birth-date with the oldest first.

First, a couple of generalisations. In chapter 1, the numerous collective public discourses available to masculine speakers were commented on, and the ways in which three male poets drew upon these to amplify the authority of their personae were examined. It was noted how carefully the poems positioned (and thus controlled) any women figures that featured in them. Similar strategies are at work in the men poets discussed in this chapter. One characteristic shared is the expectation—or, even, assumption—of a wholly masculine audience. The presence of a female interlocutor within a poem has a transformative effect, disrupting this homosocial environment and often provoking defensive self-consciousness in the poem's speaker. There is an interesting qualitative difference between this general assumption that poetry is the discourse of Wordsworth's 'man speaking to men', and the tone of much contemporary poetry by women, which may be unashamedly rooted in female experience but is far more self-conscious about the possibility of male readers.[4] In chapter 2, Jo Shapcott was shown to exploit this to address both male and female readers. Skilful ambivalence means the poems can be read as either flirtatious enticement or feminist critique. By contrast, poet Simon Armitage has said that he does not speculate about his audience: asked in an interview how he sees the role of readers in his poems about personal relationships, he responds, 'To be honest, I don't think I have ever given it a thought.'[5] A similar lack of anxiety is evident in Hugo Williams's reply to an interviewer's queries about the extent to which he felt inhibited while writing poems about his mistress: 'I think generally I don't worry about hurting people. I put making a good poem above and beyond everything and just have to take the consequences.'[6]

A second generalisation concerns the use of irony, which emerges as a popular tone in men's poetry in late twentieth-century Britain. Irony is the perfect tool for an insider critique. While it can be an effective radical force, there is something both defensive and conservative about the mode of irony deployed by these six poets. The ironist does not have to offer an alternative to the system he mocks: he finds a safe position from which to criticise, remaining enmeshed within the system. The irony deployed by these poets prefers the intellect to emotion, and is invariably low key rather than passionate. While there are differences in the quality of irony deployed by these six poets, from mild to caustic, the irony is generally used against the male speakers themselves. This could be interpreted as a pre-emptive defensive strategy.

The poets selected for this chapter are not setting out to write about masculinity, nor is this a particular feature of their writing that has been pointed out by other critics. However, the poems reveal consistent attitudes and preoccupations in their characterisation and tone. There is no attempt to draw any general conclusions about 'men's poetry' on the basis of this examination of six individuals. Gender is always inflected by class, ethnicity, sexual orientation and culture, as well as personal experience, and these poets share little beyond the fact of their sex and their careers as poets. However, the juxtapositioning of this group of poets is suggestive, since there is such an overlap in their preoccupations.

*

Masculinity, however defined is, like capitalism, *always* in crisis. And the real question is how both manage to restructure, refurbish, and resurrect themselves for the next historical turn.[7]

Solomon-Godeau's coupling is a suggestive one, particularly in the light of the current post-industrial moment and the many books published on the 'crisis of masculinity' during the last decade. Sadly, the popularity of these investigations has not been matched by similar interest from poetry critics. Gregson's book and an article by David Kennedy on masculinity in the work of Douglas Dunn and Tony Harrison constitute the field so far.

In his article, published in *Textual Practice* in 2000, Kennedy makes a point which may seem obvious but which had not been acknowledged previously: that these two poets' anxieties over class are inextricably entwined with anxieties over appropriate masculine gender roles—specifically, with anxieties about whether poetry 'is "real" work for "real" men'.[8] For Harrison, as a boy, staying in to do his Latin prep was tantamount to accepting the label 'cissie'— clear evidence that what was at stake was his masculinity, not just his class. The poem recounting this episode is called 'Me Tarzan', and the pun on Cicero's name further underlines the poem's gender concerns: 'His bodiless head that's poking out's / Like patriarchal Cissy-bleeding ro's.'[9] Kennedy suggests that Harrison's poems enact a movement 'from anxieties about sissiness to a tacit embracing of queerness as part of the male artist's project'. (p.121) Likewise, he finds in Dunn an attempt to outline a masculine poetic, 'in an environment of physicalized sociality with other men...a poetry that is built like a ship...hard, systematised and machine-like'.(p.131)

The strength of Kennedy's thesis is suggested by its pertinence to a number of other men poets he does not discuss. In Seamus Heaney's 'Digging', for example, the poet is clearly anxious about the way in which his chosen career breaks with his male forebears' occupations as physical labourers.[10] This dual concern over disrupting generational continuity between father and son, and the unmanliness of poetry, features in Harrison too. And Dunn's homosocial world, which Kennedy sees as being self-consciously created in order to forge a masculine poetic, is replicated in the six poets under consideration here. A similar theme emerged in the reading of Ted Hughes's *Birthday Letters* in the last chapter: Hughes carried the legacy of his father's war trauma, its impact so corrosive that it erupted, unbidden, in the poet's late work. On the basis of these examples, it seems as though the father's legacy exerts a crucial influence over the son–poet's creativity. Frequently too, the poems' imagined readers *are* the poets' biological fathers.

Harold Bloom's model of younger 'strong' poets wrestling with their poetic forefathers would appear to be borne out in these poets' work. Each generation has to lay claim to its right to poetic space, but the struggle is not just with poetic forefathers but also with biological fathers, as poet–sons seek to assert their right to be poets, and to have that role legitimated by their fathers. This negotiation—which may be staged as physical confrontation, but is often presented more subtly, with the right to *represent* the father standing in for a claim to status and acknowledgement—takes place exclusively between men, thus furthering the homosocial quality of men's poetry.

Both Gregson and Kennedy write optimistically of the changes that have taken place in configurations of gender, arguing that a variety of masculinities is now available, and implying that the oppositional binary model of gender roles has been dissolved. Yet neither discusses any examples of such progressive or novel versions of masculinity in poetry. While some individuals may feel freer to espouse different versions of masculine identity, there is still some way to go to achieve an acceptance of such heterogeneity within cultural institutions, poetry amongst them. Nor is there any certainty that we have yet found ways of moving beyond the dichotomies that slip so seductively into analogies for sex difference.

Indeed, these dichotomies continue to dominate mainstream discussions of masculinity. One of the most influential contributors to current debates is the psychiatrist Anthony Clare. His monograph *On Men: Masculinity in Crisis,* published in 2000, still operates within the traditional binaries: 'At the heart of the crisis in masculinity is a problem with the reconciliation of the private and the public, the intimate and the impersonal, the emotional and the rational.'[11] Clare comments on heterosexual men's need endlessly to prove, demonstrate and enact their manhood, a tendency which, in its severest cases, he calls 'phallic narcissism'.(p.203) Clare's approach illustrates the tenacity of the conventional dichotomies, and how difficult it is to move beyond them.

A more historically informed analysis can demonstrate what Solomon-Godeau has called 'the elasticity of categories of ideal masculinity',[12] while showing the one consistent factor: masculinity's

dominance over femininity. One study of contemporary masculinity particularly relevant to the poets in this chapter is Peter
Middleton's *The Inward Gaze*. One of his central claims is that
conventional conceptions of masculinity emphasise doing, rather
than being, to such an extreme extent that one of the hallmarks of
a masculine identity can be defined as resistance to introspection:

> Boys learn to be men by representing themselves as the
> subjects of violently competitive masculinity, ... thereby
> preventing analysis from addressing the process of self-repre-
> sentation because it begins up in the air of men in battle with
> one another.[13]

Middleton's sophisticated study attempts to get beyond binary oppositions by dismantling them. He argues, for example, that we need
to reconceptualise emotion as 'both rational and socially structured'
(p.13) in order to move away from its association with a chain of
qualities branded 'feminine', like irrationality, domesticity and intimacy. His analysis lays bare the extent to which the problems lie in
the existing paradigm, whose polarities Clare simply reproduces.

Middleton highlights the way in which masculinity is identified with
work and the workplace (differentiated from the home, which can also
a place of work), and points out that, since men's 'working' activities
are carried out apart from their (male) children, they (and, in turn,
masculinity) become endowed with desirable mystery.(p.41) He also
mentions 'the continuance of boyhood fantasies in so many modern
masculinities'.(p.13) One of his most suggestive insights relates to his
own personal description of the aggression that accompanied his earliest creative efforts: how the urge to write (or draw) was accompanied
in his boyhood by powerfully violent impulses and the accumulation
of an irresistible 'head of pressure'(p.2):

> Whenever I tried to write, the ball-point would dig deeper and
> deeper into the paper, incising the words and then tearing
> through. A written character with the force I wanted just
> obliterated itself in the act of writing (p.1)

This account raises possibilities about the relationship between masculinity, aggression and male creativity, suggesting some form of sublimation may be at work; it is an issue to be discussed later in this chapter.[14]

In *A History of Gay Literature: The Male Tradition*, Gregory Woods identifies three themes that recur in the work of male poets, whether homo- or heterosexual: 'Warrior, Love and Father (inseminator, not parent)'.[15] In addition to considering questions of irony and audience or readership in relation to each poet, the tenacity of these three roles will now be tested.

MATTHEW SWEENEY

Sweeney is an Irish poet. His poems recount bizarre, intense experiences, and they tend to be delivered by a dispassionate, detached narrator whose tone betrays no emotion. The poems describe ordinary people to whom extraordinary things happen, and are frequently about sudden or violent death. Many of the stories possess a quality of folk tale or myth, being both contemporary and archetypal, and lacking any detailed context.[16]

Sweeney seems particularly interested in depicting ironic versions of a contemporary warrior. His protagonists are aware of the absurdity of the role and yet are irresistibly (and often surreptitiously) drawn to it. Sweeney's treatment is satiric; the men are often portrayed as powerless or paralysed, making futile gestures for the show of it.

Sweeney's protagonists are invariably men: boys or adults. While the settings are often domestic, these male subjects are depicted as being ill at ease within this environment: they prefer to be loners and yearn for escape. One poem describes a man standing on a Donegal beach, watching the empty skyline for passing boats, waiting for the lifeboat he hopes will come 'to whisk me away'.[17] Another imagines a chained-up Irish setter breaking free to chase and frolic as he chooses; the chain is for his own safety, but it makes him howl with frustration.[18] 'Our Ikky' describes the modern-day Icarus' misguided efforts to construct a pair of wings from inappropriate bits and pieces, while his family look on, tolerant and bemused.[19] Paralysis is a frequent theme, related to both place and circumstance, especially where the men find themselves powerless.[20]

Many of Sweeney's poems are set during boyhood and adolescence.

He captures the intense self-absorption of boys living out vivid fantasies, not about sex, but about romance, heroism and travel. 'Princess' describes a lad who lives rough near the beach. He has discovered a girl's skeleton amidst some castle ruins, and he fabricates an elaborate fantasy about her: incarcerated for disobedience, she died tragically. He serves her like a devoted suitor, imagining combing her red hair and carrying gifts to her from the treasures he finds on the beach. He even decides one particular day must be her birthday, because there is a rainbow. But, characteristically, mingled with this incongruously tender romance that blurs the distinction between reality and fantasy, Sweeney inserts a macabre note. Amongst the detritus the boy gathers in tribute to his princess are two odd shoes '(one with a bony foot still in it)'.[21] The proximity of death does not seem to disturb him, and, indeed, many of these boys are quite taken with death. A similar tone slides into 'On My Own', about a young boy who breaks away from the school cross-country run to hang out by the railway:

> I think of last week, and McArdle
> headless when the train had gone.[22]

'U-Boat' describes a boy's joy at being miles away from everyone else, spending his time exploring an unknown wreck:

> I've moored my raft to the periscope
> that stays underwater. On it I keep
> my shorts and shoes, and coca-cola,
> and a Bavarian girly magazine.[23]

But his single companion is another skeleton, this time that of a drowned sailor, trapped in the wreck. These boys are depicted as being unfazed—even excited—by death. In 'Grandpa's Bed' a boy describes making out with his girlfriend on his grandfather's grave:

> While I waited, I told him
> everything about you,
> and asked his permission
> to do what we did above him.[24]

Such poems suggest a close affiliation between sex and death in the adolescent boy's fantasies. Tracing the long association between death and desire in Western civilisation, Jonathan Dollimore has written that the preoccupation 'is undoubtedly gendered...this is something that crucially involves, but goes beyond, gender'.[25] He suggests that 'it is men more than women who experience the seduction of non-being' (p.xxvi) although, disappointingly, Dollimore does not develop this idea. In Sweeney's work, the gendering of this attraction to death is enhanced by the number of poems with sea settings, in which the sea—traditionally allied to femininity—features as a dangerous but desirable element.

Where the boys are dreamily absorbed in fantasies, a markedly different tone characterises Sweeney's depiction of adult males who are depicted as feckless losers, goading themselves into ever larger gestures of failed heroism the more disastrous their circumstances. In many cases, girlfriends or wives have left them or are on the point of leaving, and the men are humiliated and bewildered. Their defiance results in pointless gestures that compensate for any real action. So the trapeze cyclist, having survived 'The Wobble' that nearly sent him plunging to his death, pushes his bike out back on to the wire, riderless, making it crash on to the rocks below.[26] Such deflationary accounts of failed glory suggest Sweeney finds the mock-heroic a suitable register for contemporary masculinity. Courting death just for the sake of it, these men's displays of hubris are merely vainglorious. One wants to have a picnic on the frozen Mullet Lake, to drive out there in a hearse, taking lots of booze and Irish music 'to charm the ghosts beneath the ice';[27] it's clear he anticipates the ice cracking midway through their festivities. The narrator of 'Flying Machines' recalls his youthful fantasies of piloting a flying boat with wry contempt:

> Me, who needs brandy to walk
> towards a smiling hostess
> up the gangplank of a DC10.[28]

It is as though these adult speakers stare at themselves in disdain. In 'Skating', the narrator chides himself for being a maudlin stay-at-home, 'stuck' in his house with his jazz and alcohol, blind to the miracle of a massive snowfall taking place outside.[29] And in 'The Cold', the drunk, self-pitying husband staggers on to the beach intending to drown himself but even fails at this task:

> ...the Atlantic sent him home again,
> not a corpse, not a ghost,
> to waken his wife
> and complain of the cold.[30]

Suicide would, to the misguided maudlin, at least be a noble act: decisive and dramatic. But instead of releasing his wife from his burdensome existence, he causes her more trouble. The sea chides him like a naughty child.

In these poems, Sweeney is alert to a strain of violence that usually issues in self-destructive behaviour, and, in his grim portraits, impotence and futility characterise masculinity. Often the violence is restrained, channelled into the curiously flat, abrupt endings to the poems. Occasionally, it surfaces: in 'Bagpipes', where the man whose wife has left him hurls himself through a window pane.[31] 'Try Biting' charts the apparently motiveless brutality of a sailor beating up a stranger: he knocks out his teeth, then steals his wallet and jeans.[32] 'Riding into Town' describes a man on horseback, concealing a sledgehammer under his coat; he rides past an orgy of violence on the streets around him, set on course for 'the statue of Our Lady of Prague', whose arms he intends to smash.[33] (This presentation of violence explicitly directed against women is far more unusual in his work than the depiction of self-directed or thwarted aggressive urges.)

One of Sweeney's themes is sudden, often accidental death. Several poems describe suicides. Many more depict seemingly arbitrary disasters in a deadpan, throwaway tone. A fisherman stranded on a rock drowns because he cannot swim; a builder falls from scaffolding; a lover dies in a fire in the London Underground; a coffin-maker is hit by a falling Sputnik; a guilty monk drowns after his boat capsizes. All these poems share a silence where the struggle of the dying man should be; they make death seem easy, almost a peaceful release. Dollimore's comment seems pertinent:

From the earliest times, death has held out the promise of a release not just from desire but from something inseparable from it, namely the pain of being individuated (separate, differentiated, alone) and the form of self-consciousness which goes with that—what philosophers like Schopenhauer call the principle of individuation.[34]

Sweeney's 'warriors' are a troubled bunch. They cannot get back to the solace of boyhood, and the adult world has no need of, or respect for, them. In such an environment, death could have its consolations.

MICHAEL DONAGHY

Michael Donaghy's *Conjure* makes the son–poet's memories of his father the lynchpin around which the collection coheres; in a sense it is a commemorative volume.[35] The verb conjure has multiple meanings: to make appear out of nothing, unexpectedly, as if by magic; to swear together, band together by oath; to call an image to mind; to call upon something (usually a spirit) to appear, by means of magic or ritual; to implore someone to do something. The way in which these definitions range between the material and the spiritual is also characteristic of the poems, which blur the boundary between the two.

The tone is set by an epigraph from *Hamlet*, taken from Horatio's speech in the opening scene, in which he tells Hamlet that the ghost appearing on the battlements has signalled that it wishes to speak with his son. But the sonority of this is undercut by the droll intervention, in italics, '*Only me, old son*', his real father's everyday voice. The mixture of an urgent, restless ghostly apparition and the familiar, harmless presence of Donaghy's old dad accurately characterises the father's personality: he is a bit of a joker, relishing pulling the rug from under people's feet. The son's feelings towards his father are a combination of leftover childhood fear and apprehension, with the adult's more knowing perspective on his father's foibles and failings. The poems are preoccupied with hauntings, in the shape not only of the father's sudden, unexpected appearances but also of memories. What startles the poet is his growing awareness of the strange doubling that occurs between the two of them, so it becomes hard for him to tell one from the other at times. Some shared similarities are easy to acknowledge, like their predilection for telling lies, creating over-elaborate excuses where simple ones (or even the truth) would do as well. So, for example, he finds himself pretending his father has died in order to explain why he hasn't done something he'd promised to do[36]—although of course this raises the suspicion that, in invoking the excuse, he wishes his father *would* die. The difficult process Donaghy charts is one of differentiation; at times the poems suggest he finds it impossible to distinguish his own experiences from those related to him by his father. In 'My Flu', for example, the delirious child finds he is dreaming one of his father's war stories.[37]

However, there are important differences between the men. His father distrusted the written word. Donaghy describes finding an envelope, after his death, but remembers that it had been sent without a letter inside: 'Maybe writing frightened you, / the way it fixed a whim.'[38] It is clear from this that the father was no poet, so the poet–son has—like Heaney and Harrison before him—to find a way of proving the legitimacy of his chosen profession. Metaphors of failed communication, and the tenuous yet persistent bond between father and son run through the collection. His father rigs up a wire as part of an elaborate excuse to get his uncle off the telephone; likewise Donaghy describes his own difficulties making a telephone connection. Later, in 'Mine', the image recurs as the thread he takes on his journey down the mine, both Theseus and the miner's son in search of his father:

> From my beginning
> to his end, a cable jerks tight, sings, twists, and frays.[39]

In this dream journey, the poem enacts the son's quest for his origins—signalled, of course, by the title's multiple meanings. He travels down the mine, retracing his father's footsteps, but the landscape becomes the London Underground of his father's memories during the Blitz. Finally Donaghy reaches the minotaur in its den, which appears to be a combination of his own nursery and his father's sickroom. The creature raises 'its fleshy, palsied, / toothless, half-blind, almost human head' only to reveal the poet's own face staring at him: 'I'm not your father, / son.' it announces self-contradictingly. It tells him, in no uncertain terms, to get a life; to stop searching in the past for origins and connections, but to make his own stories, create his own path:

> Go home, unpick the knot you've made,
> ....
> pay out whatever bloody yarn you must
> though it wind through olive grove, ruin,
> renamed road at first light where you're last seen
> walking,
> just, to the rest of your own life, whoever you are,
> and no king's daughter holding the end of your line. (p.40)

This poem feels like the resolution of the poet's quest to come to some accommodation with his father's legacy, to find a way of both acknowledging his importance and yet moving free of him. The father is shaking him off, rejecting the determinism of a suggested connection between them. The pun on 'yarn' advocates fiction, as though the father is urging his son to make up his stories of origins, rather than attempt to uncover truths. Earlier in the collection the poet had been unsure what to do with his memories, how to stop them overwhelming him: he wondered whether he should put on his father's coat, thus symbolically accepting his position as successor.[40] But the coat seemed unattractive, smelly and pathetic (almost 'weedy'). The implication of this poem, crucial in the collection, is that the son must forge his own path.

The book's last poem, 'Haunts', is spoken by the ghost-father, who himself admits the strange circularity of the relationship with his son. He remembers an occasion on which his three-year-old's voice seemed to arise 'out of radio silence', to comfort *him* in his anxiety.[41] Here, the dead father is resurrected, depicted giving his son one of his memories—not of wartime killing, but a memory that illustrates the son's importance and impact over his dad. Comforting his still living son, he gives him back the very same reassuring words, *'Don't be afraid'*, which close the book, suggesting both a benign haunting, and the son's release.

ROBERT CRAWFORD

Like Donaghy's *Conjure*, Robert Crawford's fourth collection, *Masculinity*, is explicit about its genesis in the poet's own life. Its exploration of masculinity is, as the title indicates, more self-consciously pursued than is the case with Donaghy and Sweeney. University-educated (in Glasgow and Oxford) and now an academic, Crawford came to attention as a poet preoccupied with Scottishness and questions of nationalism and literary culture. The poems in 'Masculinity' (the title of one section of the volume) are mainly written in the first person, and appear to be based on his own experiences. The poems' irony is rather like that in Sweeney's work: it is used pre-emptively, as a defence against anticipated criticisms of behavioural traits that are depicted in the poems as typical male foibles: a stubborn refusal to admit defeat, for example, or an irresistible attraction to adolescent heroes.

The poems display familiarity with gender theory, espousing the view that gender identity is culturally constructed and focusing on school as the particular location of the inculcation of lessons in masculinity. Their protagonist presents himself as always failing to make the grade as a man's man, being insufficiently talented at sport, finding himself best friends with a gay boy ('Which was fine, but left me somehow / Lonely'), and clumsily ineffectual as a charmer.[42]

Several of the poems focus on school-days, re-enacting the young lad's confusion about sexual difference. On the one hand, it all seems straightforward: the girls have one uniform, the boys another; Latin has strict rules for masculine and feminine declensions. But, in reality, things are contradictory. Both sets of uniforms are blue; but the shade differs. The Latin for 'table' is feminine, but there is a world of difference between the legs of the boy's dining-room table and the legs of a girl who sits at that table for tea. The speaker remembers himself as an inept participant in this complicated world, and the self-deprecatory, awkward air of the misfit lagging behind, the boy who does not quite measure up, persists in all the poems.

Paternal influence is seen as crucially formative. The poet describes himself as being just like his father: 'my Dad...made me // Like him an in-between, quiet man, / *Homo silens*, a missing link.'[43] This claim to be 'in-between' the two poles of gender identity ('my all-male school / And that bristling, women-only college') is an interesting one in relation to the binary thinking discussed above. Crawford tries to claim a new space for his style of masculinity, and, instead of confronting his father in a Freudian struggle, he names him as the precursor for this 'in-between' status. He does not seem to experience Harrison's or Dunn's concerns about the suitably masculine nature of poetry, but seeks to use the genre to describe a new version of masculinity. Whether this claim is substantiated in the poems is, however another matter. Crawford's persona seems to share a lot with representations of the 'New Man', raising similarly problematic issues about how to define a new version of masculinity except—in another binary—against the traditional version.

Presumably because Crawford's investigation of masculinity is so upfront, his poems are not restricted to the homosocial worlds espoused by Donaghy and Sweeney. 'PC' is an account of being interviewed 'as a New Man Poet'.[44] The interview is depicted more like a highly charged interrogation. Mention of Sharon Stone's infamous scene in the film *Basic Instinct* underlines the extent to which the poet's experience is intimidating but erotic, as a 'tough' woman journalist 'with blue, constabular eyes' fires questions at him, using the slick public discourse of the business-world ('do you have a plan to keep Family Time / Always ring-fenced in your busy lifestyle?'). The irony cuts both ways, since the poem's sly suggestion that its persona is no 'new man' beneath surface appearances (since he is relishing his private fantasy of a Sharon Stone look-alike legal adviser) can be interpreted either as mischievous triumph or satirical send-up. It also highlights another aspect of Crawford's writing on masculinity, in that the interviewer is portrayed as taking on masculine characteristics. When women figure in these poems, they tend to be briskly efficient and rather cold, even though the lightness of the poems' tone does distract from their humourlessness. The familiar binary underlies Crawford's gender poetics and exerts a sort of balance: if the man is less manly, then the woman inevitably becomes more so. This is the weakness in his attempt to define a space 'in-between'.

In keeping with the rueful, self-deprecating tone of these poems, Crawford's irony pokes fun at male weaknesses. In 'Mending the Helicopter' a man justifies not having done any of the domestic chores on the grounds that he has been too busy repairing a toy.[45]

'Reply' purports to be the woman's response: equipped with the necessary technical know-how herself, she is depicted as being far more practical than him. She has already fixed the helicopter and questions him acerbically:

> Why are you out there at night on the lawn
> Taking the whole thing to bits?[46]

Poems like this one (indeed, arguably, all Crawford's poems in this section) anticipate a female reader. (Unusually, this one also impersonates a female speaker, in a moment of gender crossing that fails to transcend conventional gender categories. See chapter 2 for further discussion of this.) If Crawford's poems differ in both their use of irony, and their expected audience, from those of the other men in this chapter, they share several of the themes identified: a recognition of the permanent attractiveness of boyhood fantasies to grown men, an interest in male filiation, and in Woods's role of 'father (inseminator not parent)'. It is as he is talking about his 'wee son's future' that the speaker of 'A Quiet Man' acknowledges the thread of continuity stretching across the (male) generations. And in 'Male Infertility', a more muted irony probes at male defensiveness with a subtlety and seriousness absent from the other poems. Its subject tries to avoid thinking about the frightening possibility that he might be infertile by sliding off into adventure fantasies. He loses himself in comforting heroic quests:

> ...the storming of the undersea missile silo,
> The satellite rescue, the hydrofoil
> That hits the beach, becoming a car.[47]

Ironically these images trigger a further involuntary memory of another adventurous escapade: but this time his unconscious has dredged up an uncannily appropriate image, '[a] speargun-carrying, tadpole-flippered frogman' who is in fact the sperm from an old sex-education film shown at school. The sperm bursts into tears, and the man starts questioning the desirability of boyhood fantasies of heroic exploits and the eternal bachelor lifestyle:

....living forever in a dinnerjacket
Fussier and fussier about what to drink,

Always, 'Shaken, not stirred.'
Chlorine-blue bikinis, roulette tables, waterskiing

Show me that scene in *Thunderball*
Where James Bond changes a nappy. (p.13.)

The poem is rare in confronting the sterility that underlies Western culture's conventional idealised depictions of masculinity. However, just at the point where Crawford seems to be ready to break the mould and acknowledge fatherhood as an integral part of masculine identity, he draws back. There are several poems about his own newborn child in this very volume, but they are placed in a different section, in an (unintended?) acknowledgement that conventional constructions of masculinity do not include paternity, only insemination. One is a song to the womb, written in Scots, which opens, 'Wee towdy mowdy creel, peat wame'.[48]

NEIL ROLLINSON

Don Paterson, the youngest of the poets in this chapter, and the most overtly 'laddish', claimed that he started writing poetry in the hope it would impress the girls; he cited 'sex, money and fame' as the primary motivations, for the ambition to make it as a poet.[49] Bearing in mind the low public profile of all but a handful of (mainly) dead poets, and the comparative poverty of most contemporary ones, it seems an unlikely, even ironic, ambition. But perhaps being a poet does endow men with a certain charisma and sexual attractiveness. Glamorised images of the Romantic poet, and of Byron ('mad, bad, and dangerous to know') contribute to this idea, as does the older tradition of the poet as composer of eloquent, seductive praises to his beloved. Published in 1996, *A Spillage of Mercury* was Rollinson's first collection, and established his reputation as a writer of sexy poems about fucking.

This description is somewhat misleading, since only a small proportion of the poems in this collection are about sex. Rollinson is more interested in men, and men's relationships with one another, than he is in women. More than half the poems in the book are about homosocial interactions: blokes talking to other blokes, or mono-loguing about their situation or feelings. There is an irreverent, satiricial edge to the treatment, and Christian or Classical materials are updated to contemporary settings and register. God and Adam feature frequently, bemoaning the lack of available females, while Jesus and his disciples are a group of thirsty guys 'doing their doctors' rounds', with the misfortune to end up at a teetotaller's wedding. Jesus obligingly provides each of the lads with their choice 'poison', before raising a toast 'to the miracle of a good drink'.[50]

Like Sweeney, Rollinson's handling of masculinity is self-conscious and ironic. These are men who respond to the urge to make grand gestures and perform super-human feats, however misguided. They are depicted as mock heroes. The speaker of 'Free Fall', who chooses not to open his parachute, describes the last moments as he plum-mets earthwards: thinking of his beloved but choosing death regardless. 'Broken Promises' is an account of another lover's moment of reckoning. Rollinson uses a spoof classicism, calling his character Demophoon, and having him return from the war to face the terri-ble outcome of his failure to come home when he said he would. Trusting him absolutely, his girlfriend has hanged herself, in the belief he is dead. By employing these mock-classical types, Rollinson implies the continuation of certain aspects of male behaviour that might once have seemed heroic but now appear self-indulgent or ridiculous.

The tone of these pieces is skilfully handled: the protagonists are left to do as they must, although it is clear their actions will lead them into trouble. The poet is an acute and wry observer of men's behaviour. In 'Giant Puffballs' the male narrator describes taking a shit in the woods, before finding and picking some mushrooms. The juxtapositioning of these two events is depicted as fortuitous, although the speaker's use of the figurative language of birth to describe the puffballs suggests otherwise. They look 'pregnant as fishbowls', he says, going on to describe his actions: 'I pull one out of its hole / gentle as a midwife…it sits in my lap / like a baby'.[51] The implication of an analogy between the man's creation—a turd—and his booty—the baby-like mushrooms—indicates a poet who likes to play with psychological theories about sexual difference.

There are also disturbing pieces about sexual obsession—one by a rapist, another by a teacher who steals girls' underwear.

Rollinson is preoccupied with non-procreative sex. Like Sweeney, many of his poems are about male fantasies, but they usually detail sexual exploits, rather than other kinds of adventure. Semen always plays a major role in these encounters. 'Ménage à Trois' is an example: it is an account of the intensified sexual passion provoked between a couple by the woman's ongoing affair with another man. As is invariably the case in Rollinson's poems, the man's confidence and authority—his masculinity—remains intact, despite circumstances that might initially imply a dent to his pride. The implication is that the woman's desire is inflamed by having two lovers, but he too seems excited by the sight of his predecessor's sperm-trails:

> You take off your dress and show me
> the stains on your skin
> like the trails of exotic gastropods;
> a body paint of semen
> which I rehydrate with my tongue.
>
> ....
>
> I suck on you greedily and slide
> my tongue where his own tongue
> must have slid long into the night.[52]

The scenario is reminiscent of Richard Dawkins's *The Selfish Gene*: two men's sperm fighting it out for a carrier, the speaker goading himself with imaginings of his rival's prowess.[53] But it is also a striking example of Sedgwick's 'homosocial triangle', in which the woman functions as a kind of decoy, enabling an erotic exchange between two men (see below for further discussion; also chapter 4, p.149).

Semen gets the lead role in 'Sutras in Free Fall' too, an account of sex in zero gravity. 'Jan' begs him to come in her mouth, which is difficult to achieve in such conditions; he comes:

> in one straight line
> like peas from a pea-shooter;
> and Jan swam after them,
> sleek as a dolphin

taking the salty beads
in her mouth.[54]

What makes Rollinson's handling of sexual material so
compelling is partly the skilled writing, and partly the way in which
he makes the women participants play the lead roles. This is a
clever manoeuvre, since it has the effect of seeming to avoid the
traditional depiction of sexual relations, in which woman was the
passive, admired object. These poems can look as though they
empower women, or tell authentic tales about female lust (not to
mention provoking the envy of male readers who have not had such
lucky encounters)—until, that is, the suspicious reader notes the
similarities between these insatiable women and the raunchy
accounts of orgies offered to porn magazines by 'readers' wives'.
At the same time, the perspective retains its masculinism, rendering the women observed objects, watched by the male lover–poet
who authors the account. This is poetry as seduction for the late
1990s: a fierce reaction against Crawford's New Man-ish humility; writing that seems determined to assert its author's potency.

It is rare to find any of the men poets discussed in this chapter
'crossing gender'. However, like Crawford, Rollinson includes one
such poem that purports to be spoken by one of his rampant lovers.
'In One of Your Filthy Poems' is placed in inverted commas to
further emphasise its authenticity. It is a witty postmodern game,
of course, inviting the reader to wonder if the poem really is penned
by one of his lovers, before noticing its stylistic similarities to
Rollinson's other work. Again, if one assumes the lover to be a
woman, this appears to place agency firmly in her control while
achieving a more appropriative feat: usurping her voice. In the
fantasy, the poet has the woman imagine herself exploring every
crevice of his body, biting him all over, taking his 'million sperm'
into her mouth, then dribbling them back 'like a bird feeding her
chick'.[55] But, tellingly, what she wants is public exposure, to fuck
in public. She, at least, has no doubt what his poems are about:
flaunting it in public, which is why she wants to appear in one:

I'll be so hot, they'll feel me come
on the clean, white pages, the smell

of our sex filling the poetry shelves
in Waterstone's, Dillon's, and public libraries
all over England. (p.33)

The innovative twist here is that, for once, a *woman's* orgasm
is employed as metaphor for the writer's creativity, although that
it is a ventriloquised piece rather invalidates any claim to see this
as empowering. However, what happens if the poem is spoken by
a male lover? His fantasy of usurping the girlfriend's bed and tearing her dress up provides another instance of Sedgwick's triangle:
the sexual excitement existing between two men.

Both this poem and 'Ménage à Trois' are, then, more startling for
the gender ambiguities they describe than for their eroticism or sexual
explicitness. In both, Sedgwick's homo-social triangle is in evidence.
In 'Ménage', it is an erotic triangle: the woman lover's body functions to give the speaker access to the other man's semen: 'this ghost
of a man drifting between us'. The prevalence of male-male interactions like these in Rollinson's work echoes Sedgwick's suggestion
that a woman often functions as a substitute for homosocial contact.

Attempts to see Rollinson as a pioneer for women's sexual freedom
founder rather quickly when one looks for variety in his female portrai-
ture. His female characters are interested in sunbathing and fucking;
they are depicted as languorously sensual, or desperate for sex. A series
of poems about Lilith presents her as a saucy temptress, driving God
so wild with desire he has to go and masturbate in the woods:

What do you think of my garden? He said.
His whole body shook. Have you ever seen orchids
as pretty as these? Lilith opened her legs.

Have you ever seen orchids as pretty as these?
Touch the petals, she whispered,
Feel how damp they are, how covered in dew.[56]

The metaphor is not new, of course; what is new is its recast-
ing as the assertive self-appreciating come-on of the woman
herself, rather than its conventional appearance as the male lover's
description.[57] But once again, the way in which Rollinson's female

speakers seem only to exist as sexual temptresses detracts from any possible authority they might wield.

If Rollinson's work in this collection provides an illustration of a male poet fulfilling Woods's role of the lover, it is interesting that his poems never describe heterosexual intercourse. Almost all of them describe oral sex, or sex in which the semen does not get where it is 'supposed' to go. Rollinson is not interested in Woods's role of the father/inseminator, but is concerned to demonstrate his lover's potency and the role of the father. Several of his poems focus on an older, paternal figure; occasionally, such a figure is explicitly named as the persona's father. 'The Way It Happens' describes an old man's death in a nursing home. As the dying man takes his last breath and closes his eyes, the poem's narrator leans forward to listen to his chest, hearing only silence. At the end of the poem he closes the curtains and prepares to leave the room:

> I pick up his cigarette
> and light it, I can feel the cool damp
> of his spittle still in the paper, the heat
> of the smoke, then even that has gone.[58]

While the poem does not name its protagonists as father and son, the intimacy of the setting makes such a relationship likely. Read as a poem about inheritance, the metaphor of the cigarette works in complex ways. It suggests the urgent need to be physically in touch with the very last evidence of this man's life-force, and the realisation that his death allows the speaker to take the man's now vacant place. The cigarette stub seems to promise continuity, something that can be passed on, but, within seconds, the link fades. It is a skilfully non-committal image, capable of being read either as a usurpatory act of triumphant accession, or as a more tender gesture, performed in order to prolong a feeling of intimacy with the dead man. Characteristically, the poem's real interest is in its speaker, not the old man, but nevertheless it suggests an interest in, and anxiety around, filiation that was present in Crawford's and Donaghy's work, and crops up again in Paterson's.

There is further evidence of this interest in 'My Father Shaving Charles Darwin', and 'The Garden'. The latter is a subtle account of the tension between an older and younger man. The speaker is the younger, guest of the elder. As the visitor his is the supporting role, but he watches the patriarch's performance with suspicion, hoping to catch him out. His host carves the roast meat with faultless skill; he conducts his younger visitor on a tour of his garden and points out the phallic shadow cast by a tree in the centre of the lawn. There is rivalry between these two men and hostility too. Once again there is a moment of failed transfer from older to younger. The speaker does not understand his host's comments about the tree shadow: when he shuts his eyes to concentrate, the image of a naked female acquaintance creeps in to distract him.

Rollinson's first collection does not have the anger, irony or urge towards violence that characterises much of the work of Sweeney (and Maxwell and Paterson, as will be demonstrated). It could be that, at this stage, the flaunting of his sexual exploits was sufficiently satisfying as to prevent or divert any impulse towards aggression.

GLYN MAXWELL

Glyn Maxwell is, like Robert Crawford, interested in masculinity.[59] Maxwell has published four sole-authored collections to date, comes from the south-east of England and is most often discussed as one of the enthusiastically postmodern British poets.[60] The poems in *Rest for the Wicked* reveal his particular interest in masculinity as a group identity, dependent on the presence and legitimisation of other men, and threatened by the intrusion of women. Like Crawford, Maxwell often depicts boys' childhood and adolescence. Many of the poems are written in the second-person singular, and this 'you' seems expansive, as though intended to reach out to others in an inclusive way. In this respect it is most unlike Carol Ann Duffy's deployment of the second person, which, as described in chapter 2, produces the impression of caustic self-critique. Maxwell's 'you' feels as though it could equally be applied to his readers. However, this inclusive intention is countered by the sex-specificity of many of the poems. Their pronouns are rarely explicitly sexed, so there is no obvious appeal to a male audience; nevertheless the tone, or the assumptions of shared knowledge, and the exclusively homosocial worlds in which the poems unfold, all contribute to this effect.

Maxwell's idiosyncratic style is compelling when it works, infuriating when it does not. He bends language to his purpose, wrenching syntax, flouting rules of grammar, convention or clarity of expression. The following brief extract from the opening poem, 'Cine', in a sequence, 'Phaeton and the Chariot of the Sun: an investigative documentary', also claims to give some insight into his working methods:

> Cine. A reel was found in a vault in a place
> I happened on in the course of a search. This reel
> was not—but is now—the object of that search
> so it's over. Which is how
>
> poetry works, by the way. Like cine film
> it yields to the bright. Like cine film it is either
> print or nothing, like cine film that nothing
> is sky. Like cine film
>
> it's made of children who run towards you and cry.[61]

The awkwardness of these lines is quite characteristic: it is as though the poet wants to leave traces of the intractability of language, its clumsiness. The foregrounding of a plain, colloquial repetitive style ('in a vault in a place /...in the course') does not make that style any less rhetorically crafted. There is a jokiness to it, as well as tremendously commanding confidence: the voice forces you to attend, and in demanding the reader persevere with such contorted syntax, Maxwell somehow wins our acquiescence. All his poems make this extensive use of deixis (context-sensitive language), drawing readers into them, but only providing titbits of revelation about setting or event; as a result, you feel disoriented, but (if the poem works) in thrall to its mesmerising, domineering style. This narrator is not to be trusted; his logic convinces via obfuscation; he will shift the terms while you are preoccupied with his syntax. For example, the analogy set out above—between poetry and cine film—actually starts out as something different: a description of the way an arbitrarily 'found' object can fortuitously become the seed for a poem. But the strength of the rhetoric is sufficiently engrossing to enable him to get away with it. In the aggressiveness of this manipulation of language and syntax, there are echoes of Middleton's speculation on the links between masculinity, representation and violence.

Maxwell's frequent use of the second person certainly implies an interest in audience, which is not surprising, since he has also worked extensively in theatre. He sets considerable store by rhythm and is acutely aware of the poem as spoken utterance—its oral and tonal qualities, and the crucial significance of word order:

> Poetry is an utterance of the body. Not the best utterance— which is pre-linguistic and made of salt water—but the best a body can do, given it has language. It is language in thrall to the corporeal.[62]

The costive feel of much of Maxwell's poetry is intentional, but its forcefulness is close to bullying, and in relation to this relish for control the frequent recurrence of cinematic and visual metaphors is suggestive. Maxwell is fascinated by time, and the possibility of controlling it. His poems can operate like a movie camera's freeze-frames, laying different scenes alongside one another to experiment with synchronicity.[63] Such techniques are associated with postmodernism, but they can also be interpreted as evidence of the poet's desire to be the director behind the camera, in absolute control.[64] It is the director who selects viewpoint and sequencing, who organises the action, who controls perspective, timing and impact. It is the director whose skill deploys image with poetic resonance, to convey something more than its literal existence.[65] The peremptory tone in Maxwell's work—a tone that commands attention and acquiescence—has more in common with the film than the theatre director since, while Maxwell is fascinated by performance and direction, he is less interested in audience response.

Maxwell's depictions of men are keenly observed, and they avoid Crawford's rueful, deprecatory tones even when the ironies are obvious. As narrator he is often also participant, although the role gives him some distance from the action. 'Wasp' is a characteristic example of his treatment of masculine aggression. It describes a group of men's reactions to a wasp nosing around the debris of their hearty meal. The wasp's persistence eventually stirs the men to act against it. One takes a swipe, and that encourages the others to get involved; they end up whipping themselves into a state of extreme agitation:

> The nasty little guy
> Chose to buzz our heads and would die because
>
> Of what it wanted and was.[66]

The tone is droll but affectionate; the narrator recognises the ludicrousness of the scene but at the same time remains loyal to his mates. He knows that the wasp is not doing any harm, even were it to eat some of the leftovers. What is at stake is the wasp's refusal to recognise that this is the men's territory; its insouciant meddling infuriates them. Later in the poem a female bee appears briefly; she is far wiser and clears off. But the men cannot resist rising to the wasp's provocation. The wasp is not sexed, but in Maxwell's poems only the female sex requires naming, so it is safe to assume the wasp is male. Its sin is to 'want what we had wanted and had'.(p.68) Maxwell's narrator is still one of the lads; he would rise to the bait, along with the rest, even though he can see that their behaviour is absurd.

The group dynamic is presented as absolutely integral to this display of ludicrous macho outrage: reactions are contagious, and the men act as one body. Maxwell invariably depicts men operating as a group and is fascinated by the seemingly effortless fluency with which this merger is accomplished. Sometimes its ends are unambiguously destructive, as in the bizarre 'A Force That Ate Itself', which describes an army that cannot stop marching, despite the fact there is no enemy and no war. In the end, having circled the world, they catch up with their tail and shoot their own men in the backs.[67] In 'Ost' violence is again described as arising out of the group's communal response, and machismo and nationalism are intertwined. A German skinhead and an Iranian *gastarbeiter* pass one another on the street. Italics indicate an unspoken exchange between them, to the effect that a physical confrontation would be inevitable if their mates were witnessing the encounter. As they are alone, they can let one another be. It is as though masculinity and chauvinism are *produced* by the group gaze. The narrator empha-sises the theatrical component of masculine bravado, by describing them as boys rehearsing with scripts, 'shitting it, / In the wings.'[68]

In these poems, men only fully inhabit their masculinity when they are part of a group, which makes shared activities vitally impor-tant. So the youthful narrator of 'The Wish' finds that his cleverness does not get him what he really wants. According to the game's rules, his mates tell him he can have but one wish: he uses it to wish for everything. But the cunning ploy backfires because, although his mates finally concede the validity of his wish, the effect of his clev-erness is to alienate him from the group: the others, with their straightforward wishes, go off and enjoy themselves, while he is left alone, waiting to find out whether his wish will be granted. By the time he is finally told it will, he realises he doesn't want that any more; the point of the game was to share a fantasy with the others.[69]

In keeping with Middleton's suggestion, Maxwell's poems depict boyhood activities retaining their appeal to adult men. 'Self-Portrait with Softball' is similar in its focus on the 'odd one out'. The poem uses the third person, despite the title (another sign of his interest in manipulating narrative distance), to describe its subject, a man who is striding purposefully across a field packed with boys play-ing ball-games, when a ball bounces into his arms.[70] The implication here is that the man has had to leave the world of boys' games. He seems to be wearing restrictive, formal clothes, as though he now has to go to work. He no longer understands the way the boys play; he expects there to be a need for him as instructor or organiser, but the boys simply regroup and start new games to get round the problem of the missing ball. These poems about boys' games form a strong contrast with Crawford's evocation of burly, sadistic sportsmasters; in Maxwell's treatment, there is a subtlety to these interactions, which is suggestive of their importance to masculine identity.

There are several poems that describe this kind of scene, in which one male is excluded from the group because he is different—and has grown up. Their theme is clearly that of loss: loss of the secu-rity and pleasure of being so intimately identified with the others. In 'The Night Is Young' the narrator describes bumping into a man who used to be 'One of the Gang'.[71] Eagerly they start reminiscing and soon:

> Were hurrying back in the years like children yelled
> Out of the light of their inexplicable game,
> Into the brooding houses to be held.(p.35)

But soon they find they have to resort to just listing the names of the other gang members. There is nothing much to be said; that time, now passed, cannot be recaptured, as the littering of pronouns suggests:

> I'd seen some, but he'd seen two I expected
> Never to see again, they were fine, they were fine,
> He mentioned, and that was that.(p.35)

Once again the language draws attention to itself because of its colloquially limited register. The disruptive line break after 'expected' is a good example of this, as it trips the reader up. But, despite its colloquial phrasing, these lines are not quite colloquial because of the transposition from active to passive voice. This highlights the fact that the anecdote is being reported at one remove and has a defamiliarising effect, despite the simple language. Something parallel is taking place on a semantic level: the metaphor implies that adulthood is an 'inexplicable game', while memories of the gang are comfortingly domestic—a strange, deliberate inversion of conventional expectations. Unusually the poem emphasises the irreversible passage of time: there are no tricks with time frames or cameras here. As he returns to his mates' table, the speaker describes:

> ...feeling about as young as the night is young

> And wanting it all, like one who has had enough.
> You don't forgive what's left of what you loved.(p.35)

These lines echo the endless, insatiable restlessness depicted with such acuity in 'Wasp'. Presumably the night is no longer young at all; the narrator's emotions are confused, and his closing epigram extends the ambiguity, implying an involuntary hostility towards his old mate, as well as towards that part of himself that still fires up at the memory of those times.

In Maxwell's poems, the bonds between men are intense, and they are destroyed by the disruptive presence of women. As a result, romance is treated with scepticism, but he depicts men throwing themselves into it with the same kind of heroic, defiant abandon that characterises all their activities. 'Stargazing' implies that men witness the vast infinitude of the galaxy, but eventually, like 'all the descended gods', give in and accept the comforting consolations of a woman's love in place of the universe's daunting scale:

> to weary of all
> that never ends, to take a human hand,
> and go back into the house.[72]

The speaker's suggestion that the starlight setting engineers romance all by itself, and makes whichever woman happens to be nearby into a suitable lover, is typical of Maxwell's cynical attitude. Coupled with the casual claim that women are not capable of understanding astronomy, it emphasises the necessity for this 'man's world' to be kept free of women. The same tone recurs in all the poems that treat men's entanglement with women.

The suggestion throughout is that men do this to themselves; their own gullibility, instinct or desire leads them into romantic relationships, however doomed. And because the narrator retains his position as friendly onlooker, insider, even participant, he avoids seeming either critical or sardonic. Nevertheless, the satire is persistent: 'So when for the once in a life I again find you' opens 'Song of the Sash', before developing into a critique of men's skill in dressing up their own desires as being in the lover's best interests.[73] Maxwell depicts an eager lover rushing off after the men who meet under the clock in 'King of the Castle Square', purportedly to seek out the 'Dirty Rascals' who run off, abandoning wives and families. The irony, of course, is that this army of seekers have themselves engineered a plausible excuse for their own regular absence, while their wives are at home, preparing their meals. So the poem's speaker dresses up his own need for freedom in the guise of winning a valuable trophy for his love.

While Maxwell's 'warriors' never actually get down to any fighting, their posturing is vital to their identity. Courtship is presented as simply another kind of military undertaking. In 'Love Made Yeah', love is depicted as dangerous territory, entailing the irrational possession of 'the Square of my reason'.[74] Hapless men tumble into the trap, their heroic bravado suddenly useless; they are 'odds-on to cop it'.(p.20) The closing shout:

> 'I am hers,
> friends, I am history!'

encapsulates the ideas played with in the poem: that women are equated with a kind of death for men—not literally but figuratively, a loss of freedom and power: a loss, ultimately, of their masculinity.

This suggestion—that in accepting a woman as lover the man somehow has to relinquish his masculinity—recurs in several of Maxwell's poems. David Kennedy has noted the importance of the 'bloke' to Maxwell's poetry; he describes the poet's idea of the bloke as

> a kind of imago adult with an emotional world undeveloped beyond, at best, his late teens. A bloke swaggers, 'curses to no effect', knows 'two dozen unfunny jokes' and, in the crudest sense, has a big heart.[75]

It is as though the bloke is some kind of inadequate compensation for the loss of boyhood solidarity. The bloke features most prominently in poems about sexual relationships. As with all his irony, Maxwell is both on his side and gently sending him up at the same time. The narrator of 'A White Car' provides an excellent illustration of this skilful positioning:

> To know this is, to know the last one
> wasn't this, and to drive towards her
> hidden, leafed address, remembering
>
> these: the first one, then the kindest

who remained kind and painting, to
recall the one with arms akimbo
threatening, with little on: these
group and hedge and agree in your knowing,
they know it too, and laugh or shrug

to watch you park a white car smiling.[76]

While the spareness of his style makes it impossible to be sure, the poem seems to be about a man who has found 'the one', the woman he wants to marry. Later, the wedding guests are shown to be a cynical bunch, inclined to laugh at the groom's conviction. The narrator's attitude is less clear; he seems to be on the bloke's side, encouraging him 'never mind how they laugh', but at the end of the poem he imagines the scene 'when this one comes, when this one means it / at the top of the stairs'. The insistence with which he sticks to the phrase 'this one' to refer to the woman who has, after all, been chosen precisely because she is *unique* is disconcerting and implies his own scepticism. The lover himself has apparently decided that this woman is 'the one' by comparing her with his ex-girl-friends. They are commemorated as a series of ciphers, each remembered in relation to one particularly memorable feature or moment, which has the effect of further depersonalising them in a humorous list.[77] The vivid vignette of a domestic row is remembered with amusement, and the woman's fury is subtly undercut by the memory that she was virtually naked at the time. Brilliantly original as an evocation of the strange ritual of the wedding reception, the poem also demonstrates Maxwell at his most characteristic: imperious, ironic and happiest amongst the lads.

DON PATERSON

Where Matthew Sweeney is preoccupied with men's deaths, Paterson's poems display an enjoyment of killing women. Accompanied by a mode of self-presentation that is scathingly sardonic, one is presum-ably intended to take such scenarios ironically. The title of the collection *God's Gift to Women* (1997), is a fine example: while the book's cover inevitably invites readers to make the author into the

subject of that phrase, the title poem describes him as helplessly ineffectual, unable to 'make it all better' for his traumatised lover.[78] In
this way Paterson plays with the distance between personae and
poet. Where Crawford's and Donaghy's poems openly explored material close to home, in this volume Paterson ranges from confession
to satire. The reader cannot be sure how seriously s/he should be
taking the poems. Paterson has said it was a great relief to him to
learn from Michael Donaghy that it was quite possible to lie in
poetry.[79] In this volume, lies and savage irony provide perfect cover
for a fully postmodern display of masculinity.

Paterson is usually discussed in relation to either his nationality
(Scottish) or his working-class, self-educated background.[80] No
one seems to have found his sexually predatory persona worthy of
comment. He works hard to make erudition sexy, and Laddism
erudite, so that whisky, sex, football are ennobled by their commem-
oration in difficult poetry. As this might suggest, the gender of his
personae plays a vital part in his work, one that is enhanced by his
determination to carve out an authoritative poetic voice. Where
Maxwell wrests language into his own idiosyncratic idiolect,
Paterson conducts his own experiments into ways of enhancing his
authority. He confesses to having learned from Sean O'Brien 'how
you can make the poetic voice sound more authoritative through
syntax'.[81] He puts his strict Calvinist upbringing to good use in the
opening piece from God's Gift to Women, delivering a spoof sermon
to his readers, or 'congregation'.[82]

Infamous for declaring he would like to punch the 'cunts' who
make up his middle-class readership, Paterson has said he is trying
to resist poetry's propensity for making 'palatable things that should
remain indigestible'.[83] What looks like an attack on middle
England's complacency distracts attention from the gender implications of this outburst. Like Ezra Pound, Paterson wants 'no more
poetry for ladies'. His themes are determinedly blokeish: 'drink,
books, sleep, sex, trains, death, sport',[84] as though his real concern
is with proving the manliness of the genre and thus relieving his
own anxieties about the effeminacy of his chosen profession. After
all, a poet like Peter Reading manages to keep his material quite
discomfortingly indigestible without concentrating on macho
themes.[85] But there is an interesting paradox here: on the one hand,

poetry's limited audience—middle-class, 'literary', white and female—frustrates him; on the other hand, the females constituting a large part of that audience act as goad and temptation. Paterson is unusually explicit about his Darwinian views on sex and poetry. He has written that men poets are 'sustained by necessary myths...money, sex and fame...very atavistic urges, primarily concerned with the propagation of the genes'.[86] In part it is this reactionary outspokenness that makes him an interesting candidate for this chapter.

The discussion that follows focuses on poems of sexual encounter, although since almost all of them do, this is hardly a selective decision. The predilection for bathos and the jokey games symptomatic of postmodernist antics are presumably meant to make these poems amusing, but the humour—because it depends on irony alone—is coercive. A series commemorating stations along a local train line provokes a stream of erotic recollections in a wry nod to Freud: '19:00: Auchterhouse' recalls enjoyable efforts to remove a splinter from Gail's bottom; '01:00: Rosemill' describes an elaborate fantasy of sex with a black woman ('girl') wearing all black. By the end of the poem his cock has become the train, 'freewheeling into Newtyle'.[87] 'Imperial' makes a pun out of one lover's virginity, opening with her frightened question, keeping the punch-line back till the last lines, where a long courtship finally results in consummation crudely signalled by mention of the blood-stained sheets.[88]

Such pieces strip bare the aggression latent within such humour: it really is a 'punch-line', suggestive of profound misogyny. 'From Advice to Husbands' opens with the epigrammatic line:

No one slips into the same woman twice.[89]

It is possible for a woman reader to find this entertaining, just as it is equally possible male readers may find the humour inadequate. But if this kind of light entertainment is froth, Paterson's tendency to cast himself in murderous roles is disconcerting. In '1001 Nights: The Early Years' his persona imagines himself as the compulsive emperor, finding his insatiable sexual appetite is matched only by the irresistible impulse to behead his deflowered virgins.[90] The poem goes on to describe how he slices off her head with a kitchen knife.

The persona clearly appeals, since it recurs in a wittily titled poem that describes the final beheading of Scheherazade, 'To Cut It Short'.[91] Here, as in 'Imperial', we are supposed to enjoy the joke without worrying that it works by making the woman into a metaphor for masculine creativity. It could be that the violence Middleton identifies as lying at the heart of men's creative desire finds its release, in these poems, as the (ostensibly ironic) poetic equivalent of the slash-movie.

The longer poems in this collection are more interesting. Here Paterson uses a voice that seems less insistently framed as a persona. With more space, his sophisticated insights into masculine identity are evident, and the ironies become complex. 'The Alexandrian Library, Part II: The Return of the Book' is a mockingly inflated account of a day in the life of the male poet, as he procrastinates endlessly: conning himself into believing he is teetering on the brink of a brilliant creative breakthrough, but spending most of his time fantasising, drinking or masturbating.[92] En route, he indulges in some of the staples of a sexist literary tradition: he gets carried away in a reverie about the librarian, whose 'nylons criss-crossing inside her starched whites / has shushed the whole place back to silence'.(p.43) The excitement enables the use of that popular metaphor, semen as ink: the pen is 'dreaming incontinently' of sexual encounters to be had in the future (p.43).

This is a far cry from Middleton's aggressive urge to rip through the white page with his pen, and from Heaney's attempt to lay claim to the manly labour of writing as 'digging'. Paterson uses the familiar metaphor with a mix of affection and mockery, but what is most interesting is the flaccidity. As the fantasy unfolds, he imagines himself proudly displaying the sheets of his completed masterpiece from his bedroom window, waving 'stained sheets' to the assembled, envious crowd. With its invented authorities and bombastic tone, the poem is clear about its status as satire and sends up the self-justificatory absorption of male creativity with wicked efficacy. 'Poem' does something similar, in a wry dig at male poets' habit of preferring their fabricated, idealised muse to any actual flesh-and-blood woman. In three lines it exclaims at the 'insolence' of the woman for actually responding to the stream of poems that yearn for her presence.[93]

More interesting than satire is the way Paterson handles emotion. These longer poems feel like exercises in confessional writing. Both are written in the first person; both tackle intimate material in revealing ways. 'A Private Bottling' is the less surprising of the two: in it the speaker's feelings about the end of a relationship get transposed on to his description of a loving, if unwisely excessive all-night ritual of sampling his way through a whole circle of malt whiskies. It is a dignified piece, full of wry self-appraisal, explicitly confronting alcohol's tendency to stimulate maudlin sentimentality, and closing with a toast 'to your sweet memory, but not to you.'[94] The speaker is frank about the way in which his carousing replaces his actual ex with an idealised version.

The poem that gives the collection its title is more startling. 'God's Gift to Women' is extraordinary for its combination of irony and what feels like genuine emotion, and for the way it moves between two foci: sometimes telling the lover's life-story, at others, his own.[95] The stark self-revelation contained in this piece is tempered by irony and the personae that dominate the collection. Paterson divulges a huge amount of personal material about the woman addressee: details of an abusive mother; a childhood in institutional care; nightmares; suicide attempts. Then he starts exploring his personal history: his weekly trips to the therapist, his 'current all-time low'(p.27); a potted Freudian account of his speedy usurpation of his father's place (p.27), and his determination never to have children (p.27). The poem feels raw, and unsteady, as though the author is not in control of its trajectory, but these qualities seem valuable, even though the sensational nature of the incidents recounted makes one question their veracity. It is difficult to know how to take all this, except as a thoroughly postmodern version of confessional writing.

'God's Gift to Women' explores the themes identified at the beginning of this chapter: male filiation, inheritance and the legitimacy of the role of poet for a heterosexual male. In this poem Paterson makes the radical suggestion that all the myths and legends about male heroism on behalf of helpless, trapped maidens actually serve as a smokescreen for the son's compulsive desire to impress his father, and win his admiration and forgiveness. Paterson writes of 'that lost soteriology' which suggests that:

> ...who slays the dragon or the wolf
> on the stage of his presexual
> rescue fantasy, makes the kill
> not just for her flushed gratitude
> but for his Father in the gods. (p.32)

The opacity of these lines conceals the boldness of the suggestion within them. Paterson is refuting the idea that male quests and heroism are performed in order to win the woman. Instead, he claims, the goad behind their actions is the need to secure the father's hard-won recognition.[96] Having earlier described his effortless supplanting of his father in his mother's affections, he goes on to claim that the hero is motivated by self-interest: what lies behind the impulse to act as saviour or rescuer is invariably a desire for personal salvation. Interestingly, the father in this poem occupies the position of God, and the distinction between them is blurred. It is the father who is the crucial imagined reader or addressee, lurking behind this piece.

Paterson's interest in filiation was evident in his first collection, *Nil Nil*, in which paternity is feared and dreaded.[97] 'The Seed' describes parenthood as 'no more than murder / by degrees'(p.17) and, while at first it is ambiguous as to whether it is parent or child who is the murderer, by the end of the poem it is clear the speaker intends both. (Such poems probably stem from the age-old anxiety that children take away creativity, wasting the male artist's seed.) Paterson's persona recalls the various methods by which he attempted to do away with his father and usurp his place but, in turn, discovers he is now the target of similar attacks from his as yet unconceived child:

> My child is hunting me down like a thief. (p.17)

The male personae in several of his poems brag of their determination to avoid paternity at all costs. Recalling his habit of having sex on the side with women who already have partners, the narrator of 'God's Gift' describes how he would take his used condoms home with him to be extra safe.[98]

Paterson's irony may be both aggressive and tiresome, but his insights into masculinity are provocative. Caustic and cynical, his poems are skilful for the way in which self-preoccupation is both indulged and mocked simultaneously. His poetic persona is an alienated and asocial bachelor: the solitary drinker, greeting the dawn by pissing from his window, recollecting shags from his past, troubled by his mortality, disgusted by procreation, preoccupied with his father. These are the poems of a particular stage in a man's life. As Paterson has moved on, so too have his poems, though the tendency to wash dirty linen in public remains a characteristic of his work.[99]

CONCLUSIONS

Peter Middleton suggests that work and the workplace play a central role in traditional conceptions of masculinity. However, in a post-industrial society, where physical labour is of marginal significance, and in which women make up half the work-force, how much store can be set by 'work' as a defining attribute of masculinity? What do these poets proffer in its place? How might their poetry be seen to outline versions of David Kennedy's masculine poetic? And how does recent cultural change affect concerns about whether poetry is a suitable job for a heterosexual 'masculine' man?

The most striking thing all six poets share is their predilection for homosocial worlds. They are interested in what happens when the boys are together: how they interrelate, age, play, fight and dream. The presence of a girl or woman disrupts the dynamics of these exclusively male environments. This focus on relations between men may sound unlike Rollinson's work, but the women who do appear in his poems tend to function as fantasy figures: consequently they do not disrupt, but actually facilitate, the persistence of a comfortably phallocentric existence. It may be that one response to anxieties about poetry's effeminacy is to emphasise (hetero)sexual activity. Rollinson's poetry certainly suggests that successful masculinity resides in (hetero)sexual (non-procreative) potency.

Paterson's depictions of women are more disconcerting, because they are more realistically framed. In his work savage misogyny, heartfelt introspection, ostentatious erudition, satire and the urge to violence make for an unsettling mix. It is the introspection that is most revealing in relation to masculinity. As Peter Middleton suggested, masculinity seems to resist introspection. Deryn Rees-Jones made a similar observation in her remarks about male confessional writing.[100] She pointed out that what is radical about it is that confession somehow contradicts conventional masculinity, which is thus exposed as being predicated upon a refusal to expose the self. It seems that Paterson is intensely conscious of this. When he risks self-exposure, he does it tongue-in-cheek, striking a series of poses with high irony. He is uncomfortable, and, consequently, he makes his reader uncomfortable.

Maxwell's interest is in homosocial bonds and the importance of the group to male identity. In his portrayal, manhood is conferred publicly; its acknowledgement depends on display and performance, as well as the agreement of a group of other men. In this respect, it contrasts markedly with the girl child's transition from girlhood to womanhood, which is invariably figured via the onset of menstruation—a physiological event over which the girl has no control, and which is private and usually concealed. Becoming a man involves the demonstrated completion of *public* feats and is a status that gets conferred by other men; because of this, masculinity *depends upon* the group.

Maxwell's preference for the mock-heroic is shared, to a degree, by Sweeney, who supplements it with a more solemn note of displacement and confusion. Sweeney's men really do seem to be devoid of a role, retreating into fantasy or impotent, often violent gestures. Crawford's 'New Man' persona marks him out from the rest, perhaps suggesting that he anticipates a female readership in a way the others do not. While he only follows established convention in defining the New Man against masculine stereotypes, in so doing he remains locked within the sex-role binary and finds himself adjusting his depiction of women, to make them more 'masculine' in turn.

In addition to the homosocial emphases of these six poets, they also share an interest in the place of the father. Only Crawford writes about actually being a father (although Paterson has written about this since *God's Gift*); for several of them, paternity seems threatening, to be avoided at all costs; their poems are the proof of their virility. Most readers would not know whether any of the others *are* fathers, since none mentions the fact in the brief biographical information in their books and in the various reference books that collate details about contemporary poets.[101] Yet father figures feature in a significant number of these poems. Rollinson describes the moment of the father's death, focusing on the son's choice: to take up his position as successor (accepting the still lit cigarette), or reject it. Paterson, ostentatiously dismissive of his father, is nevertheless frank about his importance as spectator/reader/judge of the poet–son's efforts. Crawford embraces his father as creator, he the son fashioned in his father's image, another 'in-between' man. Donaghy's collection is the one most centred on this theme. His father's death provokes questions about the burden of inheritance, and his need to let go of his father's memory and forge his own path.

It seems likely that one of the effects of recent radical developments in relation to gender roles has been to provoke poets into scrutinising their own fathers, for the versions of masculinity they espoused.[102] But while it can be explained, the one-sided nature of this preoccupation is a cause for concern. Mothers do not appear at all in these poets' work. The anxieties of Harrison and Dunn about the appropriateness of poetry for 'real men' no longer apply in that form, since masculinity itself has lost the traditional grounds for its definition. But this has left a vacuum: what does define masculinity? As a consequence, these poets are not as anxious about their status as 'real men' poets; instead, they are preoccupied with the more fundamental task of investigating what constitutes masculinity in the first place. The exclusively homosocial worlds in which this investigation takes place tells us a great deal about its subject; what it suggests about the gendering of poetry as a mode of discourse is rather more disturbing.

NOTES

INTRODUCTION
POETRY AND CRITICISM

1. Elizabeth Bishop, cited in Fleur Adcock (ed.), *The Faber Book of Twentieth-century Women's Poetry*.
2. For a fuller discussion of this phenomenon, see Lyn Pykett's essay, 'Women Poets and "Women's Poetry": Fleur Adcock, Gillian Clarke and Carol Rumens' in Gary Day and Brian Docherty, *British Poetry from the 1950s to the 1990s: Politics and Art*, Basingstoke, Macmillan, 1997, pp.253–67. Pykett discusses a special issue of *Poetry Wales*, in which women poets were asked about the relevance of their sex to their poetry; most insisted poetry should be 'gender neutral': *Poetry Wales*, vol.23, no.1, 1987.
3. Alan Robinson, *Instabilities in Contemporary Poetry*.
4. Peter Childs, *The Twentieth Century in Poetry: A Critical Survey*.
5. Keith Tuma, *Fishing by Obstinate Isles*, p.229.
6. David Kennedy, *New Relations*, p.8.
7. This is not to accuse Kennedy of a lack of interest in gender: he has recently published a fascinating article on masculinity as conceptualised by Tony Harrison and Douglas Dunn. '"*What Does the fairy DO?*", pp.115–36. See chapter 5 for a further discussion of this.
8. R. P. Draper, *An Introduction to Twentieth-century Poetry in English*. The three women are Judith Wright, Margaret Atwood and Maya Angelou.
9. Eavan Boland, 'The Woman Poet', p.45. See chapter 2 for further discussion of this issue.
10. Jane Dowson, 'Older Sisters are Very Sobering Things', pp.6–20; p.12.
11. The Women's Press published it in Britain five years later, in 1979.
12. In 1972 Margaret Byers published an essay, 'Cautious Vision: Recent British Poetry by Women'. She discussed Fleur Adcock, Elaine Feinstein,

Elizabeth Jennings, Anne Beresford, Molly Holden and Rosemary Tonks, but made some dismissive remarks about Jeni Couzyn and Libby Houston, clearly representatives of a new, politicised kind of poetry. Even though she herself was clearly not feminist, Byers expressed her disappointment at the absence of these women from contemporary anthologies and critiques. See pp.74–84 in Michael Schmidt and Grevel Lindop (ed.), *British Poetry since 1960: A Critical Survey*, Manchester, Carcanet, 1972.

13. Eavan Boland, 'The Woman Poet', p.47.

14. Helen Carr, 'Poetic Licence', p.77.

15. Nancy Miller suggests that academics use the 'authority effect' of theory to disguise the personal, subjective origins of their opinions. See *Getting Personal: Feminist occasions and other autobiographical acts*, London and New York, Routledge, 1991.

16. Philip Hobsbaum, *Metre, Rhythm and Verse Form*, p.4.

17. Suzanne Juhasz, 'The Critic as Feminist': Reflections on women's poetry, feminism, and the art of criticism', p.114. Don Paterson has suggested cynically that academics concentrate on 'difficult' poets like John Ashbery, because there is some meat for them to get their teeth into. See his interview with Raymond Friel in Robert Crawford et al. (eds), *Talking Verse*.

18. John Sutherland, 'Do I Know You, Ms Plath?', *Guardian* 27 March 2000. Sutherland explains, 'I've dined with Heaney, drunk with Blake Morrison, met Hugo Williams at conferences and hob-nobbed with Andrew Motion at publishers' parties. I don't of course "know" them, although one has that false sense of intimacy from knowing the published privacies of their poetry.'

19. Christine Battersby, 'Unblocking the Oedipal: Karoline von Gunderode and the Female Sublime'.

20. Elisabeth Bronfen, *Over Her Dead Body*.

21. Examples include Katharine Phillips and Mary Wortley Montague, both of whom were famous enough to suffer Pope's satire; Elizabeth Barrett Browning, who—during her lifetime—was far more popular and respected than her husband Robert Browning; Mary Butts, now forgotten Modernist.

22. I say particularly prone because it is not, of course, only women who suffer this fate. John Clare is a classic example of a working-class poet who was similarly erased from literary history.

23. Andy Croft, 'Some Responses are More Equal than Others', 2000, pp.51–2.

24. Rebecca O'Rourke, 'Mediums, Messages and Noisy Amateurs', p.283.

25. The shortlist included two lesbians, which certainly spiced up media coverage, but the powers-that-be played it safe and eventually chose Andrew Motion.

26. This claim is contradicted by recent anxieties about boys' lack of

interest in reading. Educationalists have suggested that the dominance of nineteenth-century romance fiction in exam syllabi discourages boys who are bored by such material.

27. Carol Ann Duffy suggests such constraints still exist; see chapter 2 for further discussion of this. Bernikow points out that, when love poetry was an exclusively male preserve, it possessed a high status; when the genre became identified with women, in the nineteenth century, their work was criticised for its sentimentality: *World Split Open*, p.6.

28. Bernikow, *World Split Open*, p.7.

29. Rebecca O'Rourke, 'Mediums, Messages and Nosey Amateurs', p.275.

30. Debbie Taylor, 'The problem with Poetry', p.9.

31. I have taken the feminist slogan to heart and assumed 'anon' was a woman in compiling these figures.

32. For an accessible introduction to her ideas, see Luce Irigaray, *Je, Tu, Nous*.

33. Don Paterson, 'The Dilemma of the Peot' [sic]. Paterson writes: 'I think one often writes sustained by necessary myths. With boys it's usually fairly straightforward, and usually involves dangling the tripartite carrot of money, sex and fame...from the end of your pencil: very atavistic urges, primarily concerned with the propagation of the genes, which have their origins in a tingling in the scrotum or the wallet. It's slightly different for girls, as they have a different part of the biological contract, and thus a different set of archetypes—ach, it'd be fun to go into this, but there isn't the space,' p.165.

34. Selima Hill, 'God's Velvet Cushions', p.30.

35. John Robert Glorney Bolton and Julia Bolton Holloway (eds), *Aurora Leigh and Other Poems*, Second Book, London, 1995, lines 90–1.

36. Carol Cosman, Joan Keefe and Kathleen Weaver (eds), *The Penguin Book of Women Poets*.

37. Cora Kaplan, *Salt and Bitter and Good: Three Centuries of English and American Women Poets*; Sandra Gilbert and Susan Gubar *Shakespeare's Sisters: Feminist Essays on Women Poets*.

38. Suzanne Juhasz, *Naked and Fiery Forms*, p.1.

39. Alicia Suskin Ostriker, *Stealing the Language*, p.239.

40. Examples include: Margaret Homans, *Women Writers and Poetic Identity*, Princeton, Princeton University Press, 1980; Mary K. De Shazer, *Inspiring Women: Reimagining the Muse: Selected prose 1979–1985*, New York, Pergamon, 1986; Adrienne Rich, *On Blood, Bread and Poetry*, New York, W.W. Norton, 1986; Marjorie Perloff, *Radical Artifice: Writing Poetry in the Age of the Media*, Chicago, Chicago University Press, 1991.

41. Claire Buck, 'Poetry and the Women's Movement in Postwar Britain', p.100.

42. Cora Kaplan, 'Language and Gender'.

43. Jan Montefiore, *Feminism and Poetry*.

44. Montefiore continues to explore the issue of separatism in women's poetry. In a recent essay on Adrienne Rich she sets out to prove the extent to which Rich's poetry draws on and responds to male predecessors. Yet it is Montefiore, not Rich, who seems to find this separatism a crucial issue; Rich herself does not claim to be uninfluenced by male poets or literary tradition. See '"Nothing to do with Eternity"? Adrienne Rich, "Feminism and Poetry"' in Mark and Rees-Jones, pp.101–18.

45. Liz Yorke, *Impertinent Voices*, p.51.

46. Examples of this 'second wave' of anthologies include Carol Rumens (ed.), *New Women Poets*, Bloodaxe, 1990; Ailbhe Smyth (ed.), *Wildish Things: An Anthology of New Irish Women's Writing*, Attic Press, 1989; Wendy Mulford (ed.), *The Virago Book of Love Poetry*, 1990; Black Womantalk (ed.), *Black Women Talk Poetry*, Blackwomantalk, 1987; Burford, MacRae and Paskin (eds), *Dancing the Tightrope: New Love Poems by Women*, Women's Press, 1987.

47. The best known is Rumens's infamous introduction to *Making for the Open*. Hostile reactions to what Rumens memorably described as 'the noisy amateurs' suggest how precarious the so-called established women poets like her must have been feeling, to fear contamination by association.

48. Lillian Mohin, *One Foot on the Mountain*, p.1.

49. Eavan Boland, 'The Woman Poet', p.44.

50. Adcock, *Twentieth-century Women's Poetry*; Sally Minogue, 'Prescriptions and Proscriptions: Feminist Criticism and Contemporary Poetry', in Minogue (ed.) *Problems for Feminist Criticism*, Routledge, 1990, pp.179–236.

51. Michèle Roberts, 'Questions and Answers', in Michelene Wandor (ed.) *On Gender and Writing*, pp.62–8.

52. See my essay, Vicki Bertram, 'Postfeminist Poetry?', pp.269–92, for further discussion.

53. Adrienne Rich, 'When We Dead Awaken'.

54. Eavan Boland, 'The Woman Poet', p.47.

55. On enrolment day for new Masters students, one expressed her misgivings about taking my course, on the grounds that she felt she ought to go for a 'broader, less partial' option.

56. Anne Stevenson, 'Defending the Freedom of the Poet/Music Under the Skin', Mark and Rees-Jones, p.3.

57. Carol Rumens, *Making for the Open*, p.xv.

58. Patience Agbabi is a good example: first rising to prominence as a performer, her second collection, *Transformatrix*, 2000, demonstrates a growing commitment to form. Seriousness and accomplishment are validated by the demonstration of expertise in poetic forms.

59. Vicki Bertram, 'Poetry to live your life by', p.61.

60. Romana Huk, 'Feminist Radicalism in (Relatively) Traditional

Forms, p.228.

61. Adrienne Rich, 'When We Dead Awaken', pp.40–1.

62. Eavan Boland, 'The Woman Poet in a National Tradition'.

63. Lillian Mohin, *One Foot*, p.1.

64. Marilyn Hacker, *Love, Death and the Changing of the Seasons*, W.W. Norton, 1995.

65. David Kennedy points this out in his analysis of the relationship between poetry and Harrison's masculinity, '*What Does the Fairy DO?*', p.123.

66. Don Paterson, 'The Dilemma of the Peot', p.162.

67. In his chapter on Heaney's conception of masculinity, Ian Gregson includes some discussion of this (specifically in relation to Heaney's essay, 'The Fire I' the Flint' which *depends* on this gendering). See Gregson, *The Male Image*.

68. David Brooks, 'Poetry and Sexual Difference'.

69. For example, Jane Dowson, *Women's Poetry of the 1930s: A Critical Anthology*, London and New York, Routledge, 1996; Jan Montefiore's *Men and Women Writers of the 1930s: The Dangerous Flood of History*, London and New York, Routledge, 1996. Alex Goody's work on Mina Loy is particularly interesting.

70. *Elizabeth Bishop: Poet of the Periphery*, Jo Shapcott and Linda Anderson (eds), Bloodaxe, 2000.

71. Bertram, *Kicking Daffodils, Feminist Review*, 'Contemporary Women Poets', issue 62, summer 1999.

72. Rebecca E. Wilson and Gillean Somerville-Arjat (eds), *Sleeping with Monsters*; Sharon Bryan (ed.), *Where We Stand: Women Poets on Literary Tradition*, New York, W.W. Norton, 1993; my own series of interviews for *P. N. Review*; occasional interviews in *Mslexia*. Creative writing guides include Susan Sellers (ed.), *Delighting the Heart: A Notebook for Women Writers*, The Women's Press, 1989; Sellers (ed.), *Taking Reality by Surprise: Writing for Pleasure and Publication*, The Women's Press, 1991.

73. Mark and Rees-Jones, *Contemporary Women's Poetry*.

74. Both have essays in the Elizabeth Bishop volume cited above; Rees-Jones is also working on a full-length study of twentieth-century women poets, *Consorting with Angels*, Newcastle-upon-Tyne, Bloodaxe, 2005.

75. Suzanne Juhasz, 'The Critic as Feminist', pp.114, 115.

76. In Bertram, '"Tidal Edges" in Contemporary Women's Poetry: towards a model of critical empathy' I tried to enact such a process. See *Women's Lives, Women's Times*, edited by Broughton and Anderson, SUNY, 1997.

77. Rebecca O'Rourke, 'Mediums, Messages and Noisy Amateurs', *Women*, p.280.

78. Anne Stevenson, 'Defending the Freedom of the Poet/Music Under the Skin', Mark and Rees-Jones (eds), p.3.

79. Rumens, *Making for the Open*, p.xvii.
80. Lynn Keller and Christanne Miller (eds), *Feminist Measures*.
81. Rachel DuPlessis, *Genders, Races and Religious Cultures in Modern American Poetry, 1908–1934*, Cambridge and New York, Cambridge University Press, 2001, p.12.
82. Critics like Ian Gregson and David Kennedy are noting the increasingly blurred line between 'lyric' and 'postmodern' poetries, so such definitions are becoming more problematic. I follow Keith Tuma's line: he points out that, even though critics have described several of these poets as postmodern writers, in terms of form their work is still fairly conventional, consisting mainly of short, self-contained lyrics. See Tuma, *Fishing by Obstinate Isles*.
83. Vicki Bertram, interview with Boland. In her published version, Boland rephrased what she initially said: 'Poetry is a superb form of experience. I don't write poems to express an experience; I write them to experience it.' p.15.
84. Ruth Padel, 'How and Why', p.13.
85. Marge Piercy (ed.), *Early Ripening*, p.2.
86. Peter Middleton, *The Inward Gaze*, p.11.
87. Rachel DuPlessis, '"Corpses of Poesy"', p.70.
88. Helen Haste, *The Sexual Metaphor*, p.39.
89. Jane Gallop, *Reading Lacan*, p.21. Peter Middleton adopts a similar strategy: 'I have used such awkward locutions as "men's modernism" and "men writers" throughout this book. Doing so underlines the possibly masculine character of many of what Genevieve Lloyd calls "cultural ideals of reason"', *The Inward Gaze*, p.11.
90. Anne Stevenson, in Marks and Rees-Jones, p.1.
91. Jan Montefiore, *Feminism and Poetry*, p.6.
92. Jane Gallop, *Reading Lacan*, pp.27, 28, 30.
93. Paul Muldoon, Oxford Poetry Lectures, January 2001. Some of these remarks were made during an interview about the forthcoming lecture, broadcast on BBC Radio 4's *Start the Week*, on 22 January 2001. Muldoon positions himself, interestingly, as the first reader, stepping onto virgin territory!
94. Sean O'Brien, *The Firebox*, p.379.
95. Tom Paulin, *Minotaur: Poetry and the Nation State*, Faber and Faber, 1992.
96. Sean O'Brien, *The Deregulated Muse*, p.256.
97. John Lennard, *The Poetry Handbook*, p.176.
98. Peter Middleton, *The Inward Gaze*, p.11.
99. I have conducted some experiments in the seminar room: giving students poems in which the poet 'crosses gender', and asking them to decide the sex of the author. Examples include Jackie Kay's 'Dance of the Cherry Blossom' and Duffy's 'Education for Leisure'. The students decide the sex of the poet on the basis of their gendering of

the speaker's sex, so most conclude that both poems are written by men. For further discussion of these issues see chapters 1 and 2; see also Alan Michael Parker and Mark Willhardt (eds), *The Routledge Anthology of Cross-Gendered Verse*, Routledge, 1996.

100. The Orange Prize 'Reading and Gender Survey', conducted March/April 1999, p.4.
101. Elizabeth Hirsch, 'Another Look at Genre', p.115.
102. Hélène Cixous, 'We Who Are Free, How Free Are We?'
103. Jane Gallop, *Feminism and Psychoanalysis: The Daughter's Seduction*, 1982, Ithaca, Cornell University Press, p.61.
104. Elizabeth Hirsch, *Feminist Measures*, p.118.
105. Gayatri Chakravorti Spivak, 'French Feminism in an International Frame', excerpted in Mary Eagleton (ed.), *Feminist Literary Criticism*, p.93.
106. Julia Kristeva, *Revolution in Poetic Language*, 1984.
107. For example, Helen Carr writes of being inundated with submissions during her time as editor of a national women's arts magazine: 'Poetic Licence', p.77.
108. Sara Mills, 'No Poetry for Ladies: Gertrude Stein, Julia Kristeva and Modernism', pp.85–107 in David Murray (ed.), *Literary Theory and Poetry*, pp.106–7.
109. At the time of writing, the commissioning editors for poetry are as follows: Faber and Faber: Matthew Hollis; Carcanet: Michael Schmidt; Bloodaxe: Neil Astley; Anvil: Peter Jay; Cape: Jason Arthur.
110. Jeni Couzyn (ed.), *The Bloodaxe Book of Contemporary Women Poets*, p.21.
111. A particularly good example of this is the tone of women poets recently commissioned by Bloodaxe: sassy and assertive, especially in relation to sexual matters. Sometimes the influence is quite significant: the cover image of a naked woman for Polly Clark's first collection, *Kiss*, was chosen by the publisher, not the poet. Similarly, while Fleur Adcock's name appears on the cover of *The Faber Book of Women's Poetry*, her commissioning editor Craig Raine exerted considerable influence over the final contents, deleting some 20 per cent of her choices.
112. Jane Dowson, 'Older Sisters', p.11.
113. Both have reviewed regularly for *Poetry Review*.
114. Betsy Erkkila, *The Wicked Sisters*.
115. See my article, 'Problems with (Girl) Friends: Contemporary Women Poets and Tensions in Female Friendship' in Heloise Brown, Ann Kaloski and Ruth Symes (eds), *Female Friendship*, Raw Nerve Books, 1999; repr. as 'Making Friends? Contemporary Women Poets' Difficulties with Friendship' in *Women's Studies International Forum*, 2000, vol.23, no.5, pp.629–44.
116. In *The Anxiety of Influence*, Harold Bloom outlined a model of

intergenerational struggle, in which the younger poet figuratively wrestles with his 'strongest' predecessor, deliberately misunderstanding him in order to overcome him and inscribe his own poems.

117. Sarah Maguire, 'Dilemmas and Developments', p.65.

118. For discussion of these issues in relation to women poets' performance work, see Bertram (ed.) 'A Round-table Discussion on Poetry in Performance: Jean Breeze, Patience Agbabi, Jillian Tipene, Ruth Harrison and Vicki Bertram', *Feminist Review*, no.62 (summer 1999) pp.24–54 and also Jean Binta Breeze, 'Can a Dub Poet be a Woman?', *Women: A Cultural Review*, vol.1, no.1, pp.47–9.

119. See, for example, 'Poetry and Paradox' in Woods' *A History of Gay Literature*, 1998. Here Woods argues that gay poets use paradox 'as weapon and shield against a world in which heterosexuality is taken for granted as being exclusively natural and healthy', p.376.

CHAPTER 1
FIRST IMPRESSIONS: GENDERING THE READING PROCESS

1. Helen Kidd, 'The Paper City: Women, Writing and Experience' in Robert Hampson and Peter Middleton, *New British Poetries: The Scope of the Possible*, Manchester, Manchester University Press, 1993, p.170.

2. Eavan Boland, 'Defining Circumstances', pp.14–16.

3. Cora Kaplan, 'Language and Gender', *Sea Changes: Culture and Feminism*, p.83.

4. Sarah Maguire, 'Dilemmas and Developments: Eavan Boland Re-examined', pp.58–66, *Feminist Review*, no.62, Summer 1999, p.64.

5. Eavan Boland, 'The Journey: Envoi', *Selected Poems*, p.90. See chapter 2 for a fuller discussion of this issue.

6. Some of the men poets considered in chapter 5 enact this 'marking' quite explicitly through metaphorical use of semen.

7. Don Paterson, *101 Sonnets*, p.xxiv.

8. The poem is Caroline Douglas's 'Blood', taken from *No Holds Barred*, a collection of work by women from all across Britain, gathered by the performers, The Raving Beauties, after the success of their first anthology, *In the Pink*. Mills's article, 'Reading as/like a feminist', pp.25–46 appears in Sara Mills (ed.), *Gendering the Reader*.

9. However, her findings echo research cited by Suzanne Juhasz, suggesting that there is a difference in the way males and females read. Juhasz quotes from David Bleich's 'Gender Interests in Reading and Language'. See '"Texts to Grow on": Reading Women's Romance Fiction', pp.239–59, *Tulsa Studies in Women's Literature*, vol.7, no.2 (Fall 1988).

10. As part of the questionnaire, Mills asked readers whether the poem was feminist. Eighty per cent of the females said yes; only one of the

males agreed. Their responses suggest that the label's effect would be to circumscribe its readership. One male reader answered, 'why categorise the feelings of being trapped by one's body as feminist?' Is he erasing the specific subject matter, or actually demonstrating his capacity to endow female experience with the capacity to transcend sex-specificity? Mills thinks it is the former, accusing him of an attempt 'to universalise the poem to human experience' (p.39). But if you accept that this sense of entrapment is partly what the poem is about, there's no need to call it feminist, since these feelings are not related to legal or political circumstances. Instead, his interpretation becomes a rare example of a specifically female situation being recognised as carrying an experience that transcends its sex-specificity.

11. Sara Mills, *Gendering the Reader*, p.5.
12. Although, as poet Clare MacDonald Shaw pointed out to me, editors often exert some control over the order in which poems are printed.
13. Michael Donaghy, 'Machines', *Shibboleth*, p.1.
14. Simon Armitage, 'Snow Joke', *Zoom!*.
15. Neil Rollinson, 'Like the Blowing of Birds' Eggs', *A Spillage of Mercury*.
16. A reader of this chapter suggested the poem could equally well be about two lesbians. To my mind the poem's syntax, manipulation of agency and imagery make this reading highly implausible. The central metaphor, with its suggestion of the destruction of an embryo, seems an unlikely figure, and the use of 'arse' and 'cunt', and the simile 'tense as a clock spring', while not impossible in a poem describing lesbian sex, all seem to me to suggest a male speaker. Something of the poem's claim to detachment also characterises Ted Hughes's tone in *Birthday Letters*. In both cases, men poets are writing about intimate relationships with women, and in both the male speakers retain their own opacity, while dissecting and publicly presenting the woman's. See chapter 4 for further discussion of this in relation to Hughes.
17. Fiona Pitt-Kethley, 'Sky Ray Lolly', *Sky Ray Lolly*, p.9.
18. Alan Robinson, *Instabilities in Contemporary British Poetry*, p.194.
19. Sujata Bhatt, 'Sujata: the First Disciple', *Brunizem*, p.9.
20. I am grateful to Poet Mahendra Solanki who helpfully interprets this vacillating tone in relation to Bhatt's complex migrations: from India, to the US, to Britain and then Germany, where she now lives. He describes a certain 'cultural unease' and an uncertainty over precisely who her audience might be, in these terms.
21. There are similarities with Jo Shapcott's 'Muse', in which the male muse is equally demanding and distracting. Sylvia Kantaris's 'The Tenth Muse'—an earlier take on the same theme—depicts a classic male chauvinist as her muse. See *The Tenth Muse*, Liskead, Peterloo Poets, 1983.
22. Kate Clanchy, *Slattern*, p.1.
23. Judith Fetterley, *The Resisting Reader*, p.xx.

24. Many pioneering women have also begun to challenge the proclaimed objectivity of such discourses. African-American lawyer Patricia Williams has produced compelling analyses of the way sexist and racist ideologies are integral to legal discourse. See *The Alchemy of Race and Rights*, Virago, 1993.

25. Luce Irigaray, *Je, Tu, Nous: Towards a Culture of Difference*, p.33.

26. Elizabeth Hirsh, 'Another Look at Genre: *Diving into the Wreck* of Ethics with Rich and Irigaray', pp.117–38 in Lynn Keller and Cristanne Miller (eds) *Feminist Measures: Soundings in Poetry and Theory*, p.120.

27. Vicki Feaver, *The Handless Maiden*, p.1.

28. This raises the vexed issue of essentialism. I am persuaded by poet Denise Riley's attitude in relation to this issue: 'Instead of veering between deconstruction and transcendence, we could try another train of speculations: that "women" is indeed an unstable category, that this instability has a historical foundation, and that feminism is the site of the systematic fighting-out of that instability.' See *"Am I That Name?" Feminism and the Category of "Women" in History*, 1988, Basingstoke, Macmillan, p.5.

29. Several examples are cited in the Introduction: reactions to *Sixty Women Poets*, supposed over-concentration on women's bodies, for one.

30. Spacks's dislike of Sexton's work—discussed in the Introduction—provides another example of a situation in which a woman's reaction seems at least partly based on her objection to feeling subsumed within a specifically female group.

31. Kate Clanchy's *Slattern* seems to fit this version of female liberation particularly well, with the title's connotations of sexual lasciviousness, and a certain raunchiness: the kind of woman who is proud of being a bit slovenly, and undomestic.

32. Patrocinio Schweickart, 'Reading Ourselves: Towards a Feminist Theory of Reading', pp.17–44 in Elaine Showalter (ed.), *Speaking of Gender*, 1989, London and New York, Routledge, p.38.

33. Alice Templeton, 'The Dream and the Dialogue: Rich's Feminist Poetics and Gadamer's Hermeneutics', Tulsa, *Studies in Women's Literature*, vol.7, no.2 (Fall 1988), pp.283–96. Her approach forms an interesting contrast with Irigaray's suggestion that poetry is essentially dialogic: see Introduction, p.35.

34. Lynne Pearce, *Feminism and the Politics of Reading*.

35. Nicole Ward Jouve, *Female Genesis*.

36. The work of Adrienne Rich offers the most famous example of such appeals. See chapter three for discussion of Grace Nichols in this respect.

37. Michèle Roberts, *The Book of Mrs Noah*, p.95.

38. Chris Baldick, *Oxford Concise Dictionary of Literary Terms*.

39. George Lakoff in Andrew Ortony (ed.), *Metaphor and Thought*, 1993, Cambridge, Cambridge University Press, pp.202–51.

40. Helen Haste, *The Sexual Metaphor*, p.56.

41. Mary Daly, *Pure Lust*, p.25.
42. Richard Bradford, *Stylistics*, p.26.
43. Gwyneth Lewis, 'Double Exposure', *Poetry Review*, vol.86, no.2 (summer) 1996.
44. Michèle Roberts, 'The long jump up to heaven', pp.25–7, *New Statesman*, 28 September 1984, p.26.
45. Paul Ricoeur, *The Rule of Metaphor*, p.7.
46. For discussion of the problems with this assumption of the transparency of language see, for example, Margaret Homans, *Woman Writers and Poetic Identity*, 1980, or Toril Moi, *Sexual/Textual Politics*, Methuen, 1985.
47. Eavan Boland, 'The Woman Poet in a National Tradition', pp.148–58, *Studies* (Dublin), summer 1987, p.152.
48. Voth Harman, 'Delivering the Mother: Three Anthologies of Birth Poetry', pp.178–88 in Vicki Bertram (ed.), *Kicking Daffodils*.
49. Ward Jouve, *Female Genesis*, p.192.
50. For some examples of lesbian poets' new metaphors, see Caroline Halliday, 'The Naked Majesty of God'.
51. Exchanges between Sheenagh Pugh and John Hartley Williams were published in *Poetry Review* during the spring and summer of 1996. See vol.86, no.2 (summer 1996), p.96 for a characteristic sample.
52. Angeline Kelly (ed.), *Pillars of the House*.
53. Metonymy and synecdoche deal only with objects/nouns, whereas metaphor can use all parts of speech. Baldick defines metonymy as 'a figure of speech that replaces the name of one thing with the name of something else closely associated with it' (*Oxford Dictionary of Literary Terms*, 1990). It is metaphor that is the most potentially innovative, because it posits totally new resemblances between ideas, whereas metonymy draws on pre-existing associations.
54. Rita Ann Higgins, *Sunny Side Plucked*, p.42.
55. Jouissance: ecstasy (sexual); coming; enjoyment (of rights, property, etc.) Definition taken from Catherine Belsey and Jane Moore (eds), *The Feminist Reader* (second edn), 1997, Glossary. Higgins's poem also gestures towards its predecessors, like John Donne's 'The Baite': where his poem casts the woman as bait, Higgins's riposte is spirited. The conventional warnings to women about the transitory quality of their beauty are transformed into the advice to make the most of the long nights of winter.by taking two lovers home on the shortest day.
56. Sujata Bhatt, 'White Asparagus', in *Monkey Shadows*, p.98.

CHAPTER 2
THROWN VOICES: DRAMATIC MONOLOGUES
BY CAROL ANN DUFFY, JACKIE KAY AND
JO SHAPCOTT

1. Both Kathleen Bell and Jane Dowson presented papers exploring the
   mode at a conference on 'Contemporary British Women Writers'
   University of Leicester, July 2000. Bell's was on U. A. Fanthorpe and
   Sheenagh Pugh: 'Writing From the Margins'; Dowson's on 'The
   Dialogic in Contemporary Women's Poetry'.
2. Alan Sinfield, *Dramatic Monologue*, p.8.
3. A good example of this—though there are many—is poet Mario
   Petrucci's prize-winning poem, 'The Confession of Borislav Herak'.
   Written in the voice of a camp commander, the poem provoked
   complaints from a Yugoslav couple when it was read out loud at a
   prize-giving ceremony. The judges defended the poem on the grounds
   that they were tired of poems about *representations* of war, experienced at one remove, and that poets should risk attempting such
   testimonials. The judges' reaction implies boredom with the safety
   and ease of most people's lives in Britain, and a yearning for engage-
   ment with more immediate, real events. However, there is obviously
   a very fine line between imaginative empathy and appropriation.
4. Nicole Ward Jouve makes a similar point in her introduction to *White
   Woman Speaks with Forked Tongue: Criticism as Autobiography*,
   Routledge, 1991. 'We have lost ourselves in the endlessly diffracted
   light of Deconstruction. I say "we" meaning all of us, but especially
   women. For we have been asked to go along with Deconstruction
   whilst we had not even got to the Construction stage.' p.7.
5. Earlier examples include poems by HD and Stevie Smith; later examples can be found in poems by Anne Sexton, Sylvia Kantaris, Judith
   Kazantzis, and Jenny Joseph.
6. Alicia Suskin Ostriker, *Stealing the Language: The Emergence of
   Women's Poetry in America*, p.210.
7. Jan Montefiore, *Feminism and Poetry*, p.56.
8. Diane Purkiss, 'Women's Rewriting of Myth', in Carolyne Larrington
   (ed.), *The Feminist Companion to Mythology*, Pandora, pp.441–57, 1992.
9. Carol Ann Duffy, *The World's Wife*.
10. Eavan Boland, 'The Woman Poet: Her Dilemma', *Stand* magazine,
    winter 1986–7, pp.43–9.
11. Emily Dickinson and Sylvia Plath have proved particularly irresistible
    targets for this style of criticism.
12. 'Defining Circumstances: an interview with Eavan Boland', *P.N.
    Review*, vol.25 (2), 14–16, December 1998.
13. Sharon Olds and Adrienne Rich are good North American examples
    of the same phenomenon. Sujata Bhatt also makes frequent use of the

first person in her poems, but her voice is far more inconsistent: uneven in its tone, moving between assertion and hesitancy in a way that does much to complicate its character. She has explained that the 'I' is not identical to her sense of herself, but is a more confident voice: 'I believe that the "I" in my poems is someone different from the "I" in my prose, and is not exactly the "I" who lives in the world. In fact, sometimes I wish that in my daily life I could be as confident as the voice in my poems.' 'Sujata Bhatt in conversation with Vicki Bertram', *P.N. Review*, vol.27, no.4 , March–April 2001, pp.36–43. p.40.

14. Cora Kaplan, 'Language and Gender', *Sea Changes: Essays on Culture and Feminism*, p.82.

15. Plath's 'Mushrooms' is a good example, in which the fungi speak, and an insignificant attribute of the species—its fast growth—is endowed with threatening power. *Collected Poems*, 1981, p.139.

16. Lesley Jeffries has suggested that Duffy's use of 'you' is intended to draw the reader into the action. See 'Point of View and the Reader in the Poetry of Carol Ann Duffy', pp.54–68 in Lesley Jeffries and Peter Sansom (eds), *Contemporary Poems: Some Critical Approaches*, 2000. In an interview, Duffy herself said that the strategy was not deliberate: 'Not at the time of writing the poem, which at that stage...is more of a dialogue with myself. The 'you' being perhaps the me that haunts the poem being addressed, or re-created, by the me who is recollecting in tranquility.' *Verse*, vol.8, no.2, 1991 p.127.

17. Duffy, *Standing Female Nude*.

18. Duffy, *Selling Manhattan*, 1987. There are 17 monologues in *Standing Female Nude*; 22 in *Selling Manhattan*, counted according to Sinfield's definition of any poem in which the first-person speaker is clearly not the poet herself.

19. This kind of poetic gender-crossing has been the subject of a recent anthology. Alan Michael Parker and Mark Willhardt, editors of *The Routledge Anthology of Cross-Gendered Verse*, Routledge, 1996, make some grand claims for its potential:

'Cross-gender verse may escape the dualism of "male" and "female" subjectivity because the poem's 'I' is never fully embodied, male or female. It is rather a blending of the two, a place which demands refining our suppositions regarding gender.' p.202.

The theory sounds exciting, but they do not come up with any convincing examples of this much-desired, much-theorised 'third place', even though they describe it later as a 'transcendent poetic gesture' (p.210). I do not think Duffy is trying to create an ungendered voice in these poems. Her love poems are a different matter: in many of these, gender remains unmarked.

20. Andrew MacAllister, 'Carol Ann Duffy: An interview', in *Bête Noire*, winter 1988, issue 6, p.70.

21. The influence of her environment during her apprentice years proba-

bly played a big part in this. She hung out with the Liverpool poets who, while iconoclastic and political, were all men; gender was not on their agenda.

22. Ian Gregson, *The Male Image*, p.160.
23. R.P. Draper, *An Introduction to Twentieth-century Poetry in English*, pp.151–3.
24. Alan Robinson, *Instabilities in Contemporary British Poetry*, p.196.
25. Carol Ann Duffy, *Standing Female Nude*, p.34.
26. Carol Ann Duffy, *Standing Female Nude*, p.35.
27. Deryn Rees-Jones, *Carol Ann Duffy*.
28. In the McAllister interview, Duffy explains that she deliberately set the poem in the past in order to avoid the risk of seeming to exploit a contemporary sex crime. See note 20 above.
29. Ian Gregson, *The Male Image*, p.160.
30. See, for example, Jane Thomas, "'The Intolerable Wrestle with Words'": The Poetry of Carol Ann Duffy', pp.78–88, *Bête Noire*, no.6, Winter 1988; Ian Gregson, *Contemporary Poetry and Postmodernism*; Deryn Rees-Jones, *Carol Ann Duffy*.
31. Although, in his history of ventriloquism, Steve Connor observes that it was only in the 19th century that ventriloquist practitioners became solely male, and—perhaps not coincidentally—the dummy was introduced. *Dumbstruck: A Cultural History of Ventriloquism*, Oxford, Oxford University Press, 2000.
32. Andrew MacAllister, Carol Ann Duffy: An interview, p.70.
33. Carol Ann Duffy, *Thrown Voices*, p.5.
34. Alan Sinfield, *Dramatic Monologue*, p.67.
35. Carol Ann Duffy, *The Other Country*, p.19.
36. Duffy, *Mean Time*, p.25. Sean O'Brien suggests that the 'edge of estrangement' in Duffy's work may stem from her childhood experience of migration south from Scotland; he describes her as 'neither uprooted or rootless, but not having taken root'. *The Deregulated Muse*, p.160. Certainly it is likely that rootlessness contributes to the ease with which she throws her voice.
37. *The Other Country*; *Mean Time*.
38. There are 9 dramatic monologues in *The Other Country*, as well as 16 poems in a first person voice, and another 10 in the second person, a kind of self-address. There are 9 dramatic monologues in *Mean Time*; 15 in a first person voice not clearly distinguishable from the poet herself.
39. Alan Sinfield, *Dramatic Monologue*, p.71.
40. Carol Ann Duffy, *The World's Wife*, p.3.
41. Angela Carter, *The Sadeian Woman*, p.5.
42. Carol Ann Duffy, *The World's Wife*, p.7.
43. Katharine Viner, 'Metre Maid', 25 September 1999, *Guardian Weekend*.
44. Jackie Kay, *The Adoption Papers*.

45. Gabrielle Griffin, 'In/Corporation? Jackie Kay's The Adoption Papers', in Vicki Bertram (ed.), *Kicking Daffodils*, pp.169–77.
46. Jackie Kay, *The Adoption Papers*, p.56.
47. Jackie Kay, *Off Colour*.
48. Jackie Kay, 'Crown and Country', *Off Colour*, p.14.
49. Jackie Kay, *Off Colour*, p.10.
50. Jackie Kay, 'The Black Chair', *Off Colour*, p.17.
51. This is not the same as suggesting the woman functions as symbol for Scottishness; Kay's poems are far too alert to the power dynamics of literary representation.
52. Jackie Kay, 'Race, Racist, Racism', *Off Colour*, p.21.
53. Sian Hughes, 'Language as Virus', pp.98–9, *Poetry Review*, vol.88, no.4, Winter 1998–99.
54. Jackie Kay, *Off Colour*, p.62.
55. This is something North American critic Rachel Blau DuPlessis has been arguing for critics to take on board. She points out that lyrics have 'often been privileged by the critical assumption of their timeless, universal emotions and nonparticipation in historical debate.' Her own work attempts to recontextualise poetic texts, in order to explore 'the cultural work done by poems'. '"Corpses of Poesy": Some Modern Poets and Some Gender Ideologies of Lyric', pp.69–95, Lynn Keller and Cristanne Miller (eds) *Feminist Measures*, pp.70–1.
56. Michael Hofmann, back cover to Jo Shapcott, *Her Book: Poems 1988–1998*, Faber and Faber, 2000.
57. The exceptions are 'Tom and Jerry Visit England'; 'Brando on Commuting', and 'Superman Sounds Depressed', pp.39, 43, 46 respectively, Shapcott, *Her Book*.
58. Ian Gregson, *Contemporary Poetry and Postmodernism*, p.239.
59. Jo Shapcott, 'Thetis', *Her Book*, p.87.
60. Interestingly, Duffy has also produced a version of the same myth; in her telling, the poem ends with a graphic description of the goddess split open by childbirth. See 'Thetis', *The World's Wife*.
61. Jo Shapcott, *Her Book*, p.97.
62. Jo Shapcott, *Her Book*, p.58.
63. Sean O'Brien, *The Deregulated Muse*, p.256.
64. Jo Shapcott, *Her Book*, p.53.
65. There are similarities here with Plath's deliberate self-display in poems like 'Lady Lazarus', satirising the ubiquity of the woman as an object of spectacle, though Shapcott's versions are obviously less sensational.
66. See, for example, 'Her Lover's Ear', *Her Book*, p.55. Other examples of the dominance of touch over sight include 'Room', p.59; 'Muse', p.58; 'Matter', p.57; 'Life', p.100.
67. Jo Shapcott, 'Mad Cow Dance', 'Tom and Jerry Visit England', 'A

Walk in the Snow', *Her Book*, pp.73, 39, 77 respectively.
68. Jo Shapcott, 'Tom and Jerry Visit England', *Her Book*, p.39.
69. Jo Shapcott, *Her Book*, pp.55–6.
70. Jo Shapcott, *Her Book*, p.52.

CHAPTER 3
CARIBBEAN COMPARISONS: GRACE NICHOLS
AND DAVID DABYDEEN

1. This is regardless of the fact that both have signalled their unease
   with such labels. Nichols's poem 'Of course when they ask for poems
   about the "realities" of black women' conveys her mistrust of gener-
   alities based on these kinds of groupings (*Lazy Thoughts of a Lazy
   Woman*, p.52). At an Asian Writing conference hosted by Dabydeen,
   University of Warwick, 1990, he expressed misgivings about the
   constraining implications of the label West Indian, in terms of prescrib-
   ing certain themes and subject matter.
2. See Nichols's mischievous poem 'With Apologies to Hamlet', whose
   opening lines 'To pee or not to pee / That is the question', are more
   characteristic of the extent and nature of her literary allusiveness.
   Lazy Thoughts of a Lazy Woman, p.6.
3. For discussion of Nichols's use of Creole, see Paraskevi Papaleonida,
   '"holding my beads in my hand": 'Dialogue, Synthesis and Power in
   the Poetry of Jackie Kay and Grace Nichols', in Vicki Bertram (ed.),
   Kicking Daffodils, pp.125–39.
4. Eavan Boland has complained of the same thing in relation to Irish literary
   tradition. See 'The Woman Poet in a National Tradition', *Studies* (Dublin).
5. Nana Wilson-Tagoe, 'Configurations of History in the Writing of West
   Indian Women', *Historical Thought and Literary Representation in
   West Indian Literature*, pp.250–1.
6. Beryl Gilroy, 'The Woman Writer and Commitment: Links between
   Caribbean and African literature', *Wasafiri*, no.10 (Summer 1989), pp.15–16.
7. See, for example, Hilary McD. Beckles, 'White Women and Slavery
   in the Caribbean', in Verene Shepherd and Hilary McD. Beckles's
   Caribbean Slavery in the Atlantic World. Beckles notes that 'the entire
   ideological fabric of the slave-based civilisation was conceived in terms
   of sex, gender and race. This was the only way that black slavery and
   white patriarchy could coexist without encountering major legal
   contradictions.' p.661. He explains that rules about white women's
   behaviour and appearance were devised in order to emphasise their
   differentiation from black women.
8. David Dabydeen, *Slave Song*, p.10.
9. See, for example, Chinweizu, 'Decolonizing African Literature',
   pp.279–88 in Walder, *Literature in the Modern World: Critical Essays
   and Documents*, Oxford, Oxford University Press, 1990.

10. I am grateful to Desmond Bermingham for this information.
11. Lauretta Ncobo (ed.), *Let It Be Told: Essays by Black Women in Britain*, p.102. This use of a collective 'we' makes her unusual; as argued in chapter 1, most British women's poetry tends to avoid the use of a collective female voice.
12. 'The fictional women who do not react self-destructively to disasters save themselves because of their strong connection with other women in their cultures.' 'Twentieth-Century Women Writers from the English-Speaking Caribbean', Laura Niesen de Abruna, in Selwyn R. Cudjoe, *Caribbean Women Writers: Essays From the First International Conference*, p.90. De Abruna concentrates on prose writers, and takes pains to point out that the interrelationships are certainly not idealised, but often describe difficult over-identifications; in this respect, Nichols's poem is different.
13. There are obvious parallels here, of course, with Toni Morrison's *Beloved*, Picador/Chatto and Windus, 1987.
14. 'Some of the publishers who rejected it, including Oxford University Press, one of the reasons they gave, even though they liked the book, was that this area, or this journey, was already covered by the poet Edward Brathwaite. Edward Brathwaite is a poet I like I but I was coming from a very female perspective, and it was exploring the whole *female* psyche, so I couldn't see their rationale at all.' 'Grace Nichols in conversation with Maggie Butcher', *Wasafiri*, no.8 (Spring 1988), p.18.
15. Edward Kamau Brathwaite, *The Arrivants: A New World Trilogy*, first published in serial form 1967–9; Oxford, Oxford University Press, 1973.
16. It is worth comparing Jean Binta Breeze's epic poem, 'A River Called Wise', for another bold example of a Caribbean woman poet's revisionist work. See Paula Burnett's discussion of the piece, 'Epic, a Woman's Place: A Study of Derek Walcott's *Omeros*' and Jean Binta Breeze's 'A River Called Wise', in Vicki Bertram, *Kicking Daffodils*, pp.140–52.
17. David Dabydeen and Wilson-Tagoe, *A Reader's Guide to West Indian and Black British Literature*, 1988, p.45. It seems they failed to notice that what the poem does is restore agency to these slave women.
18. Patrick Williams, 124/5, 'Difficult Subjects: Black British Women's Poetry' in David Murray (ed.), *Literary Theory and Poetry: Extending the Canon*, pp.108–26.
19. Grace Nichols, *Lazy Thoughts*, p.32.
20. Indenture, which became known as simply a new form of slavery, operated between 1836 and 1917. Indians were often recruited by force or kidnap, and were ignorant of where they were being taken. On arrival in the Caribbean, they were indentured to an 'owner' for five years. Planters encouraged hostility between the African and Indian populations, and attempted to socialise the latter into a more 'tractable' workforce than the former slaves had proved to be. There were acute shortages of female Indian workers, leading to intense rivalry and jealousy amongst males. (Information taken from Brinsley Samaroo,

'Two Abolitions: African Slavery and East Indian Indentureship', in Dabydeen and Samaroo (ed.), *India in the Caribbean*, pp.25–41.)

21. It is clear that the people in these songs are of Indian extraction because of the Hindu religious rituals and food referred to throughout, as well as from the fact that the plantations continue to be worked by Indo-Guyanese labourers, as opposed to Afro-Guyanese or members of other ethnic groups.

22. David Dabydeen, 'On Not Being Milton: Nigger Talk in England Today', in Ricks and Michaels (eds), *The State of the Language*, 1990, Faber and Faber, p.4.

23. David Dabydeen, 'On Not Being Milton', p.5.

24. Mark McWatt, 'Self-Consciously Post-Colonial': The Fiction of David Dabydeen', in Kevin Grant (ed.), *The Art of David Dabydeen*, 1997, Leeds, Peepal Tree Press, p.111–22.

25. David Dabydeen, *Slave Song*, p.10.

26. A similar version of the white woman as sexualised maternal figure appears in his next collection, *Coolie Odyssey*, discussed below.

27. Frank Birbalsingh, *Frontiers of Caribbean Literature in English*, p.172.

28. David Dabydeen, *Slave Song*, p.70.

29. Benita Parry, 'Between Creole and Cambridge English: The Poetry of David Dabydeen', *Kunapipi*, vol.x, no.3, 1988, p.6; reprinted in Grant (ed.), *The Art of David Dabydeen*.

30. I am grateful to Lynnette Turner for pointing this out to me.

31. Angela Carter, *The Sadeian Woman*, p.19–20.

32. Dabydeen, 'On Writing *Slave Song*', p.47.

33. See Hilary McD. Beckles, 'White Women and Slavery in the Caribbean', in Verene Shepherd and Hilary McD. Beckles's *Caribbean Slavery in the Atlantic World*, p.661.

34. David Dabydeen, 'For Mala', *Slave Song*, p.19.

35. David Dabydeen, 'Guyana Pastoral', *Slave Song*, p.21.

36. David Dabydeen, 'On Writing *Slave Song*', p.46.

37. David Dabydeen, 'On Not Being Milton', p.11.

38. Edward Kamau Brathwaite had coined the term 'nation language' as a more respectful description, in *The History of the Voice: The Development of Nation Language in Anglophone Caribbean Poetry*, New Beacon, 1984.

39. David Dabydeen, 'On Writing *Slave Song*', p.46–7.

40. David Dabydeen, 'On Not Being Milton', p.13.

41. Frank Birbalsingh, *Frontiers of Caribbean Literature in English*, p.172.

42. David Dabydeen, 'On Writing *Slave Song*', p.47.

43. David Dabydeen, *Slave Song*, p.53.

44. Carolyn Cooper, *Noises in the Blood: Orality, Gender and the 'Vulgar' Body of Jamaican Popular Culture*, 1993, p.9; cited by Denise DeCaires Narain, 'Caribbean Creole: The Real Thing? Writing and Reading the Creole in a Selection of Caribbean Women's Texts', in Susheila Nasta (ed.), 'Reading the 'New' literatures in a Postcolonial Era', *Essays and*

Studies 2000, p.107.

45. Christian Habekost (ed.), *Dub Poetry: 19 Poets From England and Jamaica*, 1987, Neustadt, Michael Schwinn. Cited by Narain, 'Caribbean Creole', p.108.

46. Narain, 'Caribbean Creole', p.121.

47. Grace Nichols, in Ncobo (ed.), *Let It Be Told*, p.97. It is worth comparing the Trinidadian poet Marlene Nourbese Philip, who is similarly preoccupied with efforts to decolonise the English language. She subjects language to systematic analysis, on the grounds that the rules that govern grammar and punctuation are just as much the invention of the colonisers as are the plantations. Her revisions are thoughtful and studied, rather than aggressive. Like Nichols, she emphasises the physicality of language and tries to reintegrate word and flesh. See 'She Tries Her Tongue', 'Discourse on the Logic of Language' and 'Universal Grammar' from *She tries her tongue, her silence softly breaks*, London, The Women's Press, 1993.

48. Grace Nichols, 'The Assertion', *The Fat Black Woman's Poems*, p.8.

49. For an infamous example of this kind of depiction of African womanhood, see Joseph Conrad's description of Kurtz' African mistress in *Heart of Darkness*. At the end of the description, he makes explicit the correlation between woman and land: 'And in the hush that had fallen suddenly upon the whole sorrowful land, the immense wilderness, the colossal body of the fecund and mysterious life seemed to look at her, pensive, as though it had been looking at the image of its own tenebrous and passionate soul.' J. M. Dent, 1974, p.104.

50. Stevie Smith and Wendy Cope have suffered a similar lack of attention. Poets whose self-presentation is comic or 'light' do not get taken seriously by the critical establishment. The work that does exist on these poets has been produced by feminist critics, and is published in feminist essay collections that remain quite separate from (and ignored by) mainstream poetry criticism, as I pointed out in the Introduction.

51. Grace Nichols, *The Fat Black Woman's Poems*, 'Thoughts drifting through the fat black woman's head while having a full bubble bath', p.15.

52. Compare Jackie Kay's poem 'Hottentot Venus', drawing attention to the derivations of this abusive white European name for the Khoikhoi people (*Off Colour*, 1998); and Marlene Nourbese Philip's use of the phrase 'prognathous jaws' in 'Testimony Stoops' (*She tries her tongue, her silence softly breaks*, London, The Women's Press, 1993.). The dictionary defines prognathous as a person having a projecting lower jaw or chin. By using these colonial coinages, the poets force readers to consider the histories hidden in language.

53. Grace Nichols, *The Fat Black Woman's Poems*, 'Invitation', p.13.

54. She made this comment at readings during the early 1990s.

55. African-American poet Maya Angelou has created similarly voluptuous female characters in her poetry. Feminist psychologist Kim Chernin has suggested that it is fear of the maternal capacities of adult

women that makes western culture opt for the underdeveloped adolescent girl's body as its ideal of female desirability. See *Womansize: The Tyranny of Slenderness*, The Women's Press, 1983.

56. Grace Nichols, *The Fat Black Woman's Poems*, p.7.
57. John Berger, *Ways of Seeing*, Harmondsworth, Penguin,1972, p.47.
58. Grace Nichols, *Lazy Thoughts of a Lazy Woman*, p.16. n.58
59. Grace Nichols, *Lazy Thoughts of a Lazy Woman*, p.32.
60. Grace Nichols, *Lazy Thoughts of a Lazy Woman*, p.25.
61. Grace Nichols, *Lazy Thoughts of a Lazy Woman*, p.37.
62. Grace Nichols, *Lazy Thoughts of a Lazy Woman*, p.11.
63. Grace Nichols, *Lazy Thoughts of a Lazy Woman*, p.10.
64. Grace Nichols, *Lazy Thoughts of a Lazy Woman*, p.47.
65. Grace Nichols, 'Hurricane', unpublished, and delivered at readings during the 1990s.
66. Grace Nichols, *Lazy Thoughts*, p.31.
67. David Dabydeen, *Coolie Odyssey*, p.10.
68. Wilson Harris, *Coolie Odyssey*, cover blurb.
69. David Dabydeen, *Coolie Odyssey*, p.34.
70. David Dabydeen, 'Rebel Love', *Coolie Odyssey*, p.35. 'Coolie' is a derogatory term for Indo-Guyanese.
71. David Dabydeen, 'The Seduction', *Coolie Odyssey*, p.30.
72. David Dabydeen, 'Miranda', *Coolie Odyssey*, p.33.
73. David Dabydeen, 'On Not Being Milton', p.13.
74. David Dabydeen, 'Coolie Odyssey', *Coolie Odyssey*, pp.9–13. In Dabydeen's reworking, the tragic dimensions of Odysseus' journeyings are foregrounded: this Odysseus no longer knows where 'home' is.
75. David Dabydeen, 'Homecoming', *Coolie Odyssey*, p.43.
76. David Dabydeen, 'The New Poetry', *Coolie Odyssey*, p.28.
77. David Dabydeen, 'New World Words', *Coolie Odyssey*,p.37.
78. David Dabydeen, 'The Sexual Word', *Coolie Odyssey*, p.32.
79. Grace Nichols's male lover in 'Configurations' also repeats the past, when he 'does a Columbus', but—in keeping with her more optimistic outlook—the woman tolerates his mimicry and is not offended by it.
80. David Dabydeen, *Turner*, p.ix.
81. David Dabydeen, *Turner*, p.21.
82. Derek Walcott, 'Another Life', p.145; from Louis James, *Caribbean Literature in English*.
83. Dabydeen makes this explicit in his preface, p.x. It is interesting that, once again (as in *Slave Song*), he makes use of an expository section to add further interpretative material to the poems.
84. The experience of the mother during slavery has been widely explored by postcolonial women writers, most famously by Toni Morrison in *Beloved*. See Judith Wilt for further examples which likewise stage a difficult meeting between slave mother and her dead child. *Abortion, Choice and Contemporary Fiction: The Armageddon of the maternal*

instinct, Chicago, University of Chicago Press, 1990. Dabydeen's treatment is very different: he employs the mother-figure as a metaphor.

85. David Dabydeen, *Turner*, p.33.

86. Karen McIntyre, 'Necrophilia or Stillbirth? David Dabydeen's *Turner* as the Embodiment of Postcolonial Creative Decolonisation', in Kevin Grant (ed.), *The Art of David Dabydeen*, p.146.

87. Another Guyanese poet, John Agard, has produced genuinely androgynous characters: Limbo Dancer defies gender categorisation along with all other forms of (colonially imported) classification. His depictions of spider Anansi assuming human forms also successfully avoid subscribing to fixed gender roles. See *Weblines*, Newcastle-upon-Tyne, Bloodaxe, 2000.

88. I am grateful to Lynnette Turner for drawing my attention to this interpretation of the painting.

89. Grace Nichols, *Lazy Thoughts of a Lazy Woman*, pp.32, 33. See also 'Behind the Mask', p.55. In this way, by varying the constituency on behalf of which she speaks, Nichols avoids the dangers she recognises in the urge to label particular groups of individuals.

90. For a description of Harold Bloom's Freudian thesis, see the introduction, p.40.

91. Derek Walcott, 'The Muse of History', quoted in Dabydeen (ed.), *Handbook for Teaching Caribbean Literature*.

92. Stewart Brown, in Dabydeen (ed.), *Handbook for Teaching Caribbean Literature*, p.100.

93. Grace Nichols, *I Is a Long Memoried Woman*.

94. Belinda Edmondson, *Making Men: Gender, Literary Authority and Women's Writing in Caribbean Narrative*. Edmondson asks, 'Does it mean the same thing for West Indian women to read Milton et al. as it does West Indian men?' She contends that the terms of writing for West Indian males 'are founded on the interpolated meanings of manhood and cultural authority that have been passed on to them from British intellectual discourse of the nineteenth century...That English "vision" of intellectual authority is the idea that intellectual labor is the realm of "real" men, "gentlemen", middle-class / upper-class Englishmen.' (p.5.) A classic example of such absorption in Victorian sensibilities is found in the work of V. S. Naipaul.

95. Caryl Phillips, interview, in Frank Birbalsingh, *Frontiers of Caribbean Literature in English*, p.195–6.

96. Jamaica Kincaid, in Frank Birbalsingh, *Frontiers of Caribbean Literature in English*, p.139. Kincaid says she felt that in England, 'You cannot express anger at your historical situation...there isn't anything about us, any reflection about our past that England or places like that used to accept.'

97. Nichols's evocations of the voluptuous Fat Black Woman are strikingly reminiscent of Angelou's depiction of similarly sensuous large

women, see note 55. 'On Poems and Crotches' is dedicated to Shange. There are also thematic parallels with Toni Morrison's work. However the turn to North American writers may be partly explained by the lack of visibility and networks between Caribbean women writers: often they did not know of one another's work.

CHAPTER 4
THE INTIMATE AUTHORITY OF TED HUGHES'S *BIRTHDAY LETTERS*

1. See, for example, Andrew Motion, 'A Thunderbolt from the blue: this book will live forever', *The Times*, 17 January 1998; Seamus Heaney, 'A wounded power rises from the depths', *Irish Times*, 31 January 1998; Sarah Maguire, 'An Old Fresh Grief', *Guardian Books*, 22 January 1998.
2. 'Whitbread completes clean sweep for Ted Hughes', *Guardian*, 27 January 1999.
3. Ian Sansom, 'I was there, I saw it', *London Review of Books*, 19 February 1998.
4. This readership is, of course, not necessarily the same as that audience familiar with the poetry of Plath and/or Hughes. It is much larger, and will be unaware of the extent to which the *Birthday Letters* are, as I go on to show, rewritings of Plath's poems.
5. The film *Betty Blue* provides another famous contemporary version of the same story.
6. Sylvia Plath, *Collected Poems*, p.295.
7. 'Night-Ride on Ariel', p.175; 'The Bee God', p.152, both from Ted Hughes, *Birthday Letters*.
8. Ted Hughes, 'Black Coat', *Birthday Letters*, p.102.
9. Sylvia Plath, 'Man in Black', *Collected Poems*, p.120.
10. Ted Hughes and Frances McCullough (eds), *The Journals of Sylvia Plath*. See entry for 23 April, 1959.
11. Louise Glück, 'Invitation and Exclusion', *Proofs and Theories*, pp.113–23.
12. Vicki Bertram, 'Defining Circumstances: An interview with Eavan Boland', *P. N. Review,* vol.25, no.2, 14–16 December 1998.
13. Consider Adrienne Rich's description of the poet's task: 'if the imagination is to transcend and transform experience it has to question, to challenge, to conceive of alternatives, perhaps to the very life you are living at that moment. You have to be free to play around with the notion that day might be night, love might be hate; nothing can be too sacred for the imagination to turn into its opposite or to call experimentally by another name.' 'When We Dead Awaken: Writing as Re-Vision', *On Lies, Secrets and Silence*, p.43.
14. Louise Glück, 'Invitation and Exclusion', p.123.

15. Ruth Padel, 'Telling not Showing', *Independent on Saturday Magazine*, 31 January 1998, p.7.

16. It is a characteristic I identify in Neil Rollinson's work and, to a lesser degree, Don Paterson's too. See chapter 5 for a fuller discussion of this.

17. Deryn Rees-Jones, 'Consorting with Angels: Anne Sexton and the Art of Confession', *Women: A Cultural Review*, vol.10, no.3 (winter 1999), p.285.

18. Plath kept her marriage secret at first, out of fear that the Cambridge or Fullbright authorities would remove her scholarship if they knew she had become a wife. It is easy to forget how difficult it was for women to be taken seriously—as intellectuals, or writers—during these years.

19. John Sutherland, 'Do I know you, Ms Plath?', *Guardian*, 27 March 2000. Sutherland uses the phrase to include Plath's work, but I disagree with this suggestion.

20. Ted Hughes, 'Crow Tries the Media', *Crow*, p.46. The exact quotation is 'words/Waving their long tails in public / with their prostitute's exclamations'.

21. Ted Hughes, *Crow*. See 'Two Eskimo Songs', p.93; 'Crow Hears Fate Knock on the Door', p.23; 'Crow's Account of St. George', p.32; 'Fragment of An Ancient Tablet', p.85. Surprisingly, Gregson reads *Crow* as 'a brilliant examination of the damage caused by the attempts of masculinity to define itself against, and establish its independence from femininity'. (p.82) and comments, 'What is most importantly missing is the creative and regenerative spirit of the feminine.' (p.82). This seems to overlook the frequent associative link made in the poems between femininity, violence and death. Ian Gregson, *The Male Image*.

22. Neil Corcoran, *English Poetry Since 1940*, p.119.

23. See, for example, Ted Hughes, 'Crow's Nerve Fails', *Crow*, p.47.

24. Alison Wertheimer, *A Special Scar: The Experiences of People Bereaved by Suicide*, Routledge, 1991.

25. Ted Hughes, *Birthday Letters*, p.11.

26. Ted Hughes, *Birthday Letters*, p.173. My point about the syntax of pronouns refers to the last six lines of the poem.

27. Ted Hughes, *Birthday Letters*, p.18.

28. Ted Hughes, 'St Botolph's', *Birthday Letters*, pp.14–15.

29. Ian Gregson, *The Male Image: Representations of Masculinity in Post-war Poetry*, 1999. Gregson suggests that, until *Wodwo*, Hughes is preoccupied with the masculine struggle to establish an identity separate from the 'possessive control' of the phallic mother (Hughes, in *Shakespeare and the Goddess of Complete Being*). According to Gregson, from *Wodwo* onwards, Hughes's work claims that 'a systemic rejection of the feminine...inflicts dire psychic consequences on Western culture.' (p.80) In the poet's late work, Gregson identifies a version of eco-feminism in Hughes's idealisations of the Goddess figure.

30. Ted Hughes, *New Selected Poems 1957–1994*, p.31. For further examples of the fear associated with what is out of sight, beneath water or

land, see 'Mayday on Holderness' 'Ghost Crabs', 'Pike'.

31. Ted Hughes, 'Fragment of an Ancient Tablet', *Crow*, p.85.
32. Nicole Ward Jouve, 'The Missing Men and the Women's Sentence', *Female Genesis: Creativity, Self and Gender*, p.93.
33. Ted Hughes, 'Dust As We Are', *New Selected Poems 1957–1994*, p.269.
34. Ted Hughes, 'Dust As We Are', *New Selected Poems 1957–1994*, p.269.
35. Ted Hughes, 'Out', *New Selected Poems 1957–1994*, p.73. Gregson also discusses Hughes's poems about his father, and comments on the way Hughes feels himself 'a sort of scapegoat' for his father's war suffering. *The Male Image*, pp.70–2.
36. Ted Hughes, 'Two Tortoiseshell butterflies', *New Selected Poems 1957–1994*, p.223. In *Crow* the revulsion at life is so strong that Nature is its butt, and Mother the cause of the unending pain of existence.
37. Ted Hughes, 'Eclipse', *New Selected Poems 1957–1994*, p.228.
38. Ted Hughes and Frances McCullough (eds), *The Journals of Sylvia Plath*, p.xiv.
39. Ted Hughes, *Birthday Letters*, p.164.
40. Sylvia Plath, *Collected Poems*, p.264.
41. Sylvia Plath, *Collected Poems*, p.22.
42. 11 March 1956. Ted Hughes and Frances McCullough (eds), *The Journals of Sylvia Plath*, p.134.
43. The tone is similar to that of Plath's 'The Snowman on the Moor', *Collected Poems*. p.58.
44. 'The Fifty-Ninth Bear', pp.94–105, *Johnny Panic and the Bible of Dreams*.
45. Ted Hughes, 'The 59th Bear', *Birthday Letters*, pp.89–95, p.94.
46. Ted Hughes, *Birthday Letters*, 'You Hated Spain', pp.39–40. Sylvia Plath, *Collected Poems*, p.47.
47. In this he is like the speaker of Plath's 'Electra on Azalea Path', who 'borrow[s] the stilts of an old tragedy', *Collected Poems*, p.117.
48. Eve Kosofsky Sedgwick, *Between Men: English Literature and Male Homosocial Desire*, p.21.
49. Ted Hughes, *Birthday Letters*, p.139.
50. Ted Hughes, *Birthday Letters*, p.184.
51. Ted Hughes, *Birthday Letters*, p.103.
52. Ted Hughes, *Birthday Letters*, p.159.
53. Hughes first published this opinion in 'Sylvia Plath and her journals', *Winter Pollen: Occasional Prose* (ed.) William Scammell, Faber and Faber, 1995, pp.177–90. He described the 'root system of her talent' as 'a deep and inclusive inner crisis' (p.179), composed of her father's death, her own attempted suicide and 'rebirth' into art.
54. Ted Hughes, *Birthday Letters*, p.103. Part of the anger against Otto could

be Hughes's own father's displaced anger against the older fathers who demanded their participation in war and hence their sacrifice.

55. Lynda K. Bundtzen, 'Mourning Eurydice: Ted Hughes as Orpheus in *Birthday Letters*', *Journal of Modern Literature*, XXIII, 3–4, summer 2000, pp.455–69.

56. Ted Hughes, *Birthday Letters*, p.193.

57. A similar shift in focus is enacted in separate poems by both Don Paterson and Jamie McKendrick: retelling ancient myths, they twist the emphasis away from the prize of the maiden, on to the scene of rivalry and contest between father and son. See 'God's Gift to Women' and 'Matador', discussed in chapter 5.

58. Ted Hughes, *Birthday Letters*, p.143.

59. Ted Hughes, *Birthday Letters*, p.153.

60. See for example, entries for 27 December 1958, and throughout January 1959. Ted Hughes and Frances McCullough (eds), *The Journals of Sylvia Plath*.

61. Sylvia Plath, *Collected Poems*, p.129.

62. Jacqueline Rose, *The Haunting of Sylvia Plath*, p.128–9.

63. Jacqueline Rose, *Haunting*, p.xiv.

64. Sybille Bedford, *A Compass Error*, 1968 and Virago, 2000, p.18.

65. Ted Hughes, *Birthday Letters*, p.145.

66. Sylvia Plath, *Collected Poems*, p.194.

67. Ted Hughes, *Birthday Letters*, p.146. Frequently in *Birthday Letters*, Plath's poems are figured as appearing to her effortlessly, out of thin air. This has the effect of further reducing her own agency as their author.

68. Sylvia Plath, *Collected Poems*, p.194. This metaphor is in the last stanza of the poem.

69. Louise Glück, 'Invitation and Exclusion', p.123.

70. Christina Patterson, 'Ted on Sylvia, for the record', *Guardian*, 18 August 2001, p.3.

CHAPTER 5
IRON(IC) JOHN: MEN POETS ON MASCULINITY

1. Gregory Woods, *A History of Gay Literature: The Male Tradition*, 1997, p.376.

2. While this deduction assumes some continuity between personae and poet, it seems reasonable in the absence of any evidence to the contrary, and on the grounds that, post-Stonewall, gay male poets now tend to signal the fact of their sexual orientation quite explicitly, building it into their aesthetic (e.g. Frank O'Hara, Thom Gunn, Mark Doty, John Ashbery, Edwin Morgan and Gregory Woods).

3. Published in 1999, Gregson's study includes discussion of Robert Lowell, Ted Hughes, Seamus Heaney, Paul Muldoon, C. K. Williams,

Derek Walcott, John Berryman, John Ashbery and Frank O'Hara, as well as a chapter on women poets' representations of men.

4. Women's greater sensitivity to, and awareness of, the possibility of male readers stems from their sharper consciousness of the *difference* of their own gender. Men are not continually reminded of the fact of their gender. As one describes it, 'When I look in the mirror…gender is invisible to me because that is where *I* am privileged. I am the norm. I believe that most men do not know they have a gender.' Michael Kimmel, quoted in Peter Middleton, *The Inward Gaze*, p.44. In Virginia Woolf's *A Room of One's Own*, Granada, 1977, p.78, Woolf's exaggerated anxiety lest a man be hidden behind the curtain is more than a rhetorical gesture. It suggests how markedly the presence of men as auditors affects the manner and the matter of women's communications. Describing her experience of reading an unusual first novel by one Mary Carmichael, she suddenly draws to a halt:

> determined to do my duty by her as reader if she would do her duty by me as writer, I turned the page and read…I am sorry to break off so abruptly. Are there no men present? Do you promise me that behind that red curtain over there the figure of Sir Charles Biron is not concealed? We are all women you assure me? Then I may tell you that the very next words I read were these—'Chloe liked Olivia…' Do not start, Do not blush. Let us admit in the privacy of our own society that these things sometimes happen. Sometimes women do like women.

5. Robert Crawford et al. (eds), *Talking Verse*, p.26.
6. 'On leaving my mistress', article by Emma Brockes, *Guardian*, 27 October 1999, p.16.
7. Abigail Solomon-Godeau, 'Male Trouble' in Maurice Berger, Brian Wallis and Simon Watson (eds), *Constructing Masculinity*, p.70.
8. David Kennedy, '"*What does the fairy DO?*" The staging of antithetical masculine styles in the poetry of Tony Harrison and Douglas Dunn', *Textual Practice*, vol.14, no.1, 2000, p.115.
9. Tony Harrison, *Selected Poems*, p.84.
10. Seamus Heaney, 'Digging', *Death of a Naturalist*, Faber and Faber, 1966, p.13.
11. Anthony Clare, *On Men: Masculinity in Crisis*, p.212.
12. Abigail Solomon-Godeau, 'Male Trouble', p.73.
13. Peter Middleton, *The Inward Gaze*, p.231.
14. Violence is a characteristic noted by Jane Stabler in her interview with Simon Armitage; she comments on the barely contained force or energy described in his poems. He responds by saying that he tries to refer to violence 'through exclusion or refraction. To run alongside' rather than to collude with it. Robert Crawford et al. (eds), *Talking Verse*, p.24.
15. Gregory Woods, *A History of Gay Literature: The Male Tradition*, 1997, p.376.

16. Sean O'Brien also makes this observation, *The Deregulated Muse*, p.201.
17. Matthew Sweeney, 'North', *Blue Shoes*, p.6.
18. Matthew Sweeney, 'Dog on a Chain', *Blue Shoes*, p.4.
19. Matthew Sweeney, 'Our Ikky', *The Bridal Suite*, p.23.
20. Matthew Sweeney, 'A Daydream Ahead', *Blue Shoes*, p.12.
21. Matthew Sweeney, 'Princess', *The Bridal Suite*, p.12.
22. Matthew Sweeney, 'On My Own', *Blue Shoes*, p.19. Deborah Randall has also written several poems about boyhood, with strikingly similar themes. See *The Sin Eater*, Newcastle-upon-Tyne, Bloodaxe, 1989.
23. Matthew Sweeney, 'U-boat', *Blue Shoes*, p.23.
24. Matthew Sweeney, 'Grandpa's Bed', *The Bridal Suite*, p.16.
25. Jonathan Dollimore, *Death, Desire and Loss in Western Civilisation*, 1998, p.xxvii.
26. Matthew Sweeney, 'The Wobble', *The Bridal Suite*, p.23.
27. Matthew Sweeney, 'A Picnic on Ice', *The Bridal Suite*, p.45.
28. Matthew Sweeney, 'Flying Machines', *Blue Shoes*, p.42.
29. Matthew Sweeney, 'Skating', *The Bridal Suite*, p.47.
30. Matthew Sweeney, 'The Cold', *Blue Shoes*, p.1.
31. Matthew Sweeney, 'Bagpipes', *The Bridal Suite*, p.21.
32. Matthew Sweeney, 'Try Biting', *The Bridal Suite*, p.10.
33. Matthew Sweeney, 'Riding into Town', *The Bridal Suite*, p.11.
34. Jonathan Dollimore, *Death, Desire and Loss in Western Culture*, p.xx.
35. Michael Donaghy, *Conjure*. Some of the poems in this volume have already been published in other collections ('Caliban's Books' appeared in *Penguin Modern Poets 11*, along with 'Letter', which is also about his father).
36. Michael Donaghy, 'The Excuse', *Conjure*, p. 3.
37. Michael Donaghy, 'My Flu', *Conjure*, p.13.
38. Michael Dongahy, 'Letter', *Penguin Modern Poets 11*, p.27.
39. Michael Donaghy, 'Mine', *Conjure*, p.39.
40. Michael Donaghy, 'Not Knowing the Words', *Conjure*, p.4.
41. Michael Donaghy, 'Haunts', *Conjure*, p.46.
42. Robert Crawford, 'A Quiet Man', *Masculinity*, p.2.
43. Robert Crawford, 'A Quiet Man', *Masculinity*, p.2.
44. Robert Crawford, 'PC', *Masculinity*, p.10.
45. Robert Crawford, 'Mending the Helicopter', *Masculinity*, p.8.
46. Robert Crawford, 'Reply', *Masculinity*, p.9.
47. Robert Crawford, 'Male Infertility', *Masculinity*, p.13.
48. Robert Crawford, 'Whisht', *Masculinity*, p.62.
49. 'The Dilemma of the Peot' (ed.) Curtis, *How Poets Work*, p.165.
50. Neil Rollinson, 'The Miracle of Drink', *A Spillage of Mercury*, p.28.
51. Neil Rollinson, 'Giant Puffballs', *A Spillage of Mercury*, p.7.
52. Neil Rollinson, 'Ménàge a Trois', *A Spillage of Mercury*, p. 42.
53. Richard Dawkins, *The Selfish Gene*, Oxford, Oxford University Press,

1989.

54. Neil Rollinson, 'Sutras in Free Fall', *A Spillage of Mercury*, p.50.

55. Neil Rollinson, 'In One of Your Filthy Poems', *A Spillage of Mercury*, p.33. Don Paterson makes similar postmodern play in a poem that describes how a man inadvertently vidcos himself wanking to a porn movie. See 'Postmodern', *God's Gift*, p.51.

56. Neil Rollinson, 'Lillith', *A Spillage of Mercury*, p.18.

57. Don Paterson employs a similar image in '*From* Advice to Young Husbands', comparing a woman's genitalia to an unfolding river-lotus, *God's Gift*, p.53.

58. Neil Rollinson, 'The Way It Happens', *A Spillage of Mercury*, p.39.

59. This interest is singled out in the blurb to his fourth collection, 'Its focus is men—and boys "who are going to be boys, who have had to be men"' ('The Boys at Twilight'). The poems sort the men from the boys: boys at play, men at war, boys grown up, men reverting, men in love and poetry and politics, running countries, ruining things.' Glyn Maxwell, *Rest for the Wicked*, 1995.

60. See, for example, '"England Gone": The Rhetorical Imagination and Ideas of Nation in the Poetry of Simon Armitage and Glyn Maxwell', pp.55–78 in David Kennedy, *New Relations: the refashioning of British Poetry 1980–94*; and Ian Gregson, *Contemporary Poetry and Postmodernism: Dialogue and Estrangement*.

61. Glyn Maxwell, 'Phaeton and the Chariot of the Sun: An investigative documentary', pp.93–109, *Rest for the Wicked*.

62. Glyn Maxwell, 'Strictures', *Strong Words: Modern Poets on Modern Poetry*, edited by W. N. Herbert and Matthew Hollis, p.256, Newcastle-upon-Tyne, Bloodaxe, 2000.

63. See for example, 'Did I Imagine That', *The Mayor's Son*, p.72; 'How Many Things', *The Mayor's Son*, p.40; 'Tale of a Chocolate Egg', *The Mayor's Son*, pp.96–112.

64. Maxwell's interest in forms of representation other than the printed page is clear from sequences like 'Phaeton and the Chariot of the Sun: Fragments of An Investigative Documentary', with its preoccupation with angle, film footage and point of view.

65. Poets have been slow to embrace filmic potential. Tony Harrison has produced some superb mergers of film and poetry. See, for example, his television films *The Blasphemer's Banquet* and *Black Daisies for the Bride*. For further discussion of these, and other poets' work with film, see my essay, 'Words on Film: Collaborative work between poets and film-makers' in Andrew Roberts and Jonathan Allison (eds), *Contemporary Poetry, Culture and Value*, Edinburgh, Edinburgh University Press, 2002.

66. Glyn Maxwell, 'Wasp', *The Mayor's Son*, p.68.

67. Glyn Maxwell, 'A Force That Ate Itself', *Rest for the Wicked*, p.88.

68. Glyn Maxwell, 'Ost', *Rest for the Wicked*, p.90.

69. Glyn Maxwell, 'The Wish', *Rest for the Wicked*, p.15.

70. Glyn Maxwell, 'Self-Portrait with Softball', *Rest for the Wicked*, p.16.
71. Glyn Maxwell, 'The Night Is Young', *Rest for the Wicked*, p.35.
72. Glyn Maxwell, 'Stargazing', *Rest for the Wicked*, p.29. There is an interesting similarity to Simon Armitage here; his collection, *CloudCuckooLand* (Faber, 1997) portrays the night-sky ruminations of a solitary man as a necessarily lone, male quest.
73. Glyn Maxwell, 'Song of the Sash', *Rest for the Wicked*, p.33.
74. Glyn Maxwell, 'Love Made Yeah', *Rest for the Wicked*, p.20.
75. David Kennedy, *New Relations*, p.71.
76. Glyn Maxwell, 'A White Car', *Rest for the Wicked*, p.85.
77. Compare Nick Hornby's *High Fidelity* (London, Indigo, 1996), with its witty depiction of the male predilection for list-making.
78. Don Paterson, *God's Gift to Women*, 1997. The title poem starts on p.25.
79. Robert Crawford et al. (eds), *Talking Verse*, p.194.
80. See Sean O'Brien, *Deregulated Muse*, p.261 for the first; also Ian Sansom, 'Excess Its Own Reward', pp.44–5, *Poetry Review*, vol.87, no.2 (summer 1997).
81. Cited by Peter Sansom, 'Excess Its Own Reward', p.45.
82. God's Gift, 'Prologue', *God's Gift to Women*, p.1.
83. Crawford et al. (eds), *Talking Verse*, p.193.
84. Crawford et al. (eds), *Talking Verse*, p.197.
85. Further examples of 'undigestible' poetry might include Joolz and the African-American Sapphire, as well as some of the experimental poets.
86. Paterson, 'The Dilemma of the Peot', from *How Poets Work*, Tony Curtis (ed.).
87. *God's Gift*, '19:00: Aucterhouse' p.52; '01:00: Rosemill', p.35: both from Paterson, *God's Gift*.
88. Don Paterson, 'Imperial', *God's Gift*, p.37.
89. Don Paterson, '*From* Advice to Husbands', *God's Gift*, p.53.
90. Don Paterson, '1001 Nights: The Early Years', *God's Gift*, p.8.
91. Don Paterson, 'To Cut It Short' *God's Gift*, p.19.
92. Don Paterson, 'The Alexandrian Library, Part II: The Return of the Book', *God's Gift*, pp.42–50.
93. Don Paterson, 'Poem', *God's Gift*, p.38.
94. Don Paterson, 'A Private Bottling', *God's Gift*, p.18.
95. Don Paterson, 'God's Gift to Women' *God's Gift*, p.25. Because of Paterson's propensity for invented personae, there is of course no certainty that the narrator is himself. However, there is a different quality to this piece, which leads me to hazard equating the poem's voice with its author.
96. Don Paterson is not the only poet to make this claim. Jamie McKendrick's 'Matador' depicts Theseus realising he deliberately didn't raise the sails—the sign of his successful mission prearranged with his father—so as to ensure his father's suicide. Father–son rivalry

and tension is clearly a crucial issue for many male poets.

97. See *Nil Nil*, pp.5, 6, 7, 17, 20, 24 for examples.

98. *God's Gift*, p.28. Ian McMillan's 'Tempest Avenue' offers a novel alternative to this fear that children will impede a poet's creativity. The poem opens with a description of its speaker laying his sleeping son back into his cot. Its last stanza appropriates the same imagery to describe his act of writing the poem: 'And I am being careful, so careful/with these words, laying them/gently into this poem, turning to the door', *Dad, the Donkey's On Fire*, Newcastle-on-Tyne, Bloodaxe, 1994, p.17.

99. 'Letter to The Twins' is a case in point: an apparent praise-song to women that sticks the knife into 'her who said she was your mother', *London Review of Books*, vol.25, no.8, 17 April 2003.

100. See chapter 4 for fuller discussion of the gendering of confession. Paterson's self-exposure sets him apart from several other contemporary men writers who divulge personal information about significant others in their lives, while keeping their own privacy. Compare Hanif Kureshi, *Intimacy*, 1999; Hugo Williams, *Billy's Rain*; Craig Raine, *A La Recherche du Temps Perdu: A Poem*.

101. In fact, all except Rollinson have children. The absence of any mention of them in their biographies is is in striking contrast to the blurb descriptions of many women writers, which tend to include information about their marital status and offspring. Incidentally, in his study of homosexual poetry, Gregory Woods suggests that it is quite common to come across the kind of usurpation of the female reproductive potential evident in Paterson's and Rollinson's work. He goes so far as to claim that 'it may be one of the prime functions of the arts in general, to placate male uterus-envy', *Articulate Flesh*, p.85. On the basis of the analysis in this chapter, it seems as though the tendency is not restricted to homoerotic poetry.

102. Further examples include Michael Hofmann's 'My Father at Fifty', p.265, in Michael Hulse et al. (eds), *The New Poetry* (Bloodaxe, 1993), and 'Greenhouse' by Simon Armitage. Speaking of 'Greenhouse', in an interview, Armitage spoke of the importance of his relationship with his father, and how he has 'tested my shoe size in his footprints', Crawford et al. (eds), *Talking Verse*, 1995, p.21.

BIBLIOGRAPHY

Adcock, Fleur (ed.), 1987, *The Faber Book of Twentieth-century Women's Poetry*, London, Faber and Faber.

Armitage, Simon, 1989, *Zoom!*, Newcastle-upon-Tyne, Bloodaxe.

Baldick, Chris, 1990, *Concise Dictionary of Literary Terms*, Oxford, Oxford University Press.

Battersby, Christine, 1994, 'Unblocking the Oedipal: Karoline von Gunderode and the Female Sublime', in Sally Ledger, Josephine McDonagh, and Jane Spencer (eds), *Political Gender: texts and contexts*. Hemel Hempstead: Harvester Wheatsheaf.

Beckles, Hilary McD. 2000, 'White women and slavery in the Caribbean', in Veren Shepherd and Hilary McD. Beckles (eds), *Caribbean Slavery in the Atlantic World*, Oxford, James Curry Publications.

—— 1989, *Natural Rebels: A Social History of Enslaved Black Women in Barbados*, London, Zed Books.

Berger, Maurice, Wallace, Brian, and Watson, Simon (eds), 1995, *Constructing Masculinity*, London and New York, Routledge.

Bernikow, Louise (ed.), 1979, *The World Split Open: Women Poets 1552–1950*, London, The Women's Press.

Bertram, Vicki, 1996, 'Postfeminist poetry? "one more word for balls"', in James Acheson and Romana Huk (eds), *Contemporary British Poetry: Essays in Theory and Criticism*, New York, State University of New York Press.

—— 1997, '"Tidal Edges" in Contemporary Women's Poetry: Towards a Model of Critical Empathy', in Trev Broughton and

Linda Anderson (eds) *Women's Lives, Women's Times*, New York, State University of New York Press.

—— (ed.), 1997, *Kicking Daffodils: Essays on Twentieth Century Women Poets*, Edinburgh, Edinburgh University Press.

—— 1999, "'Poetry to live your life by': Mimi Khalvati in conversation", *P. N. Review*, vol.26, no.2 (November-December).

—— 1999, 'Performance Poets', in *Feminist Review, Contemporary Women Poets*, no.62, summer.

Bhatt, Sujata, 1988, *Brunizem*, Manchester, Carcanet Press.

—— 1991, *Monkey Shadows*, Manchester, Carcanet Press.

—— 2000, *Augatora*, Manchester, Carcanet Press.

Binder, Wolfgang, 1997, 'An Interview with David Dabydeen', in Kevin Grant (ed.), *The Art of David Dabydeen*, Leeds, Peepal Tree Press.

Birbalsingh, Frank, 1996, *Frontiers of Caribbean Literature in English*, contains interview with Dabydeen reprinted in Kevin Grant (ed.), Macmillan Educational.

—— 1997, 'Interview with David Dabydeen', in Kevin Grant (ed.), *The Art of David Dabydeen*, Leeds, Peepal Tree Press.

Bloom, Harold, 1973, *The Anxiety of Influence*, Oxford and New York, Oxford University Press.

Boland, Eavan, 1980, *In Her Own Image*, Dublin, Arlen House.

—— 1986-7, 'The Woman Poet: Her Dilemma', *Stand Magazine*, winter 1986–87.

—— 1987, *The Journey and Other Poems*, Manchester, Carcanet.

—— 1987, 'The Woman Poet in a National Tradition', *Studies* (Dublin), vol.76., summer.

—— 1998, 'Defining Circumstances: An Interview with Eavan Boland', *P.N. Review*, vol.25, no.2, December.

Bradford, Richard, 1997, *Stylistics*, London and New York, Routledge.

Bronfen, Elisabeth, 1992, *Over Her Dead Body: Death, Femininity and the Aesthetic*, Manchester, Manchester University Press.

Brooks, David, 1985, 'Poetry and Sexual Difference', *Meanjin*, vol. 44, no.1, March.

Buck, Claire, 1996, 'Poetry and the Women's Movement in Postwar Britain', in James Acheson and Romana Huk (ed.), *Contemporary British Poetry: Essays in Theory and Criticism*,

New York, State University of New York Press.

Bundtzen, Lynda K, 2000, 'Mourning Eurydice: Ted Hughes as Orpheus in Birthday Letters', *Journal of Modern Literature*, xxiii, 3–4 (summer 2000), Indiana University Press.

Carr, Helen, 2000, 'Poetic Licence', in Alison Mark and Deryn Rees-Jones, *Contemporary Women's Poetry: Reading/Writing/ Practice*, Basingstoke, Macmillan.

Carter, Angela, 1979, *The Sadeian Woman: An Exercise in Cultural History*, London, Virago.

Childs, Peter, 1999, *The Twentieth Century in Poetry: A Critical Survey*, London and New York, Routledge.

Cixous, Hélène, 1993, 'We Who are Free, How Free are We?', *Critical Inquiry*, vol.19, no.2.

Clanchy, Kate, 1995, *Slattern*, London, Chatto & Windus.

Clare, Anthony, 2000, *On Men: Masculinity in Crisis*, London, Chatto & Windus.

Clark, Polly, 2000, *Kiss*, Newcastle-upon-Tyne, Bloodaxe.

Cooper, Carolyn, 1993, *Noises in the Blood: Orality, Gender and the 'Vulgar' Body of Jamaican Popular Culture*, London and Basingstoke, Macmillan Educational.

Cosman, Carol, Keefe, Joan and Weaver, Kathleen (eds), 1980, *The Penguin Book of Women Poets*, Basingstoke, Penguin.

Couzyn, Jeni (ed.), 1985, *The Bloodaxe Book of Contemporary Women Poets*, Newcastle-upon-Tyne, Bloodaxe.

Crawford, Robert, 1990, *A Scottish Assembly*, London, Chatto & Windus.

Crawford, Robert, Hart, Henry, Kinloch, David and Price, Richard (eds), 1995, *Talking Verse*, St Andrews and Williamsburg, Verse.

—— 1996, *Masculinity*, London, Cape.

Croft, Andy, 2000, 'Some Responses are More Equal than Others', *Thumbscrew*, no.16, summer, Oxford.

Dabydeen, David, 1984, *Slave Song*, Mundelstrup, Denmark, Dangaroo.

—— 1986, 'On Writing Slave Song', *Commonwealth Essays and Studies*, vol.8, no.2, spring.

—— and Samaroo, Brinsley (eds), 1987, *India in the Caribbean*, London, Hansib.

—— 1988, *Coolie Odyssey*, Hansib, Dangaroo.

—— and Wilson-Tagoe, Nana (eds), 1988, *A Reader's Guide to West Indian and Black British Literature*, Warwick, Hansib and Rutherford Press.

—— (ed.), 1988, *Handbook for Teaching Caribbean Literature*, Oxford, Heinemann Education Books.

—— 1990, 'On Not Being Milton: Nigger Talk in England Today', in Christopher Ricks and Leonard Michaels (eds), *The State of the Language*, London, Faber.

—— 1994, *Turner*, London, Cape.

Daly, Mary, 1984, *Pure Lust*, London, The Women's Press.

Dawes, Kwame, 1997, 'Interview with David Dabydeen', in Kevin Grant (ed.), *The Art of David Dabydeen*, Leeds, Peepal Tree Press.

Day, Aidan, 1996, *Romanticism*, London and New York, Routledge.

De Caires Narain, Denise, 2000, 'Caribbean Creole: The Real Thing? Writing and reading the Creole in a selection of Caribbean women's texts', in Susheila Nasta (ed.), *Reading the 'new' literatures in a postcolonial era, Essays and Studies*, The English Association, Cambridge, Boydell and Brewer.

DeShazer, Mary K., 1986, *Inspiring Women: Reimagining the muse*, New York and Oxford, Athene /Pergammon Press.

Donaghy, Michael, 1988, *Shibboleth*, Oxford, Oxford University Press.

—— and Motion, Andrew, Williams, Hugo (eds), *Penguin Modern Poets, volume 11*, 1997, London.

—— 2000, *Conjure*, London, Picador.

Dowson, Jane, 1999, '"Older Sisters are Very Sobering Things": Contemporary Women Poets and the Female Affiliation Complex', in Vicki Bertram (ed.), *Feminist Review, Contemporary Women Poets*, no.62, summer.

Draper, R. P., 1999, *An Introduction to Twentieth Century Poetry in English*, Basingstoke, Macmillan.

Duffy, Carol Ann, 1985, *Standing Female Nude*, London, Anvil Press.

—— 1986, *Thrown Voices*, London, Turret Books.

—— 1987, *Selling Manhattan*, London, Anvil Press.

—— 1988, 'An interview with Andrew McAllister', 69–77, *Bête*

Noire, issue 6 (winter).
—— 1990, *The Other Country*, London, Anvil Press.
—— 1993, *Mean Time*, London, Anvil Press.
—— 1999, *The World's Wife*, London, Picador/Macmillan.
DuPlessis, Rachel, 1990, *The Pink Guitar: Writing as Feminist Practice*, New York and London, Routledge.
—— 1994, '"Corpses of Poesy": Some Modern Poets and Some Gender Ideologies of Lyric', in Lynn Keller and Cristanne Miller (eds), *Feminist Measures: Soundings in Poetry and Theory*, Michigan, University of Michigan Press.
Eagleton, Mary (ed.), 1991, *Feminist Literary Criticism*, London and New York, Longman.
Edmondson, Belinda, 1999, *Making Men: Gender, Literary Authority and Women's Writing in Caribbean Narrative*, Raleigh, NC, Duke University Press.
Erkkila, Betsy, 1992, *The Wicked Sisters: Women Poets, Literary History, and Discord*, Oxford, Oxford University Press.
Feaver, Vicki, 1994, *The Handless Maiden*, London, Cape Poetry.
Feminist Review special issue (ed.) Vicki Bertram, 1999, 'Contemporary Women Poets', *Feminist Review*, no.62 (Summer).
Fetterley, Judith, 1978, *The Resisting Reader: A Feminist Approach to American Fiction*, Bloomington, Indiana University Press.
Gallop, Jane, 1985, *Reading Lacan*, Ithaca, Cornell University Press.
Gilbert, Sandra and Gubar, Susan (eds), 1979, *Shakespeare's Sisters: Feminist Essays on Women Poets*, Bloomington, Indiana University Press.
Glück, Louise, 1999, 'Invitation and Exclusion', in *Proofs and Theories*, Manchester, Carcanet Press.
Grant, Kevin (ed.), 1997, *The Art of David Dabydeen*, Leeds, Peepal Tree Press.
Gregson, Ian, 1996, *Contemporary Poetry and Postmodernism: Dialogue and Estrangement*, London, Macmillan.
——1999, *The Male Image: Representations of Masculinity in Post-war Poetry*, London, Macmillan.
—— 2000, 'Living Dolls and Broken Machines: Caricatural Effects in Ian McMillan, Carol Ann Duffy and Geoff Hattersley', in

Lesley Jeffries and Peter Sansom (eds), *Contemporary Poems: Some Critical Approaches*, Huddersfield, Smith/Doorstep Books.

Habekost, Christian (ed.), *Dub Poetry: 19 Poets From England and Jamaica*, 1987, Neustadt, Michael Schwinn.

Halliday, Caroline, 1990, '"The Naked Majesty of God", Contemporary Lesbian Erotic Poetry', in Mark Lilly (ed.) *Lesbian and Gay Writing: An Anthology of Critical Essays*, Basingstoke, Macmillan.

Haste, Helen, 1993, *The Sexual Metaphor*, Brighton, Harvester Wheatsheaf.

Higgins, Rita Ann, 1996, *Sunny Side Plucked: New and Selected Poems*, Newcastle-upon-Tyne, Bloodaxe.

Hill, Selima, 2000, 'God's Velvet Cushions', in Alison Mark and Deryn Rees-Jones (eds), *Contemporary Women's Poetry: Reading /Writing/Practice*, Basingstoke, Macmillan.

Hirsh, Elizabeth, 1994, 'Another Look at Genre: *Diving Into the Wreck* of Ethics with Rich and Irigaray', in Lynn Keller and Cristanne Miller (eds), *Feminist Measures: Soundings in Poetry and Theory*, Ann Arbor, University of Michigan Press.

Hobsbaum, Philip, 1996, *Metre, Rhythm and Verse Form*, London and New York, Routledge.

Hughes, Ted, 1972, *Crow*, London, Faber.

—— and McCullough, Frances , 1982, *The Journals of Sylvia Plath*, New York, Random House/Ballantine Books.

—— 1995, *New Selected Poems 1957–1994*, London, Faber.

—— 1998, *Birthday Letters*, London, Faber.

Huk, Romana, 1997, 'Feminist Radicalism in (Relatively) Traditional Forms: An American's investigation of British poetics', in Vicki Bertram (ed.), *Kicking Daffodils*, Edinburgh, Edinburgh University Press.

Hulse, Michael, Kennedy, Frances and Morley, David (eds), 1993, *The New Poetry*, Newcastle-upon-Tyne, Bloodaxe.

Irigaray, Luce, 1993, *Je, Tu, Nous: Towards a Culture of Difference*, London and New York, Routledge.

Jackson, Stevie and Jones, Jackie (eds), 1998, *Contemporary Feminist Theories*, Edinburgh, Edinburgh University Press.

James, Louis, 1999, *Caribbean Literature in English*, London and New York, Longman.

Jeffries, Lesley and Sansom, Peter (eds), 2000, *Contemporary Poems: Some Critical Approaches*, Huddersfield, Smith/Doorstep Books.

Juhasz, Suzanne, 1976, *Naked and Fiery Forms: Modern American Poetry by Women: A New Tradition*, New York and San Francisco, Harper Colophon Books.

—— 1977, 'The Critic as Feminist: Reflections on Women's Poetry, Feminism and the Art of Criticism', *Women's Studies*, vol.5.

—— 1994, 'Adventures in the World of the Symbolic: Emily Dickinson and Metaphor', in Lynn Keller and Cristanne Miller (eds) *Feminist Measures: Soundings in Poetry and Theory*, Ann Arbor, University of Michigan Press.

Kaplan, Cora, 1986, 'Language and Gender', in *Sea Changes: Essays on Culture and Feminism*, London, Verso.

Kay, Jackie, 1991, *The Adoption Papers*, Newcastle-upon-Tyne, Bloodaxe.

—— 1993, *Other Lovers*, Newcastle-upon-Tyne, Bloodaxe.

—— 1998, *Off Colour*, Newcastle-upon-Tyne, Bloodaxe.

Keller, Lynn and Miller, Cristanne (eds), 1994, *Feminist Measures: Soundings in Poetry and Theory*, Ann Arbor, University of Michigan Press.

Kelly, A. A., 1987, *Pillars of the House: An Anthology of Verse by Irish Women from 1690 to the Present*, Dublin, Wolfhound Press.

Kennedy, David, 1996, *New Relations: The Refashioning of British Poetry, 1980–1994*, Bridgend, Seren.

—— 2000, '"What does the fairy DO?" The staging of antithetical masculine styles in the poetry of Tony Harrison and Douglas Dunn', *Textual Practice*, vol.14, no.1.

Kristeva, Julia, 1984, *Revolution in Poetic Language*, New York, Columbia University Press.

Lakoff, George, 1993, From Andrew Ortony (ed.) *Metaphor and Thought*, Cambridge University Press.

Larrington, Carolyne (ed.), 1992, *The Feminist Companion to Mythology*, London, Pandora.

Lennard, John, 1996, *The Poetry Handbook*, Oxford, Oxford University Press.

Lochhead, Liz, 1984, *Dreaming Frankenstein*, Edinburgh, Polygon.

Longley, Edna (ed.), 2000, *The Bloodaxe Book of Twentieth Century Poetry*, Newcastle-upon-Tyne, Bloodaxe.

McAllister, Andrew, 1988, Carol Ann Duffy: an interview, in *Bête Noire*, winter 1988, Issue 6.

McIntyre, Karen, 1997, 'Necrophilia or Stillbirth? David Dabydeen's Turner as the embodiment of Postcolonial Creative Decolonisation', in Kevin Grant (ed.), *The Art of David Dabydeen*, Leeds, Peepal Tree Press.

McKendrick, Jamie, 1997, *The Marble Fly*, Oxford, Oxford University Press.

McWatt, Mark, 1997, 'His Tree-True Face: Masking and Revelation in David Dabydeen's Slave Song', 15–25, in Kevin Grant (ed.), *The Art of David Dabydeen*, Leeds, Peepal Tree.

Maguire, Sarah, 1999, 'Dilemmas and Developments: Eavan Boland Revisited', in *Feminist Review*, no.62, Summer.

Mark, Alison and Rees-Jones, Deryn (eds), 2000, *Contemporary Women's Poetry: Reading/Writing/Practice*, Basingstoke, Macmillan.

Maxwell, Glyn, 1990, *Tale of the Mayor's Son*, Newcastle-upon-Tyne, Bloodaxe.

—— 1992, *Out of the Rain*, Newcastle-upon-Tyne, Bloodaxe.

—— 1995, *Rest for the Wicked*, Newcastle-upon-Tyne, Bloodaxe.

Middleton, Peter, 1992, *The Inward Gaze: Masculinity and Subjectivity in Modern Culture*, London, Routledge.

Mills, Sara, 1989, 'No Poetry for Ladies: Gertrude Stein, Julia Kristeva and Modernism', in David Murray (ed.) *Literary Theory and Poetry: Extending the Canon*, London, Batsford.

Mills, Sara, 1994, 'Reading as/like a feminist', in *Gendering the Reader*, Brighton, Harvester Wheatsheaf.

Mohin, Lillian (ed.), 1979, *One Foot on the Mountain: An Anthology of British Feminist Poetry 1969–1979*, London, Onlywomen Press.

Montefiore, Jan, 1987; revised and reprinted 1994, 2003, *Feminism and Poetry: Language, Experience, Identity in Women's Writing*, London, Pandora.

Mulford, Wendy, 1990, '"Curved, Odd...Irregular". A Vision of Contemporary Poetry by Women', *Women: A Cultural Review*, vol.1 no.3 (winter).

Ncobo, Lauretta (ed.), 1987, *Let it Be Told: Essays by Black Women in Britain*, London, Pluto Press.

Nichols, Grace, 1983, *I Is A Long Memoried Woman*, London, Karnak House.

—— 1984, *The Fat Black Woman's Poems*, London, Virago.

—— 1989, *Lazy Thoughts of a Lazy Woman*, London, Virago.

O'Brien, Sean, 1998, *The Firebox: Poetry in Britain and Ireland after 1945*, London and Basingstoke, Picador, Macmillan.

—— 1998, *The Deregulated Muse*, Newcastle-upon-Tyne, Bloodaxe.

O'Rourke, Rebecca, 1990, 'Mediums, Messages and Noisy Amateurs', *Women: A Cultural Review*, vol.1 no.3 (winter),

Orange Prize for Fiction, 1999, *Reading and Gender Survey*, London.

Orbach, Susie and Eichenbaum, Luise, 1988, *Bitter Sweet: love, envy and competition in women's friendships*, London, Arrow.

Ostriker, Alicia Suskin, 1987, *Stealing the Language: the Emergence of Women's Poetry in America*, London, The Women's Press.

Padel, Ruth, 2000, 'How and Why', in Alison Mark and Deryn Rees-Jones (eds), *Contemporary Women's Poetry: Reading/Writing/ Practice*, Basingstoke, Macmillan.

Parry, Benita, 1997, 'Between Creole and Cambridge English: The Poetry of David Dabydeen', in Kevin Grant (ed.), *The Art of David Dabydeen*, Leeds, Peepal Tree Press.

Paterson, Don, 1993, *Nil Nil*, London, Faber.

—— 1996, 'The Dilemma of the Poet', *How Poets Work* (ed.) Tony Curtis, Bridgend, Seren.

—— 1997, *God's Gift to Women*, London, Faber.

—— (ed.), 1999, *101 Sonnets from Shakespeare to Heaney*, London, Faber.

Patterson, Christina, 2001, 'Ted on Sylvia, for the record', in *Saturday Review, Guardian*, 18 August.

Pearce, Lynne, 1997, *Feminism and the Politics of Reading*, London and New York, Arnold: Hodder Headline Group.

Philip, Marlene Nourbese, 1994, 'Dis Place   The Space Between', Lynn Keller and Cristanne Miller (eds), *Feminist Measures: Soundings in Poetry and Theory*, Ann Arbor, University of Michigan Press.

Piercy, Marge (ed.), 1987, *Early Ripening: American Women's Poetry*

Now, London, Pandora.

Pitt-Kethley, Fiona, 1986, *Sky Ray Lolly*, London, Chatto & Windus.

—— 1989, *The Perfect Man*, London, Sphere Books.

Plath, Sylvia, 1975, *Letters Home: Correspondence 1950–1963*, London, Faber.

—— 1977, *Johnny Panic and the Bible of Dreams*, London, Faber.

—— 1981, *Collected Poems*, London, Faber.

Rees-Jones, Deryn, 1999, *Carol Ann Duffy*, Plymouth, Northcote House.

Rich, Adrienne, 1980, 'When We Dead Awaken: Writing as Re-Vision', in *On Lies, Secrets, and Silence: Selected Prose 1966–78*, London, Virago.

Ricoeur, Paul, 1978, *The Rule of Metaphor: Multi-disciplinary Studies in the Creation of Meaning*, London, Routledge.

Roberts, Michèle, 1986, *The Mirror of the Mother*, London, Methuen.

—— 1987, *The Book of Mrs Noah*, London, Methuen.

Robinson, Alan, 1988, *Instabilities in Contemporary British Poetry*, Basingstoke, Macmillan.

Rollinson, Neil, 1996, *A Spillage of Mercury*, London, Cape.

Rose, Jacqueline, 1991, *The Haunting of Sylvia Plath*, London, Virago.

Rumens, Carol (ed.), 1985, *Making for the Open: the Chatto book of post-feminist poetry 1964–84*, London, Chatto & Windus.

Samaroo, Brinsley, 1987, "Two Abolitions: African Slavery and East Indian Indentureship", in David Dabydeen and Brinsley Samaroo (eds), *India in the Caribbean*, London, Hansib.

Sansom, Peter, 1997, 'Excess Its Own Reward' (review of Don Paterson's *God's Gift to Women*), in *Poetry Review,* vol.87, no.2, summer.

Schweickart, Patrocinio P., 1989, 'Reading Ourselves: Toward a Feminist Theory of Reading', in Elaine Showalter (ed.) *Speaking of Gender*, London and New York, Routledge.

Sedgwick, Eve Kosofsky, 1985, *Between Men: English Literature and Male Homosocial Desire*, New York, Columbia University Press.

Shapcott, Jo, 1998, *My Life Asleep*, Oxford, Oxford University Press.

Shepherd, Verene and Beckles, Hilary McD. (eds), 2000, *Caribbean Slavery in the Atlantic World*, Oxford, James Currey.

Sherman, Charlotte, 1995, *Sisterfire: Black Womanist Fiction and Poetry*, London, Women's Press.

Sinfield, Alan, 1977, *Dramatic Monologue*, London, Routledge.

Solomon-Godeau, Abigail, 1995, 'Male Trouble', in Maurice Berger et al. (eds), *Constructing Masculinity*, London and New York, Routledge.

Stevenson, Anne, 2000, 'Defending the Freedom of the Poet / Music Under the Skin', in Alison Mark and Deryn Rees-Jones (eds), *Contemporary Women's Poetry: Reading/Writing/Practice*, Basingstoke, Macmillan.

Sutherland, John, 2000, 'Do I know you, Ms Plath?', *Guardian*, 27 March.

Sweeney, Matthew, 1989, *Blue Shoes*, London, Secker & Warburg.

—— 1997, *The Bridal Suite*, London, Cape.

Taylor, Debbie, 2000, 'The Problem with Poetry', *Mslexia* no.6 (summer/autumn).

Templeton, Alice, 1988, 'The Dream and the Dialogue: Rich's Feminist Poetics and Gadamer's Hermeneutics', *Tulsa Studies in Women's Literature*, vol.7, no.2, Fall.

Tuma, Keith, 1998, *Fishing by Obstinate Isles: Modern and Postmodern British Poetry and American Readers*, Evanston, Northwestern University Press.

Viner, Katherine, 1999, 'Metre Maid' (article on Carol Ann Duffy), *Guardian Weekend*, 25 September.

Voth Harman, Karin, 1997, 'Delivering the Mother: Three Anthologies of Birth Poetry', in Vicki Bertram (ed.), *Kicking Daffodils*, Edinburgh, Edinburgh University Press.

Wandor, Michelene (ed.), 1983, *On Gender and Writing*, London, Pandora.

Ward Jouve, Nicole, 1998, *Female Genesis: Creativity, Self and Gender*, Cambridge, Polity Press.

Welsh, Sarah Lawson, 1997, 'Experiments in Brokenness: The Creative Use of Creole in David Dabydeen's *Slave Song*', in Kevin Grant (ed.), *The Art of David Dabydeen*, Leeds, Peepal Tree Press.

Wills, Clair, 1993, *Improprieties: Politics and Sexuality in Northern*

Irish Poetry, Oxford, Oxford University Press.

Wilson, Rebecca E. and Somerville-Arjat, Gillean (eds), 1990, *Sleeping with Monsters: Conversations with Scottish and Irish Women Poets*, Edinburgh, Polygon.

Wilson-Tagoe, Nana, 1998, *Historical Thought and Literary Representation in West Indian Literature*, Talahassee, University Press of Florida.

Woods, Gregory, 1987, *Articulate Flesh: Male Homo-eroticism and Modern Poetry*, New Haven, Yale University Press.

—— 1998, *A History of Gay Literature: The Male Tradition*, New Haven, Yale University Press.

Woolf, Virginia, 1977, *A Room of One's Own*, London, Granada.

Yaeger, Patricia, 1989, 'Towards a Female Sublime', in Linda Kauffman (ed), *Gender and Theory: Dialogue on Feminist Criticism*, Oxford, Blackwell.

Yorke, Liz, 1991, *Impertinent Voices: Subversive Strategies in Contemporary Women's Poetry*, London and New York, Routledge.

ACKNOWLEDGEMENTS

I should like to thank the Leverhulme Trust and the Arts and Humanities Research Board for funding some of the research leave that has made this book possible. Colleagues from the School of Humanities at Oxford Brookes University also generously supported my requests for study leave on several occasions. A number of individuals have kindly read drafts of this material, and given me invaluable feedback: in particular, Deana Rankin, Trev Broughton, Lynne Pearce, Gregory Woods, Helen Bruder, Alison Donnell, Lynnette Turner, Jane Dowson and Alice Entwistle. Colleagues Nigel Messenger and Paul O'Flinn offered consistent support and proved exemplary role models of how to be an academic today without abandoning a sense of proportion, justice and wry humour. All my friends have offered encouragement over the years, including the Leeds' Women Writers class, the *Kicking Daffodils* team and participants, the Brookes MA in Modern Poetry seminar group, and colleagues from *Feminist Review*. I should also like to thank Michael Donaghy and Neil Rollinson, for generously allowing me to reproduce their work here. Much love to Sarah, Jo, Jacqui and Marian for their precious friendship and good company always. And thanks to Tom, with whom I have discovered such joy, and who has been helpful, positive, and loving throughout the writing of this book.

'Machines' by Michael Donaghy (originally published in *Shibboleth*, 1988, OUP) reproduced by kind permission of the author. 'Snow Joke' by Simon Armitage (originally published in *Zoom!*, 1989, Bloodaxe) reproduced by kind permission of the author. 'The Blowing of Birds' Eggs' (originally published in *A Spillage of Mercury*, 1996, Cape) reproduced by kind permission of the author. Sujata Bhatt's 'Sujata:The First Disciple' from *Brunizem*, 1988 and 'White Asparagus' from Monkey Shadows, 1991, both published and here reproduced with permission from Carcanet

Press Ltd. 'Men' by Kate Clanchy, from *Slattern*, (Chatto & Windus,1995) reproduced with the permission of Macmillan, London. Rita Ann Higgins' 'The Did-You-Come-Yets of the Western World' published in *Sunny Side Plucked: selected poems* by Bloodaxe, 1996. Fiona Pitt-Kethley's 'Sky Ray Lolly' was published in 1986 by Abacus, in her collection of that title.

Excerpts from Duffy's work are reproduced by kind permission of Anvil Press Poetry. Those from 'You Jane', 'Whoever She Was', 'Standing Female Nude' are taken from *Standing Female Nude* by Carol Ann Duffy, published by Anvil Press Poetry in 1985. Excerpt from 'Psychopath' is taken from *Selling Manhattan* by Carol Ann Duffy published by Anvil Press Poetry in 1987. Excerpt from 'Talent Contest' is taken from *The Other Country* by Carol Ann Duffy, published by Anvil Press Poetry in 1990. Excerpts from poems by Jackie Kay are taken from *Off Colour*, published by Bloodaxe Books, Newcastle-upon-Tyne, 1998. Excerpts from poems by Jo Shapcott are taken from *Her Book: Poems 1988–1998*, Faber and Faber, 2000.

Lines from the collections *Slave Song*, *Coolie Odyssey* and *Turner*, by David Dabydeen are reproduced with thanks to Curtis Brown Ltd. London, on behalf of David Dabydeen, Copyright © David Dabydeen, 1984, 1988, 1994 respectively. Extracts from the work of Grace Nichols are taken from *i is a long memoried woman* (Karnak House, London, 1983), *The Fat Black Woman's Poems*, copyright © Grace Nichols 1984, published by Virago, London and *Lazy Thoughts of a Lazy Woman,* copyright © Grace Nichols 1989, published by Virago, London.

Lines from 'The Rabbit Catcher' are taken from *Collected Poems* by Sylvia Plath, published by Faber and Faber in 1981.

Lines from 'A Quiet Man', 'Reply', 'PC', 'Male Infertility', 'Whisht' from *Masculinity* by Robert Crawford, published by Jonathan Cape, 1996, and from 'Grandpa's Bed' from *The Bridal Suite*, by Matthew Sweeney, published by Jonathan Cape, 1997 and used by permission of the Random House Group Limited. Extracts from 'Flying Machine', 'U-Boat' and 'The Cold' are published in Matthew Sweeney's *Selected Poems*, Cape, 2002. Extracts from poems by Don Paterson are published in *God's Gift to Women*, Faber and Faber, 1997. Lines from poems by Glyn Maxwell are reproduced from *Rest for the Wicked*, published by Bloodaxe Books, 1995. Lines from 'Mine' by Michael Donaghy are taken from *Conjure* (Picador, Macmillan) 2000. Lines from Neil Rollinson's poems are from *A Spillage of Mercury* (Cape, 1996) and are reproduced with the kind permission of the author.

I have made every reasonable effort to trace copyright holders and seek their permission, where required. In some cases this has not been possible. I should be grateful for any assistance with this matter.

INDEX